wearing GOD

ALSO BY LAUREN WINNER

Girl Meets God: On the Path to a Spiritual Life

Real Sex: The Naked Truth about Chastity

*Mudhouse Sabbath: An Invitation to
a Life of Spiritual Disciplines*

Still: Notes on a Mid-Faith Crisis

wearing GOD

Clothing, Laughter, Fire, and Other Overlooked Ways of Meeting God

LAUREN F. WINNER

HarperOne
An Imprint of HarperCollinsPublishers

*Grateful acknowledgment to the following for permission
to use their previously published works:*

Jeanne Murray Walker's "Staying Power," published in *Helping the Morning*
(Seattle, WA: WordFarm, 2014), is used by permission of the author.
"But Not With Wine" is from *The Selected Poetry of Jessica Powers*
published by ICS Publications, Washington, D.C. All copyrights,
Carmelite Monastery, Pewaukee Wl. Used with permission.

In order to protect the privacy of church members and friends,
some of the names and identifying details of people who
appear in this book's vignettes have been changed.

HarperCollins books may be purchased for educational, business, or
sales promotional use. For information please e-mail the Special Markets
Department at SPsales@harpercollins.com.

HarperCollins website: http://www.harpercollins.com

FIRST HARPERCOLLINS PAPERBACK EDITION PUBLISHED IN 2016

Designed by Ralph Fowler
The leaf ornament throughout this book is part of the text font family
Type Embellishments. Used by permission.

ISBN 978–0–06–176813–2

Library of Congress Cataloging-in-Publication Data
Winner, Lauren F.
Wearing God : clothing, laughter, fire, and other overlooked ways
of meeting God / Lauren F. Winner. — first edition.
pages cm
Includes bibliographical references and index.
ISBN 978–0–06–176812–5 (hardcover)
1. Image of God. 2. Spirituality—Christianity. 3. Spiritual life—Christianity.
4. Christian women—Religious life. I. Title.
BT103.W56 2015
231.7—dc23   2015001455

18 19 20   LSC(H)   10 9 8 7 6 5 4 3

For Sarah

Were we, in our effort to give an account of God, to make use only of expressions that are literally true, it would be necessary for us to desist from speaking of Him as one that hears and sees and pities and wills to the point where there would be nothing left for us to affirm except the fact of His existence.

—THE SADIA GAON

*Everything I see of the heavens,
I know by the earth.*

—PATTIANN ROGERS

Contents

wearing GOD

The God Who Runs
after Your Friendship

*The best metaphors always [give] both a
shock and a shock of recognition.*

—SALLIE MCFAGUE

O n some days, I know instinctively that God is closer to me than my nearest neighbor. On other days, God seems distant and inscrutable, but some days God is neighborly, and close at hand. One fine morning I see a jackdaw out my window on the branch of the tree, and for a week or so I think about how God is like a bird. And sometimes I fear God, and sometimes I don't give God a passing glance, and then I feel I should think about God more.

Sometimes, a hymn gets caught in my hair, and I sing it all week long, off and on, without ever thinking hard about what it says about God.

Some days God feels like an abyss. Some days God feels like the father I always wanted, and some days God seems like the father I actually have. Some days I know that God is whatever gives me solace, and wherever I abide. On some days, maybe many days, I don't picture God at all.

If you, like me, picture God in lots of different ways, or if sometimes God seems easy to speak about, and on some days you have no words for God, and sometimes you feel that there are too many words for God, so many that the abundance stumps you—if that is the case, then you are pretty much right in line with how the Bible invites us to imagine God: in some very singular ways; in dizzyingly hundreds of ways; sometimes, in no way at all.

I started thinking about all this a few years ago when two circumstances converged in my life. The first circumstance was that I found myself newly fascinated by the Bible. I had always been a member of one or another religious community—first synagogues, then churches—that loved the Bible, that encouraged individual and corporate study of the Bible, that held up the Bible as the word of God. I had diligently (and sometimes not so diligently) tried to get on board with this, but in all honesty for many years I was just not that interested in Bible reading. I liked prayer books. I liked to study church history. I found the Bible boring. And then, at about thirty-three, about five years ago, Cupid came and shot me with a Bible arrow and I got very interested in the Bible for the first time. I became like an infatuated schoolgirl, obsessed. I began to see that one of the amazing things about the Bible is that it's so multi-layered. Even when I think I "understand" a biblical story, even when I think I've gotten to "the" kernel of insight the story holds—it turns out there is something more there, something I haven't yet seen. As a rabbi with the wonderful name Ben Bag Bag once said of the Talmud, "Turn it and turn it, for everything is in it. Look deeply into it, and grow old with it, and spend time over it, and do not stir from it, because there is no greater portion." Turn it and turn it—there is always more to see. This amazes me. This is why the Bible is different from *Pride and Prejudice* or *Little Women*. There is a lot to see in *Pride and Prejudice* and *Little Women*. There is much to see. But I do not for a minute believe that even the best novel endlessly overflows in the same way that the Bible does. This amazes me, this endless overflowing.

All that began to happen about five years ago: I began to be awake to the scriptures. At around that time, I was also in a particular spot in my friendship with God. Simply put, I had felt very far away from God for some years. It was a long season, salty and bitter, but it did not last forever. During the months in which I was emerging from that season—the months in which I was beginning to realize that God had been there all along; that maybe what had felt to me like God's absence was actually a tutorial in God's mystery; that maybe it was my imagination, not God, that had faltered—during that emergence, I began to notice God darting hither and thither, and I began to notice that I was darting hither and thither near God, and I began to realize that my pictures of God were old. They were not old in the sense of antique champagne flutes, which are abundant with significance precisely because they are old—when you sip from them you remember your grandmother using them at birthday dinners, or your sister toasting her beloved at their wedding. Rather, they were old like a seventh-grade health textbook from 1963: moderately interesting for what it might say about culture and science in 1963, but generally out of date. My pictures of God weren't of Zeus on a throne, the Sistine Chapel God. Instead, my pictures were some combination of sage professor and boyfriend, and while sage professor and boyfriend might, as metaphors, have some true and helpful things to say about God, I found that neither of them had much to say about this new acquaintance I was embarking on, or being embarked on. All this intersected, not coincidentally, with my newfound wakefulness to the scriptures, and it led me on a search: what pictures, what images and metaphors, does the Bible give us for who God is, and what ways of being with God might those pictures invite?

The Bible has a great deal to say about this. Your church might primarily describe God as king, or light of the world, or ruler of all. In my church, we tend to call God Father, or speak of God as shepherd or great physician. When we are really going out on a limb, we pick up Matthew and Luke's avian image and pray to God the mother hen tending her brood. Most churches do this—hew closely to two or three favored images of God, turning to them in prayer and song and sermons. Through repetition and association, these few images can become ever richer: there was once a time when I didn't have many thoughts or feelings about God as great physician, but now I have prayed to that God with Carolanne, whose husband is pinned down by Parkinson's, and Belle, who so much wants to keep this pregnancy, and Albert, who is dogged by depression, and because of those prayers, and the fears and hopes and miracles and disappointments they carry, God-as-physician seems a richer image than I first understood.

Yet the repetition of familiar images can have the opposite effect. The words become placeholders, and I can speak them so inattentively that I let them obscure the reality whose place they hold. I repeat them, I restrict my prayer to that small cupful of images, and I wind up insensible to them.

Unlike my church, with its four favored metaphors, the Bible offers hundreds of images of God—images the church has paid a great deal of attention to in earlier centuries, although many are largely overlooked now. Drunkard. Beekeeper. Homeless man. Tree. "Shepherd" and "light" are perfectly wonderful images, but in fixing on them—in fixing on any three or four primary metaphors for God—we have truncated our relationship with the divine, and we have cut ourselves off from the more voluble and variable

There are many metaphorical names for God in the biblical literature . . . but playing a privileged role amongst them are anthropomorphic titles. These personify God, and it seems that the biblical writers were pressed to use anthropomorphism to do justice to a God whose acts they wished to chronicle. This is a God who cajoles, chastises, soothes, alarms, and loves, and in our experience it is human beings who preeminently do these things. Early Christian theologians saw in this plentitude of divine titles a revelation of the manner in which God, while remaining one and holy mystery, is in diverse ways "God *with us*."

—Janet Martin Soskice

witness of the scriptures, which depict God as clothing. As fire. As comedian. Sleeper. Water. Dog.

There are plenty of psychological and even medical reasons why our images of God matter. Scholars have found correlations between the ways a person imagines God, on the one hand, and, on the other hand, eating disorders, shame, and alcoholism. People who primarily imagine God to be distant and judging, as opposed to intimate and loving, tend more toward psychopathology and have a higher rate of gun ownership. I recently read that, according to a study done at the University of Miami, "among HIV patients better immune functioning is found among those who have an image of God that is more compassionate and loving than those who have images of God as more judgmental and punitive. . . . Changes in God image changes t-cells in randomized trials."

There are also social and political consequences to our images of God. As theologians Mary Daly and Judith Plaskow have pointed out, the characteristics we attribute to God will always be those characteristics we value most highly in our own society: we will value what we take God to be (and perhaps, conversely, it's what we value that we take God to be). So if we say that a core characteristic of God is mercy, we will value merciful people. If we imagine God as one who nurtures, we will value nurturing. If we pray to a God who is a property owner (as in the parables of the vineyard), we will admire people who own houses and land. If we focus instead on God as a homeless man (as in Matthew 8:20 and Luke 9:58), we might accord homeless people more esteem.

Underneath all that psychological and sociological ruminating, there are spiritual questions: How do our images of God—and our resulting images of ourselves (sheep?
vassals?)—invite us to become (or interfere with our becoming) the people God means us to be?

How do our images of God draw us into worship, rever-
ence, adoration of God?

How do our images of God help us greet one another as
bearers of the image of God?

How do we pray to the God who is king or shepherd? Or
dog? How does the God who is king or shepherd pray in us?

If the kind of self-knowledge we seek is precisely knowledge of ourselves, unsheathed, before God, what self-
knowledge do we gain when standing (kneeling) before the
God who is a tree, a glass of living water, a loaf of bread?
(And what kind of bread? Might things change if we pause
to really think about bread, all the many kinds of bread
there are, how different they taste, what different memories
they conjure?)

Where, in the variegated topography of life with God, do
the images we hold of God invite us to go?

The Bible's inclusion of so many figures for God is both
an invitation and a caution. The invitation is to discovery:
discovery of who God is, and what our friendship with
God might become. The caution is against assuming that
any one image of God, whatever truth it holds, adequately
describes God. As Janet Martin Soskice has noted in her
reading of Deuteronomy 32—which identifies God as a father "who created you," and as the "Rock that bore you . . .

the God who gave you birth"—the Bible's habit of stacking many different metaphors for God on top of one another, like a layer cake, is itself instructive, a reminder that we cannot wholly locate God within any one image. "Both paternal and maternal imagery are given in quick succession," writes Soskice, "effectively ruling out literalism, as does the equally astonishing image of God as a rock giving birth."

None of these images—rock, shepherd, vine—captures the whole of God because, as Benjamin Myers puts it, "God is too full, too communicative, too bright and piercing" to be easily spoken of. The euphony of biblical speech about God—about what God is like and how we, with our finite minds, might imagine God—is a summons to revel in God's strange abundance. I go to the Metropolitan Museum of Art for an afternoon, and when I come out, I try to describe it to you, but all I am really describing is this blue Turkish bowl or that Flemish painting or possibly the sandwich I ate in the café at lunchtime. There is (to again borrow from Myers) "too much" there to describe. And yet, I sat in front of that blue bowl for an hour, and I sketched it, and I paid attention to it (and I also paid attention to myself in its presence). What I can say about the bowl is, if partial, also true and enlivening. The Bible gives us this surfeit of images in order to "rule out literalism," and the Bible gives us these images because each image holds a different way (maybe many different ways) into our life with God. Each image invites a different response from us, a different way we might be with and for God.

One of my favorite sermons is one preached by Rabbi Margaret Moers Wenig, many years ago, on the Jewish holiday of Yom Kippur. Yom Kippur is the holiest day of the Jewish calendar—it is the Day of Atonement, the day of penance, when Jews fast and pray and beseech God to forgive them for the wrongs they have committed in the past year. Rabbi Wenig's sermon was an extended metaphor: *God is like your grandmother, and she yearns for you to visit her. When we speak of repentance, that is what we are speaking of—paying a visit to God, just as you might visit your grandmother, after a long time away.*

I was a high school student, not especially fond of either of my grandmothers, when I heard the rabbi of my synagogue, in his Yom Kippur sermon, borrow Rabbi Wenig's metaphor. Following Wenig, my rabbi suggested that the process of repenting is like going to see your grandmother, whom you had been ignoring.

Rabbi Wenig's picture of God stayed with me for a long time. Every now and again, sometimes for reasons I could discern and sometimes for no discernible reason, her picture came to mind: that God was a grandmother whom I had not visited lately, who was perhaps deeply sad about my absence, who longed for my visit and would welcome

All images are necessarily partial.

—Marcia Falk

me any time I came. God was a grandmother at whose table I might pass an afternoon having conversation and a piece of pie. Maybe the time with my grandmother would be uncomfortable, or maybe it would feel exactly like coming home, or maybe I would be bored or feel guilty, or maybe I would feel grateful and suffused with love. Visits with God feel all of those ways, just as visits with my grandmothers, both now dead, sometimes felt.

Over a period of several decades—during which time I joined the Episcopal Church and was ordained to the priesthood—Rabbi Wenig's grandmother God sometimes seemed to be nearby. And when I was emerging from that salty season of feeling estranged from God, I decided I would like to read the sermon. It turned out it was easy to find. It had been widely anthologized, justly so. Some of the versions I found had no citations, but some versions had footnotes, and what astounded me most when I actually read the sermon was not that Rabbi Wenig managed

Every meaningful metaphor implies some *differences* between the thing and that to which it points. When a metaphor suggests something quite the opposite of what we think, it can evoke a negative reaction that might actually help us clarify the objects under consideration. . . . To be useful, a metaphor for God needs to evoke [two] reactions *at the same time:* "Oh, yes, God *is* like that," and, "Well, no, God is *not* quite like that."

—Carolyn Jane Bohler

to exactly describe repentance without ever using the verb "repent," though that did astound me; and not how drawn I felt to the God she evoked, though that astounded me, too. What astounded me most was that many of the images in Rabbi Wenig's sermon came from scripture and liturgy. Wenig's suggestion that God might grow older is, for example, drawn from a centuries-old prayer that describes God as a young man and as an old man, "with the hair on thy head now gray, now black." Grandmother God's explicit longing for Her children was inspired by God's declaration in a Rosh Hashanah prayer that "my heart longs for [my dearest child], / My womb aches for him" (the prayer in turn draws on Jeremiah and Ezekiel). God's loving declaration that we should not be afraid, because God will be with us even when we are gray-headed and aging, came straight from Proverbs 3:25 and Isaiah 46:4.

I had always assumed that Wenig had made up the image of God as a grandmother—that she had invented it from whole cloth. The footnotes showed me that I was wrong. Certainly, Rabbi Wenig's sermon is creative, and certainly it did in part come from her imagination, but it also came from the Bible and other classical Jewish texts. The

No one image or model, however elusive or rich, can do more than offer glimpses and hints toward the divine.

—Nicola Slee

footnotes gave the sermon a bit of weight I had not allowed it to have before. Rabbi Wenig's God was not dreamed up by one lone person in the late twentieth century. It was grounded in the ways the people of God had long imagined God and long prayed to God. And it was also grounded in Rabbi Wenig's own daily life, in her life as a daughter or granddaughter who knew what it was like to stay away and not visit.

Returning to God after dallying far away is, indeed, somehow like visiting my grandmothers. It was hard to visit them. I felt that I should like them, but in fact I didn't like them very much; and I felt that I should feel guilty about this, but I didn't feel much guilt. They were a little scary. I didn't know how to become close to them. I thought—I still think—that I disappointed them. Yet spending time with them was sometimes surprising and wonderful. Sometimes there was rum cake. Sometimes there was real connection. Once or twice, I felt that my paternal grandmother understood me better than anyone ever would. Once, she and I danced to Frank Loesser's "Fugue for Tinhorns" in my father's living room. Now I am older, and I like to visit them. It is now a sad, great pleasure to go to their graves, which are two hundred yards apart in Riverside Cemetery in Asheville, North Carolina.

"God is lonely tonight, longing for her children," writes Rabbi Wenig.

> "Come home," she wants to say to us. "Come home." But she won't call. She is afraid that we'll say no. She can anticipate the conversation: "We are so

busy. We'd love to see you but we just can't come. Too much to do." God knows that our busyness is just an excuse. She knows that we avoid returning to her because we don't want to look into her age-worn face. It is hard for us to face a god who disappointed our childhood expectations: She did not give us everything we wanted. She did not make us triumphant in battle, successful in business, and invincible to pain. We avoid going home to protect ourselves from our disappointment and to protect her. We don't want her to see the disappointment in our eyes. Yet, God knows that it is there and she would have us come home anyway.

I have now read Rabbi Wenig's sermon dozens of times. It never fails to stir me, and it often leads me to pray. God as the grandmother I have neglected is not a metaphor that I just think about. It is a metaphor that beckons me to go somewhere toward and with God.

The biblical images for God that you will encounter in this book are perforce selected—they are the images that have particularly resonated with me as I have meandered through the Bible. My attention is often grabbed by images and metaphors that can be found in my daily life—clothing but not shepherds, fire but not kings. I have heard in countless sermons that, however unfamiliar twenty-first-century city folk are with shepherds, the original readers and hearers and pray-ers of the Bible saw shepherds all the time, and knew all about the qualities of a good shepherd and the characteristics of sheep; to call God "shepherd"—or for that matter vine, vintner, or king—was to describe God with images drawn from people's quotidian repertoires. I don't live in a society in which I have daily contact with, or even daily thoughts about, shepherds or kings, but many other biblical images for God are still very much part of my daily life. One of the invitations of this book—and, I think, of the Bible—is this: you can discover things about God by looking around your ordinary, everyday life. An ordinary Tuesday— what you wear, what you eat, and how you experience the weather—has something to offer you about God. There is a method here, and it is Jesus's method. Jesus, after all, special-ized in asking people to steep themselves in the words of the

We should exercise that far higher privilege which appertains to Christians, of having "the mind of Christ;" and then the two worlds, visible and invisible, will become familiar to us even as they were to Him (if reverently we may say so), as double against each other; and on occasion sparrow and lily will recall God's providence, seed His Word, earthly bread the Bread of Heaven, a plough the danger of drawing back; to fill a bason and take a towel will preach a sermon in self-abasement; boat, fishing-net, flock or fold of sheep, each will convey an allusion; wind, water, fire, the sun, a star, a vine, a door, a lamb, will shadow forth mysteries.

—Christina Rossetti

scriptures and then to look around their ordinary Tuesdays to see what they could see about holiness and life with God. This is not merely entertaining wordplay to give overactive minds something pious to do. It is the Bible's way of making us aware of God and of the world in which we meet God.

One word you will encounter in this book, for example, is "friend." There isn't a chapter dedicated to God as friend, but throughout the chapters, you will find the formulation of pursuing or deepening your friendship with God, of making yourself available to friendship with God. This metaphor

The child became a man and the man became a preacher whose sermons were full of commonplace things: seeds and nets, coins and fishes, lilies of the field, and birds of the air. Wherever he was, he had a knack for looking around him and weaving what he saw into his sermons, whether it was sparrows for sale in the marketplace, laborers lining up for their pay, or a woman glimpsed through a doorway kneading her family's bread. . . . "The kingdom of heaven is like this," he said over and over again, comparing things they knew about with something they knew nothing about and all of the sudden what they knew had cracks in it, cracks they had never noticed before, through which they glimpsed bright and sometimes frightening new realities. . . . Every created thing was fraught with divine possibility; wasn't that what he was telling them? Every ho-hum detail of their days was a bread crumb leading them into the presence of God, if they would just pick up the trail and follow.

—Barbara Brown Taylor

comes from the writers of the Old Testament, who speak of Abraham and Moses as the friends of God, and it comes from the Gospel of John, where Jesus tells his disciples that they are no longer his servants but his friends.

Although the language of people's friendship with God is woven through scripture, I first really heard the idiom from Sam Wells, who was the dean of Duke Chapel during my first few years at Duke Divinity School. It seems to me that this formulation is one of Sam's favorite ways of approaching God, but maybe my memory exaggerates its preponderance in his writing precisely because the image so needled me at first. Sam would say something about God's having given us everything we need to be God's friends, and I would wonder, "Who am I to be a friend of the Almighty, of my maker and redeemer?" It seems almost disrespectful, given God's grandeur and transcendence, to speak of my "friendship with God."

But I kept hearing the language from Sam, and then I began noticing that he was not the first interpreter of scripture to use this idiom. Theologians through the ages—Irenaeus, Gregory of Nyssa, Thomas Aquinas—have spoken of all of us, not just biblical heroes, as friends of God. Theodoret of Cyrus, a fifth-century bishop, said that friendship with God is the entire goal of the Christian life. Eventually, I decided to try the language myself, not because it had suddenly become easy or natural, but precisely because it had not: it is one of my working theories in the spiritual life that when a prayer (or a parable, or phrase from the Bible, or a question posed in a sermon, or a picture in a museum, or a passage in a book) rubs you the wrong way but you find yourself unable to set down the rankling thing and move on, the rankling might in fact be the Holy Spirit's way of getting your attention, of fixing your eyes and asking you to look more closely at the prayer or parable or painting or phrase—to discover what it holds for you, if only you'd be willing to explore it, and yourself, deeply enough.

So—with the awkward intentionality of one who is trying suddenly to call her fiancé's parents, formerly Mr. and Mrs. Browning, "Mom" and "Dad"—I began to practice and ponder my *friendship* with God. In sermons I preached, in conversations I had with students, in my own interior monologues, and in prayer, I adopted Sam's metaphor (I realize it came first from Isaiah and 2 Chronicles and Jesus, but I will always think of it as Sam's)—this more intimate way of limning what I sought in the spiritual life, and maybe what God seeks from me.

As I began to write and speak about friendship with God, I tried, through two kinds of ponderings, to understand more fully what it might mean to be God's friend (and these are the same kinds of ponderings you will encounter throughout *Wearing God*). First, what did Christians in

God is friendship.

—Aelred of Rievaulx

earlier eras have to say about being friends with God? Second, what could my own life, which is full of friendship, tell me about friendship with God?

As with many of the images I explore in this book, the saints of the tradition—preachers and mystics, theologians and pastors—had a great deal to say on the subject. In their company, with their books and sermons on my lap, I began to see how much a simple three-word idiom might hold.

I was especially drawn to Thomas Aquinas's discussion of friendship in his great treatise, the *Summa Theologiae*. Friendship requires intimacy, said Aquinas: we see the friend as an "other self." That is a beautiful notion, but it simply led me back to the question I had when I first heard Sam Wells speak of our friendship with God—if to have a friend is to have an "other self," can I possibly claim the Creator of all as a friend? The *Summa,* it turns out, is interested in this question. In the *Summa,* Aquinas examines friendship through the writings of Aristotle, who, centuries before, had argued that true friendship required mutuality, reciprocity, and equality—three things that don't seem to exist between God and human beings. So, says Aquinas, if Aristotle's description of friendship is correct, can we possibly be friends with God? Then Aquinas answers his own question: in a straightforward way, there is indeed no equality between God and me, between God and you. There is no mutuality or reciprocity either. But there is Jesus, and Jesus is a bridge. Jesus's life and work create a sort of mutuality. There is no mutuality or reciprocity between us and God, but (as the theologian Mindy G. Makant has put it), "Jesus makes it so. Jesus calls us his friends, and just as Genesis reports that God's speaking makes creation so, Jesus' words that we are his friends make it so."

When I took up the language of "friendship with God," then, I was not just adopting a nice phrase. My use of Sam's idiom, and my studious attempts to plumb the idiom, became diagnostic, showing me the limits of my own appreciation of all that Jesus is and does. If I were going to understand myself as a person in a friendship with God—if I were going to understand God as my friend—I had to accept, and expect, that my theological imagination would be changed, deepened, stretched.

But the task of receiving God as friend, and receiving myself as one who might be a friend to God, is not just cerebral. To be embraced by this metaphor, there are certain spiritual practices I should take up. The fourth-century preacher John Chrysostom said that two groups of people are especially friends of God: saints and the poor. One way to pursue our own friendship with God, said Chrysostom, would be to pursue friendship with the people who are already God's friends. We should pray, in order to become friends of the saints, and we should practice hospitality and generosity, in order to become friends of the poor. It is through those disciplines—prayer and generosity—that we might become friends of the One who, in Chrysostom's rendering of Jesus's words in John 15, said to his disciples, "I ran after your friendship."

Reading Aquinas and Chrysostom has helped me understand what friendship with God might entail, but so has reading my own life. What do I know about friendship from close to four decades of being, or trying to be, a friend?

I know that friendship both requires and breeds honesty—perhaps foremost honesty with myself. When I am lying to myself (as I have been known to do, usually about something important—otherwise why bother?), I am not available for friendship.

I know that friendship is rich and delightful. I know that I could live anywhere if I had two or three real friends.

I know that friendship is often supported by institutions and the structures they provide. A few years ago, the rector of the church where I served as a priest associate left for another job. The moment she announced she was leaving, I began to dread the ways our friendship would suffer—and it has. It hasn't disappeared, but now it is entirely dependent on our free time and our admittedly plentiful affection for each other. We manage to meet for a cocktail about every four months, which is better than nothing but a lot more fragile than when we not only adored each other but also shared common work and common concern for a parish. Likewise, I do not look forward to the day I stop teaching at the women's prison with my friend Sarah. I have buckets of affection for her, too, but it is a relief that we have something to talk about other than current events and our petty domestic squabbles; we also plan syllabi together, and think together about what our students need from us, and argue about which books to assign. Friendship benefits from the support of institutions: classes taught together, church bazaars planned together.

Also, I know I am an uneven, inconstant friend. Friendship has probably been the category of relationship most sustaining in my life, and I have been lucky to have the most interesting, most faithful friends in the world (you will meet some of them in the pages of this book). But I am sporadic. I can go months without calling. I sometimes give extravagantly to my friends, but if there were a balance sheet—which, thankfully, there is not—I am pretty sure it would show that I take more than I give. And yet I also know I have grown as a friend. I am less inconstant than I once was. I have begun to set aside other things, ratchet down other priorities, so that I have more time to practice friendship.

All this, it turns out, can be said of my friendship with God. All this frames my life with God in a way that shows

One of the aims of prayer is to grow in friendship with God. If this is the case, then let's consider what constitutes a friendship, and then try to pray in accordance with that. One of the things about friends is that they want the same thing for each other. Not that they necessarily both want ice cream at the same time, but that the well-being of one person is tied to the well-being of the other. This doesn't just mean that God wants what we want, but that we want what God wants out of friendship for God. That is a basis for intercessory prayer. If God's deepest longing is for the well-being of the world, then God wants the well-being of Bosnia, and we pray for that out of friendship with God.

—Roberta Bondi

me certain things I might not have seen without the frame of friendship. My friendship with God is supported by institutions like daily prayer and church. My friendship with God is strengthened when, instead of just relying on our nebulous affection for each other, I join in the work that God loves—the pursuit of justice, the work of hospitality. My friendship with God requires and provokes honesty. Also, I am uneven. I am inconstant. Yet I have begun to grow as a friend. I am less inconstant than I once was.

I like living with the metaphor "friendship with God." It is still not an entirely comfortable idiom for me, but I am more and more persuaded that it is uncomfortable precisely because it calls me to account for my own unevenness. I am more and more persuaded that it is an idiom I should practice precisely because I find it unsettling.

In this book, we will explore several overlooked biblical idioms for God. We will look at what the Bible itself suggests about these idioms, and what our daily lives have to say about them, and what various preachers and pray-ers and writers from earlier eras made of them. Your guide in this exploration is a bookworm who can happily get lost for a few days on a research trail, and I sometimes bring the words of anthropologists or historians or literary critics to bear on our ruminations. (Since the library of insights from those who have gone before us, and from contemporary scholars and preachers, is so rich, I have set additional gems at the bottoms of many pages. These quotations are there for stimulation and contemplation. Feel free to stop and linger over them, or skip them, or add your own musings.) Because I hope the book will help you sit down with God in a place the two of you have never visited before, each chapter concludes with a prayer. The final aim of this book is not to persuade you to stop thinking about God as your shepherd and start thinking about God as a cardigan sweater or One who weeps. The aim, rather, is to provoke your curiosity, and to inspire your imagination, and to invite you farther into your friendship with God.

A Short Note on Gender and Language for God

My God, my God, thou art a direct God, may I not say a literal God, a God that wouldst be understood literally and according to the plain sense of all that thou sayest? but thou art also (Lord, I intend it to thy glory, and let no profane misinterpreter abuse it to thy diminution), thou art a figurative, a metaphorical God too, a God in whose words there is such a height of figures, such voyages, such peregrinations to fetch remote and precious metaphors, such extensions, such spreadings, such curtains of allegories, such third heavens of hyperboles, so harmonious elocutions, so retired and so reserved expressions, so commanding persuasions, so persuading commandments, such sinews even in thy milk, and such things in thy words, as all profane authors seem of the seed of the serpent that creeps, thou art the Dove that flies. O, what words but thine can express the inexpressible texture and composition of thy word.

—JOHN DONNE

How we talk about God matters: that is one of the core assumptions underpinning this book. How we talk about God matters because how we talk always matters: language does more to us and for us than we know. And so I have one final word, by way of introduction, a word about gender and how we speak about and imagine God. Although it's both common sense and a matter of Christian doctrine that the triune God is not male, we often speak as though God were. (For example, the first draft of the end of the previous sentence read, "we often speak about God as though He were.") Thus certain questions about men and women, about maleness and femaleness, and about masculinity and femininity hover about the whole project of noticing overlooked biblical images of God: given the diversity of biblical imaginings of God (father, nursing mother, warrior, pregnant rock, husband, mother bear, dew), is it faithful to speak, in English, of God as "He"? What are the criteria by which we decide what is faithful? Church tradition? The impact gendered speech has on the women who constitute 60 percent of church attendees on any given American Sunday (or on the zillions of women who do not)? Given that language arranges power, how shall we speak about the One who unseats the mighty and lifts up the humble?

For the first fifteen years of my Christian life, I almost always used masculine pronouns for God, and used them with great comfort: *He, Him, His.* As far as I could tell, this was the language the church had always used, the language the church had discerned spoke best of God—and when it comes to preserving what the church has discerned, my instincts run pretty conservative.

But after about a decade and a half of speaking about God in this way, I began to sense that, just as limiting ourselves to two or three images for God (king, shepherd, and so forth) truncates our imagination of who God is (and who we, as people bearing God's image and kin to God, are), so too habitually referring to God with masculine pronouns subtly teaches us to imagine the triune God as something God is not—male or exclusively masculine. It thereby distorts our imaginations. And, I began to feel, my distorted imagination was distorting even my prayers.

It turns out the assumption that had been underpinning my use of masculine pronouns—that the church had always, discerningly and univocally, used masculine language for God—was inaccurate. The Syriac church, for example, spoke of the Holy Spirit in the grammatical feminine for four hundred years. Upon reflection, it seems obvious that the church hasn't always said He, Him, and His, because the church hasn't always spoken (doesn't always speak) English. Different languages give different options, and this linguistic diversity is not theologically incidental: noting that different languages gender "spirit" differently (masculine in Latin, neuter in Greek, and feminine in Syriac), the early church father Jerome said this very linguistic diversity tells us that "in the deity there is no sex."

About four years ago, I made a conscious decision to try to set aside third-person singular pronouns for God, except when they appeared in prayers and hymns written by someone else or scripture translated by someone else. That is to say, I didn't edit out every "He" from my public recitation of liturgy from the Book of Common Prayer ("Let us give thanks to the Lord our God. It is right to give him thanks and praise"; "Happy are they [whose] . . . delight is in the law of the Lord; . . . they meditate on his law day and night"). But I tried otherwise to remove third-person singular pronouns from my speaking and writing about the Lord. This irked me aesthetically—saying "God's self" instead of "Himself" felt about as natural as speaking backward would—but more than I wanted oral and aural loveliness, I wanted to try to speak in a way that was more consistent with what I knew about God. Simply put, God is not male, so why speak of God exclusively with masculine pronouns? Also, the awkwardness itself seemed usefully true—to abandon all third-person singular pronouns with reference to God was to remember how different God is: why shouldn't our speech about God be a little strange? The occasional dictional acrobatics of speaking without "He" came to be a theologically instructive marker—a reminder not only that God is "not male," but also that God is different from us, and requires different kinds of speech.

So I undertook a retraining of my speech, and as I retrained, I noticed several things. First, I began to hear the extent to which my community's prayers, hymns, and sermons are saturated with masculine language. One Tuesday, I was gathered with the rest of the altar party outside of the divinity school chapel, about to go into worship, and I heard all the masculine language the student praying for us, the altar party, used. I heard all the pronouns in our opening hymns (one of my absolute favorites, "All Creatures of Our God and King": "O praise Him! Alleluia!" "The flowers and fruits that in thee grow, / Let them His glory also show"). I heard the masculine formulations in the opening acclamation ("Blessed be His kingdom . . ."). I had never really heard these things before. I wondered how they sounded to God.

Second, I noticed in my own prayer life that (because I have for so many years spoken of God exclusively as "He") I tend to hear the word "God" not as somehow beyond gender or as betokening the diversity of divine life; rather, I hear it as male. The antidote to this formation is, perhaps, not to wholly rid one's speech about God of third-person pronouns, but to sometimes use feminine pronouns and sometimes masculine pronouns. I thought, when I began writing this book, that exploring the Bible's euphony of God images would make things easier. After all, it seems clear that some of the Bible's images for God are masculine and some are feminine—surely "father" is a masculine image that calls for the pronoun "He," and surely "nursing mother" is a feminine image that calls for "She." Yet even that is less straightforward than it might at first blush appear: unless by "mother," we mean "a caregiver with ovaries" (in which case God is not one, nor is anyone who has had an oophorectomy), then men can mother, and when we address the first person of the Trinity as Father, we are not suggesting that the first person of the Trinity is a man.

My approach in this book has been to refrain generally from the use of third-person singular pronouns when the antecedent is divine, but to use gender-specific pronouns— sometimes "He," sometimes "She"—in instances where it seems apt, instructive, playful, or prayerful to do so.* Like calling God a friend, calling God "She" sometimes feels very uncomfortable to me, but I persist with it because I believe it is the Holy Spirit doing the uncomforting, and that the uncomforting is holy and blessed.

But I remain comfortably old-fashioned in another way. I still capitalize my pronouns for God. These capitalized pronouns might jar the eye. They are another way of noting that God is not like us; God is the only One whose pronouns we capitalize.

---

*In an essay on feminine language for the divine, English liturgist Janet Morley reminds readers not to call God "She" only when speaking of a God who is loving and warm. "It is particularly important to use female language when dealing with problematic aspects of God's nature. . . . it really will not do for me to call God 'she' only when I mean what is tender and unproblematic." The God who is She, in other words, is not only or necessarily a nurturer (both because men can be nurturing, and because many women are not).

Clothing

*I saw that He is to us everything that is good
and comfortable for us: He is our clothing
that for love wrappeth us, claspeth us, and all
encloseth us for tender love, that He may never
leave us; being to us all-thing that is good.*

—JULIAN OF NORWICH

H ave you ever had the experience of reading something and automatically assuming you know what it means—indeed, you are so certain of the meaning that it does not occur to you that you are doing any interpretation? And only later do you learn that there are other equally plausible (or more plausible) meanings in what you've read? Maybe you walk by a certain house every day and it is obvious to you that it is red, and it doesn't occur to you that someone else might reasonably see it as green, and then it turns out that almost everyone sees it as green, and it hasn't occurred to them that the house might be red?

That is my experience with the garments of skin God stitched for Adam and Eve right before they were exiled from the garden of Eden.

Here is what the scriptures tell us: the man and the woman have eaten the forbidden fruit, stitched fig leaves together to cover their newfound vulnerability, and hidden from God. God has discovered their wrongdoing, and pronounced punishments upon them. Then God is just about to banish Adam and Eve from Eden—but in a gracious and merciful response to their sinfulness, God first dresses them properly. "The LORD God made garments of skin for Adam and his wife and clothed them."

I have known about those garments, and the fig leaves they replaced, since childhood Sunday school—and I have always understood the description in Genesis to mean that God clothed Adam and Eve *with their own skin*. In my imagining, they needed skin in order to live in the non-Eden world, and so God gave it to them, right before expelling them from the garden. (I never really stopped to think what their bodies looked like before they got their skin—if you'd asked me about it, I suppose I would have pictured something like those jangly skeletons from grammar school Halloween coloring pages. I would have said that Adam and Eve didn't need skin in the garden. In the garden, all their organs and bones and blood held together by themselves with no need for a protective cloak. What do you need protection from in the garden of Eden?)

It was not until recently, when I read Gary Anderson's book *The Genesis of Perfection,* that I realized a more straightforward interpretation might be that Adam and Eve had skin from the start, and that after the Fall, God clothed them in garments of animal skin—which would be sturdier and warmer than their self-fashioned fig-leaf garments. Anderson suggested this, and I ran it by three different clergy friends, who all said it had never occurred to them that the verse meant anything other than leather tunics. My friend Cathie said she has always imagined God making clothing out of fur. "Bearskin or rabbit," she said. "Something warm and hardy and beautiful."

I was relieved to find out from Anderson that I am not the only person to think that the garments in question were Adam and Eve's own skin. Many rabbis have also read

Genesis 3:21 that way, seeing the garments of skin as not
"a separate piece of clothing to be put on like a jacket but
as human flesh itself."

So there are at least two different ways of reading what
is happening when God clothes Adam and Eve, and I find
that I now need both interpretations. In the human skin interpretation, there is the wonderful implication that Adam
and Eve become fully human only upon leaving the garden.
The Fall is the Fall—but it is also the culminating step in
Creation. This was, perhaps, the logic of God's Creation
all along: to become fully human, Adam and Eve had to

The expulsion was indeed the finishing touch to the creation
of human beings. . . . What Adam and Eve did in the Garden
of Eden was . . . supposed to happen. Indeed, it has happened
in every generation since. Children disobey their parents and,
in so doing, complete their own creation. Adam and Eve are
duped, not by the snake, but by God. They were lovingly
tricked into committing the primal act of disobedience that
alone could ensure their separation from God, the individua-
tion, and their expulsion from [childhood's] garden. Yet just
because such is the way of the world does not mean there is no
psychic damage. . . . For our own good we have been tricked
into leaving our parents' home, into separating from God. . . .
The necessary price for becoming an autonomous adult is the
unending pain of separation.

—Lawrence Kushner

leave Eden, and God clothed them with their humanity as they left.

But I also like my friends' less idiosyncratic and more widespread interpretation—that God made Adam and Eve dresses of rabbit fur, trousers of bearskin. This interpretation underlines the mercy in God's response to Adam and Eve's sin. Indeed, God's clothing them is the first disclosure of something we see over and over in the Bible: God's deep, abiding interest in working with and for human beings. God is so committed to working with us and for us that God works inside our own limitations, even the limitations of our sin. Sometimes God's clothing Adam and Eve is taken as evidence that nakedness is bad, that we should be ashamed of our naked bodies. But perhaps God's dressing Adam and Eve does not speak to anything other than God's care. I find myself picturing what Cathie pictures: God bent over, stitching fur garments for Adam and Eve. I imagine that God is sad while stitching, and I imagine God's gift as one of utter tenderness: *I know you have to leave, but here is one last thing I can do for you before you go.*

All these changes did the Merciful One effect:
Stripping of His glory and putting on a body;
For He had devised a way to reclothe Adam,
In that glory which Adam had stripped off.

—Ephrem of Syria

Ever since God clothed Adam and Eve in their full humanity, clothes have not only protected us from the elements and kept us warm; they have also profoundly shaped our identity and our sense of self. It is not surprising, then, that clothing is an image that runs all the way through scripture from the first mention in Genesis to Revelation, where the gathered community of worshippers is clothed in robes made white by being laundered in the blood of the Lamb. To my eye, the image sitting at the center of all the Bible has to say about clothing is Paul's startling statement in Galatians 3: "As many of you as were baptized into Christ have clothed yourselves with Christ." God doesn't just clothe us with skin (or rabbit fur); God clothes us with God's own self.

This seems a pretty radical thing for Paul to say. Intriguingly, scholars believe that this metaphor is original to the Pauline writings. In the ancient world, it was not unusual to speak, as do 1 Peter 5 and Colossians 3, of "putting on" virtues—this was a common rhetorical device, used

For our salvation, He put on a man and dwelt in him.

—The catechism of Theodore of Mopsuestia

to encourage people to adopt or practice various worthy qualities. But nowhere in ancient literature does there appear to be a "clear parallel," writes New Testament scholar Roy R. Jeal, to the Pauline "rhetoric of being clothed with a *person*."

And not just any person: God.

Maybe it's that clothes figure more centrally in my daily life than kings or shepherds, but I find the notion of God as clothing to be endlessly suggestive. I have some sense of what my clothes do to and for me each day, how they act upon me, what they mean for my life and identity. What might it mean to understand myself as clothed in God? What does it mean to imagine God as a warm winter coat? As a handmade bespoke suit? As a beloved cardigan sweater, purchased in Galway on your honeymoon—chunky purple wool, with fisherman's knots?

As God's chosen ones, holy and beloved, clothe yourselves with compassion, kindness, humility, meekness, and patience. Bear with one another and, if anyone has a complaint against another, forgive each other; just as the Lord has forgiven you, so you also must forgive. Above all, clothe yourselves with love, which binds everything together in perfect harmony.

—Colossians 3:12–14

And all of you must clothe yourselves with humility in your dealings with one another.

—1 Peter 5:5

I have come to a large department store in Raleigh to see what I might see in Galatians 3, if I read it among actual clothes—if I read it among the racks of jersey dresses and boiled wool jackets and burnout velvet tops. I sit down on the floor next to the entrance to the dressing rooms; my back is against the wall, my corduroy tote bag beside me, my Bible on my lap. I half hope I look innocuous, and I half hope someone will ask me what I'm doing.

The first thing I notice is a large poster of a woman strutting down a runway in an outfit I could never afford and would not be caught dead in if I could. She seems to be wearing seven-inch heels. Appropriately enough, the caption at the bottom of the poster reads "The Height of Fashion."

"Fashion" is a noun, calling to mind Paris runways, models in Jean Paul Gaultier creations, *Elle* and *Marie Claire* magazines. But "fashion" is also a verb. It means "to mold or to shape." We fashion dough into the shape of a bread loaf; we fashion clay into a pot or a bowl. Indeed, the word "fashion" had that meaning—the action of making or shaping something—before it became a noun designating clothing, and "fashion" came to designate apparel precisely because clothing shapes us. This is why some of us enjoy clothes so much, why we love changing our clothes and trying out a different look—every time we change into a different kind of clothing, we can play at being a different kind of self.

My own closet holds three distinct kinds of outfits, clothes that bespeak three different personas. There are the quite formal work clothes—the dresses from Talbots, the black interview suits, the slightly Jackie O jackets. I bought these when I was first starting out as a professor, and although at the moment I'm in a phase where I don't wear them very often, when I do they make me feel very adult; they make me comport myself in a somewhat more adult, formal way.

Hanging next to the suits are the vintage clothes—dresses from the 1930s, polyester novelty shirts from the 1970s. These craft a much hipper persona, which is probably no less fraudulent than the crisp, adult persona offered by the suits, since really I am not even remotely hip. I have a very specific association with the 1970s novelty shirts. I began to buy them after spending a weekend at a history conference with the historian Bethany Moreton. Dr. Moreton, who has been wearing just such a shirt every time I've laid eyes on her, is a brilliant scholar (author of the wonderful *To Serve God and Wal-Mart: The Making of Christian Free Enterprise*) and a passionate activist, and she seems at ease around other people, more at ease than I will ever be. I wish I were more like her, and when I wear these shirts I am playing, a little, at being smarter and more politically engaged than I actually am. I am trying to channel her a bit, in hopes that the shirts will cease to be a costume and will in fact transform me into a more brilliant, more appealing, more Bethany-esque person.

Then there are the clothes in my closet that I actually wear. These are a series of shapeless black dresses, put aside occasionally for a black V-neck sweater and a pair of black velvet pants. (On courageous mornings, I enliven all the onyx with an orange or cranberry cardigan.) I have sometimes joked that I wear all these black dresses because I am in denial about no longer living in New York. But in fact these dresses capture the persona that is probably closest to who I actually am—the absentminded professor who simply throws these things on, half the time with the cardigan inside out, before hopping on her tricycle and triking to school. I am slightly ashamed of being this person, and that is why I enjoy buying and holding on to the other kinds of outfits. When I get sick of the dotty academic who lives more in her head than in her body, I can put on the Talbots suit or the vintage novelty shirt and, briefly, become someone else.

If to change clothes can be to change one's sense of self; if to change clothes is to change one's way of being in the world; if to clothe yourself in a particular kind of garment is to let that garment shape you into its own shape—then what is it to put on Christ?

Alexander MacLaren was a nineteenth-century Baptist minister in Manchester, England. In his commentary on Romans, I read this: "It takes a lifetime to fathom Jesus; it takes a lifetime to appropriate Jesus, it takes a lifetime to be clothed with Jesus. And the question comes to each of us,

Our body became your Garment;
Your spirit became our robe.

—Ephrem of Syria

have we 'put off the old man with his deeds'? Are we daily, as sure as we put on our clothes in the morning, putting on Christ the Lord?"

I take out a note card and copy down MacLaren's words. I will tape the card to my closet door.

I become professional or hip, depending on what I am wearing. I feel different when I am wearing different clothes. I act different. I let my Talbots suits and my vintage shirts remake me in their image. I want to let Jesus do the same.

Clothing doesn't just shape identity. It also communicates something about our identity to the people we meet. I am not just trying to convince *myself* that I am a professional when I wear those Talbots suits—I am also trying to say to my colleagues and students: *I am a grown-up, I belong here, I take this work seriously, please take me seriously.*

The way clothing shapes one's sense of self and shows something to others comes home to me when I walk into my church for the funeral of a longtime member and see three bereaved daughters, and their own daughters, clad in elegant black. In an earlier era, those women would have worn black for months, and the sons and grandsons would have worn black armbands. The daughters' black dresses are doing precisely the kind of fashioning I was thinking about at the department store—they are helping shape the dead woman's family into mourners. I remember this from my own mother's death a decade ago: stepping into that black dress and jacket, putting on the black stockings and heels—yes, I felt sad before I put on the black dress, but I was not yet a *mourner*. It was only when I looked in the mirror and saw myself in the black dress and heels that I knew I was truly bereaved. In centuries past, they called the practice of wearing black clothes "wearing mourning."

The black garb of bereavement does something more than help craft or fashion a survivor's grief. It also communicates that grief to others. This seems especially true when we think of the older practice of wearing mourning for months. The black dress of a widow or an orphan wordlessly conveyed that the wearer was in mourning. And the mourning garb made a demand on the mourner's community, on every single passerby—the demand to acknowledge the mourning and treat the mourner appropriately. Early-twentieth-century etiquette doyenne Emily Post explained this to readers of her 1922 guide, *Etiquette in Society, in Business, in Politics and at Home:*

> If you see acquaintances of yours in deepest
> mourning, it does not occur to you to go up to them
> and babble trivial topics or ask them to a dance
> or dinner. If you pass close to them, irresistible
> sympathy compels you merely to stop and press
> their hand and pass on. A widow, or mother, in the
> newness of her long veil, has her hard path made as
> little difficult as possible by everyone with whom she

comes in contact, no matter on what errand she may be bent. A clerk in a store will try to wait on her as quickly and as attentively as possible. Acquaintances avoid stopping her with long conversation that could not but torture and distress her. She meets small kindnesses at every turn, which save unnecessary jars to supersensitive nerves.

Once in a great while, a tactless person may have no better sense than to ask her abruptly for whom she is in mourning! Such people would not hesitate to walk over the graves in a cemetery! And fortunately, such encounters are few.

Ninety years later, Meghan O'Rourke made the same point in a memoir about her mother's illness and death. Five days after her mother died, O'Rourke was on a New York subway:

A man elbowed me aside . . . and I felt bruised and angry; if I had been wearing mourning clothes, I furiously thought, he would have taken greater care. I longed for rituals not only to indicate I was still in mourning but also to have a nonpsychological way of commemorating and expressing my loss. Without ritual, the only way to share a loss was to talk about it—foregrounding the particularities of my own emotions, my own bereavement. At times . . . this sharing felt invasive. . . . In those moments, I wanted a way to show my grief rather than tell it.

Had O'Rourke been wearing a black veil or dress, her clothes would have displayed her grief silently, inviting the people who shared her subway car to respond to her in a particular way.

This notion of communicative clothing—and the idea that, as with a garment, Christians might wordlessly speak something of Jesus—is appealing. One often hears (in evangelical churches) about "lifestyle evangelism" or (in mainline churches) about St. Francis, apocryphally bidding people to preach the Gospel always, using words only when necessary. Most of this chat about mute evangelizing revolves around the profound and enticing things we might each tacitly say, with our inspiring soup kitchen service or our serene deportment. Yet in the Christian life, we are often the passerby; the one in a position to notice, and respond to, someone else's sartorial speech. To return to Alexander MacLaren's formulation, the question comes to each of us, daily: when I see

For thousands of years human beings have communicated with one another first in the language of dress. Long before I am near enough to talk to you on the street, in a meeting, or at a party, you announce your sex, age, and class to me through what you are wearing—and very possibly give me important information (or misinformation) as to your occupation, origin, personality, opinions, tastes, sexual desires and current mood. . . . By the time we meet and converse we have already spoken to each other in an older and more universal tongue.

—Alison Lurie

my friend, clad in the finery of Christ, what do I allow her clothing to say to me? What do I allow it to impress upon me? What gestures do I allow it to compel?

Still, there are days in the calendar of faith when each of us is that 1920s widow with her voluble veils. I like to imagine that occasionally people I encounter know from my vesture that my affections are Godward; that sixteen years ago in a small chapel in England, I took off the old clothes of sin and was garbed in Jesus. I aspire to more such days, although I am not sure they are the kind of thing that can be sought. They might instead be something to ask for, and to hope to receive. What we are asking for, of course, is not clothing that is more articulate, but that our disposition—which is indeed on display, often to a greater extent than we wish—would be more congruent with the Jesus whom we wear.

C lothing not only creates bonds between individuals, such as the understanding between the bereaved

Through their wearing apparel, people can
say subtle or important things that they
could not or would not utter directly.

—Linda Baumgarten

mourner and her neighbor. It also creates communities and sustains communal identity. This is why all the students at the girls' school where I recently served as interim chaplain often wore Saint Mary's School sweats; clothing emblazoned with their school's name marked them as members of a student body, as members of a particular academic community. This is why the sorority sisters I passed on Franklin Street last week were all wearing matching shirts, identical except for the color (each gal sported a different shade of sherbet); the shirts helped constitute their relationship as "sisters." This is why my own sister dressed herself and her daughter in matching outfits for a formal photograph a few years ago: the dresses mark and support their familial identity. Clothing makes community.

There is an underside, of course—as clothing creates community, it also creates borders and boundaries between people. Each week I teach at a women's prison. Half of the students are incarcerated, and half are students enrolled at Duke Divinity School. My co-teacher Sarah and I work hard to level as many distinctions as we can between the two student groups, so that they might come to understand themselves, for a brief two hours every week,

In every culture, clothing not only is utilitarian but also symbolizes a person's or group's identity.

—Sarah A. Chase

as fellow students learning together, equal in our classroom if nowhere else in society. To that end, we remind our Duke students that their classmates do not have access to computers, and we ask them to handwrite their papers. We remind our Duke students that the incarcerated women cannot Google the Dukies and find their secrets shared in publicly available court records or newspaper accounts, and we ask the women from Duke to refrain from seeking out their classmates' criminal justice histories online. These measures help create a sense of community and equality in a classroom marked by deep political, economic, and social distinctions. But there is one visible boundary in our classroom that Sarah and I can't do anything about—half the students (and the two teachers) come to class each week wearing whatever cute skirts and cardigans and earrings struck our fancy that morning. The other half of the class is wearing seafoam-green uniforms. When speaking for themselves as a group, the incarcerated women often say, "Those of us in green . . ." The uniforms are a forceful reminder of the capacity of clothing to reinforce social and political divisions.

The prison provides an illustration, too, of the ability of clothing to blur those distinctions. Each week, about thirty minutes into class, the prison has "count." During count, we all stay put while two correctional officers go through the campus counting each body, making sure every incarcerated woman is where she is supposed to be. In our classroom, where there are as many guests to the prison as residents, the officers count clothing. They are looking not for twelve women but for twelve bodies clothed in seafoam green. Last week one of the Duke students happened to wear a sweater that matched the uniforms precisely. The officers got confused—they kept counting an extra incarcerated body than should have been in that room. Finally the incarcerated women counted off out loud—one, two, three—and the officers left. Clothing had, for a brief moment, blurred the distinctions between imprisoned and free.

Prison is not the only place where clothing underlines socioeconomic distinctions. For many centuries, countries in the Western world had sumptuary laws that dictated, for example, that only the wealthy could wear clothes with lace or gold thread. In our current era, clothing recreates class divisions all the time: consider the way girls at elite boarding schools solidify their social and class status by wearing Uggs, Tori Burch riding boots, Vineyard Vines dresses, and Barbour jackets.

But clothing need not always create borders between people. Clothes can also minimize divisions. That is one of the chief arguments for school uniforms: in addition to reducing friction between parents and teens every morning and reducing violence in schools (especially in schools where, without uniforms, clothing might mark gang membership), school uniforms "serve as a social and economic equalizer" among students, and create environments where income is not advertised by shirts and slacks, and friendship and learning are possible across class lines.

Another social division clothing can either make or unmake is gender. Clothing helps make someone, and mark someone as, feminine or masculine. (This is true today, of course, but it was also true when Paul wrote to the Galatians: for example, married women wore a garment called a stola, "a large sleeveless overgarment with narrow shoulders," which was a mark of virtue and modesty. As my colleague Brittany Wilson explained to me when I stopped her in the hallway, this garment was part of what marked Roman women, in life and in art, as "distinctly not male.") Alternatively, clothing can erode social norms around masculinity and femininity. This is why folks in earlier decades were so anxious about women wearing slacks, and why the question "Who wears the pants in this relationship?" packs such a punch.

Paul addresses this in Galatians: "There is neither Jew nor Greek, there is neither slave nor free, there is no male and female, for you are one in Christ Jesus." To understand Christ as clothing is to understand a certain holy gender-bending. I do not think it is a coincidence that Paul's declaration that we, the baptized, have been clothed in Christ comes right before Paul's equally famous insistence that "we are all one in Christ Jesus": Christ is the clothing that has the power to say no male and female. In fact, all three of the distinctions that Paul explicitly names as undone by Jesus—male/female, Jew/Greek, slave/free—are distinctions that, at various points in history, have been created in part through clothing. For example, in the Middle Ages, the church demanded that Jews wear special sartorial markers: as the Fourth Lateran Council of 1215 declared, in order to prevent "pious Christians" from having sex with Jews or "Saracens," "such persons of either sex, in every Christian

province and at all times, are to be distinguished in public from other people by the character of their dress." And
many slave societies have attempted to set apart slaves by
their clothing: in ancient Rome, lawmakers tried to distinguish enslaved women from free women by dress. Even in
societies where slavery was racialized and enslaved people
more easily identifiable by skin color (and, indeed, their free
kin more easily mistaken for slaves), slaveowners clothed
slaves distinctively: in the eighteenth-century Caribbean, for
example, it was typical for planters to order the linen from
which they would have slaves' clothing made "dyed a distin-
guishing color to help identify slaves."

On Paul's terms, Jesus is not the kind of clothing that
creates social divisions but the kind of clothing that un-
does them. Jesus is not a Vineyard Vines dress or a Barbour
jacket; He is the school uniform that erases boundaries between people. Or at least that is the kind of clothing Jesus
wants to be. When those of us clothed in Him trespass
boundaries in His name, we allow Him to be that school
uniform; when we put up walls in the name of Jesus, we are
turning the Lord into an expensive designer dress.

It is late on Thursday night; I got home from the prison
about an hour ago. Lying in bed, I see a window and two
closets. My husband often leaves the closet doors open,
which drives me insane. As I lie here, my thoughts bounce
from the mundane to the holy and back again: what will
I wear to work tomorrow? (Predictably, I feel that I have
"no clothes" even as I do not have space for all the clothes
I obviously do have.) Should I purchase a seafoam-green

cardigan and wear it every Thursday night as a minuscule, condescending act of solidarity with my incarcerated sisters in Christ? How can I remove the clothes that set me apart from other people and instead wear God? How can I even ask these questions while lying in this bedroom that I just renovated, paying a carpenter several hundred dollars to build more closets? Do I participate in the holy reordering, the boundary breaking, that Paul speaks of in Galatians? If the answer to that last question is no, can I say with any integrity that I am in fact wearing Jesus?

I am in my red chair reading a monograph about Emily Dickinson and clothing. The author, Daneen Wardrop, explains the nineteenth-century garments (the tippet, the basque) that turn up in Dickinson's poems; she discusses Dickinson's performing seamstress duties for her household; she analyzes the importance of bonnets and lace to Dickinson's writing. It is an absorbing study; I make all kinds of notes. In the book's conclusion, Wardrop asks her reader a question: "How do we tell ourselves apart from what we wear, in the end?" Wardrop goes on to make disturbing observations about the ways that nineteenth-century clothing shaped women's bodies—bustles created a "faux derriere," petticoats limited women's ability to walk. This clothing was so constricting that women eventually got up a movement for "reform dress." Reformers wanted to get rid of corsets and long skirts and replace them with clothes that allowed women to more easily move (and breathe). Perhaps the most famous proposal of the movement was the (never very popular, but highly symbolic and hotly debated) "bloomer costume"—essentially a short dress with a pair of trousers gathered at the ankle, named for the activist Amelia Bloomer.

Wardrop's analysis is making me think about Jesus—is Jesus the constricting corset, or is Jesus the bloomers that give women freedom of movement?

Just as I am beginning to preach a sermon in my head about how some Christians have worn Jesus as a corset and others have worn Jesus as reform dress, I come to this: "the body interacts and changes places with apparel as we wear it, changing ruffle to ankle, in the vision of one motion. We let it affect the way we move, the way we interact, the way we shape affection, the means by which we negotiate others' opinions of our social standing, the way we cognize our own body."

Wardrop intends only to exegete Emily Dickinson—she is not trying to exegete Paul. But in her analysis, I hear Paul telling me something about my life with Christ. When I was baptized, I was clothed in Christ, and the God who is

**The Lord Jesus Christ himself . . . is said
to be the clothing of the saints.**

—Origen

clothing is the God who wants to shape me more and more into the image of Jesus. I need to let Jesus, my clothing, affect the way I move. I need to let Jesus affect the way I interact, the way I shape affection, the means by which I negotiate others' opinions of me. I need to let Jesus affect the way I perceive my own body. What if I could say "My body interacts and changes places with Jesus as I wear Him"?

G od clothes. God is our clothing. And, finally, God draws us into the act of clothing, by instructing us to clothe others. Consider the Epistle of James. The famous

"See the day-spring from afar
Usher'd by the morning star!"
Haste; to him who sends the light,
Hallow the remains of night.
Souls, put on your glorious dress,
Waking into righteousness:
Cloth'd with Christ aspire to shine,
Radiance he of light divine;
Beam of the eternal beam,
He in God, and God in him!
Strive we him in us to see,
Transcript of the deity.

—Charles Wesley

"faith without works" passage speaks specifically of our obligation to clothe people:

> What good is it, my brothers and sisters, if you say you have faith but do not have works? Can faith save you? If a brother or sister is naked and lacks daily food, and one of you says to them, "Go in peace; keep warm and eat your fill," and yet you do not supply their bodily needs, what is the good of that? So faith by itself, if it has no works, is dead.

Jesus makes the same point in Matthew 25, when he tells his disciples that every time they clothe a cold, naked person, they are in fact clothing Him, and every time they ignore someone who needs clothes, they are ignoring Him:

> Then the King will say to those on his right, "Come, you who are blessed by my Father; take your inheritance, the kingdom prepared for you since the creation of the world. For I was hungry and you gave me something to eat, I was thirsty and you gave me something to drink, I was a stranger and you invited me in, I needed clothes and you clothed me, I was sick and you looked after me, I was in prison and you came to visit me."
>
> Then the righteous will answer him, "Lord, when did we see you hungry and feed you, or thirsty and give you something to drink? When did we see you a stranger and invite you in, or needing clothes and

clothe you? When did we see you sick or in prison and go to visit you?"

The King will reply, "Truly I tell you, whatever you did for one of the least of these brothers and sisters of mine, you did for me."

Then he will say to those on his left, "Depart from me, you who are cursed, into the eternal fire prepared for the devil and his angels. For I was hungry and you gave me nothing to eat, I was thirsty and you gave me nothing to drink, I was a stranger and you did not invite me in, I needed clothes and you did not clothe me, I was sick and in prison and you did not look after me."

They also will answer, "Lord, when did we see you hungry or thirsty or a stranger or needing clothes or sick or in prison, and did not help you?"

He will reply, "Truly I tell you, whatever you did not do for one of the least of these, you did not do for me."

Jesus offers this command to clothe other people as a basic norm, a test even, for discipleship and hospitality. God clothes us, and then God invites us to join God in the business of clothing others. When I remember God's clothing Adam and Eve in Genesis 3, I realize that to donate onesies to your neighborhood baby clothes drive, or to purchase a wardrobe for a refugee family that your church has adopted, or to take a formerly incarcerated woman shopping for professional clothing is not just to participate in charitable good work. To do those things is to involve yourself in the choreography of divine action. It makes you a mimic of God, and it shapes you more and more into God's image.

Since, in Paul's account, there is an intimacy between Jesus and clothing, when we give someone trousers or a shirt or a down vest, we are doing more than just offer-

Several years ago, having miscarried a cherished pregnancy on the day after Christmas, I found myself seemingly screwed to my bed with depression, unable to work, read or pray. I was, however, able to talk on the phone. Day after day I wore out my friends, especially my friend Kay. The year before, Kay had left behind a job, salary and colleagues to spend a year in prayer and silence. Violating her dearly bought solitude again and again, I cried on the phone, "I am so depressed that I can't even pray. I try to pray, but I can't." A few days later, a package arrived from Kay. It contained a simple beige jumper and a note that read, "I have prayed in this dress every day for a year. You don't have to pray. Just wear it. It is full of prayers." I did wear that dress. I wore it and wept in it, and cried out Why? to God in it. I let the prayers in that dress pray for me when my mouth was dry and full of ashes. And when I became pregnant again, I continued to wear that dress. Kay loves long, loose clothes, and her dress was spacious enough to accompany me nearly to the end of my ninth month. Her prayers were spacious enough, too, to gather up my fear and grief and anger. And my joy, when it came.

—Stephanie Paulsell

ing clothing. In some oblique, metaphorical, yet quite real way, we are offering Jesus Himself. And in a strange circle, it is Jesus who receives this offering, for when we give people clothing, we are not just caring for the people; circuitously, but straight through Matthew 25, we are also caring for God, as God tenderly cared for us before telling us we had to leave the garden.

I t is October. I have been sitting in my red chair a lot lately, praying those verses from Genesis 3 where God clothes Adam and Eve and then sends them out into the world. I have been using a mode of prayer developed in the sixteenth century by Ignatius of Loyola. Ignatian prayer is all about hearing God speak to you through the scriptures. You pick a passage of scripture—I find that narrative passages are the best fit for Ignatian prayer—and, using all your senses, you imagine the story and scene. What does the garden of Eden look like? What is the soundscape? What do you smell when you breathe in deep through your nose? What's the temperature? How does the air feel on your arms?

And then, as you find the scene in your imagination, you imagine yourself as a character in the story. Maybe you are Eve, or Adam, or the serpent, or the tree, or a toucan who is looking in on it all. Maybe you are one of the rabbits whose fur became Adam and Eve's first clothing. Maybe you are just you, somehow transported to the garden. Imagine yourself in the story; allow yourself to encounter

the place and to encounter God in that place, and see what
God has for you, in that place, in that story. I am praying
Genesis 3 and picturing God making clothes for me. The
air is thick with shame and with love. I am sitting here in
one of my ubiquitous shapeless black dresses. In my prayer,
I am thinking about bodies and shame.

There is a lot of shame shot through this Genesis story,
of course: Adam and Eve's shame about eating from the
forbidden tree; what seems to be their shame about their
bodies. I am feeling in the garden the shame I carry about
my own body. I so rarely even name this shame to myself;
layers and layers of feminist politics and willed insistence
that I love my body as it is keep me, most of the time, from
a direct encounter with the shame.

But the shame is there. It weighs exactly twenty pounds.
It is about ten years old. The body I would feel unashamed
of, the body I believe I could delight in, is twenty pounds
thinner—what my body looked like a decade ago.

Clothing plays an ambiguous role in this dance of my
body and shame. I clothe my body to hide the parts I most
hate, and yet the clothes themselves bespeak the shame,
because if I were thinner, I would wear something else,
not this shapelessness, not these cat's-eye glasses and cow-
boy boots that pull attention from my hips to my eyes or
my toes.

And there is another layer of shame here: it never seems
to end, for women, this tricky dance, "the long struggle
to be at home in the body, this difficult friendship." This
additional layer of shame presented itself when I started
running two months ago. I did not start running to lose

weight or to reshape my body. I started running because the dance class I had been taking conflicts with my teaching schedule this term; and in time I realize I am running because I am tired of feeling defeated by my body (I want to feel strong); and in time I realize I am running because I am angry at my husband, and I need somewhere for the anger to go. But regardless of my high-minded insistence that I am not running *in order* to reshape my body, a small reshaping happens. My calf muscles change. My stomach changes, a little. I don't keep a scale in the house, but I bet I have lost three pounds, or five. I feel delighted by these changes. I put on a neon yellow running shirt so that the cars can see me in the early light, and it hugs my body, and I feel delighted. And then I feel ashamed of my delight—this is not good feminism; I am not supposed to care about this. I am supposed to love my body because God made it and called it good, not because I lost five pounds; I am supposed to love it regardless of whether I lose or gain those pounds because this is the body God gave me and it is the body I will be for eternity and this body does good and faithful things, like study and pray and teach and cook and eat and, yes, even run. This difficult friendship, this constant shame.

Perhaps, if I sit inside Genesis 3 long enough, I might come to know that God is not hidden from my body, my body that holds delight and shame. Perhaps I will come to know that God is in fact intimately pressed up against my body, as near as a camisole or a neon running shirt. That God is as close to my shame as this shawl is to my shoulders. That God is pressed up against *all* the corrosive shame in my life—not just the shame I feel about my body, but all my whatever-else shame, all the many pockets of curdling shame and regret I carry. While I feel cloaked with shame, God is tenderly stitching me a suit of clothes. The clothing is God's own self.

I suspect that if I could receive this, something small but important would change. I suspect that the way I inhabit myself would be different if my spinning, whirling brain could receive this, if my heart could receive it, if my *body* could receive it. If I could know that God wants to nestle up close to the places of my shame, as close as clothing— then the shame would dissolve. Anything God wants to nestle against is not shameful, so if I actually believed that God wanted to be close to my curdling, the shame would dissolve, and I would be slightly less hidden from God, or from myself.

"You are always in God's sight comely, always in God's sight lovely, always in God's sight as though you were perfect. For ye are complete in Christ Jesus, and perfect in Christ Jesus. . . . Always do you stand completely washed and fully clothed in Christ." Those are the words of Charles Spurgeon, the great nineteenth-century English preacher,

Clothing is our most intimate environment.

—Susan M. Watkins

taking up Paul's sartorial idiom to describe how beautiful redeemed men and women appear to God.

Always in God's sight lovely. Always.

I will try believing that for one day.

A PRAYER

Awake, I beseech thee, O my soul, and let the fire of a heavenly love be kindled in thy heart, and wisely consider the beauty which Thy Lord God hath bestowed upon thee. . . . For doth not He who maketh thee to abide in Him, and hath condescended to dwell in thee, clothe thee, cover thee, adorn thee with Himself? *As many of you,* saith the Apostle, *as have been baptized into Christ, have put on Christ.*

What praise, what thanksgiving wilt thou rightly bestow upon Him, who hath clothed thee with so great beauty, exalted thee to so great honour, that thou canst say with all joy of heart, *The Lord hath clothed me with the garments of salvation, He hath covered me with the robe of righteousness.* It is the highest joy of the angels of God to contemplate Christ, and lo, of His boundless condescension He so far inclineth unto thee, as to be pleased to clothe thee with Himself.

—Anselm of Canterbury

Smell

The sight of You delights, Your smell is
sweet, Your mouth is holy. . . .
Your eyes are merry with delight at all who kiss You,
Your lips distill the fragrance of life,
While balsam flows from Your fingertips.
Who can set eyes on You and not
breathe in Your fragrance? . . .
How lovely are You in every way.
Even Your mouth's murmur tells of Your Father.
How gorgeous is Your beauty, how sweet
[Your] smell . . . O infant God!

—ANONYMOUS SYRIAC HYMN

My students know I am interested in Christian kitsch—my office is littered with Jesus paint-by-numbers from the Eisenhower era and I run a perpetual contest for the most sentimental St. Francis paraphernalia. Once in a blue moon, a devoted student brings a contribution to the cause: last month, it was a candle from an Illinois-based company called His Essence. The founders of the company, Bob and Karen Tosterud, take their inspiration from Psalm 45:8: "All your robes are fragrant with myrrh and aloes and cassia." Interpreting this as a reference to how Jesus's robes will smell when He returns, the Tosteruds have "carefully combine[d] these ingredients and the result is a fragrance which serves as a reminder of His Presence." Their other offerings include the Resurrection candle, based on Nicodemus's myrrh and aloe (see John 19:39–40), and the Adoration candle, inspired by the three wise men's frankincense and myrrh. The Tosteruds hope the candles will help those who light them "Sense Him in a new way." My student brought me a Servanthood candle (John 12:3): "Mary took about a pint of pure nard, an expensive perfume; she poured it on Jesus's feet and wiped his feet with her hair. And the house was filled with the fragrance of the perfume." I didn't tell the student that I already knew about His Essence candles (I've actually been burning them for years). I did tell her she could write a paper about smelling as a spiritual practice, if she wished.

Senses and sensory perception pervade the Bible. People see and gaze. Joseph sees his brothers' hunger; Mary Magdalene sees that the stone had been moved away from the tomb. People hear. People listen, to one another and to God—or sometimes fail to listen and are chastised. People praying the psalms can taste the Lord's sweetness.

It is not just people whom the Bible depicts as sensory perceivers. Both Old and New Testaments speak of God as one who shares sensory perception with us. As the King James has it,

> He that planted the ear, shall he not hear? he that formed the eye, shall he not see?

In contrast to idols who "have ears, but do not hear; noses, but do not smell . . . have hands, but do not feel," God "looks on the earth and it trembles" and "touches the moun-

When a man's senses are perfectly united to God, then what God has said is somehow mysteriously clarified. But when there is no union of this kind, then it is extremely difficult to speak about God.

—John Climacus

tains and they smoke." God's eyes are upon the righteous and God's ears are attentive to their cry. Even the names of minor characters in scripture remind people that God hears and sees. Six people get the name Elishama—"God heard." Hazael, "God has looked," was king of Aram. The name Shemaiah(u), "God has listened," appears over and over.

What about the sense of smell? In the West, we have learned to be visual people who overwhelmingly privilege sight, and, to a lesser extent, hearing. This sensory hierarchy is millennia old. Aristotle ranked the senses, putting smell squarely in the middle, between the "intellective"

And by his smelling in awe of the Lord, and not by [what] his eyes see, will [the Messiah] judge, and not by [what] his ears hear, will he decide.

—Isaiah 11:3

The ear is sometimes deceived in hearing sounds, which are only imaginary; the eye, too, sees things in motion, which in reality are at rest; the sense of smell alone is not deceived.

—Ibn Ezra, commenting on Isaiah 11:3

We ought to attend, first of all, to the metaphor in the verb *smell,* which means that Christ will be so shrewd that he will not need to learn from what he hears, or from what he sees; for by *smelling* alone he will perceive what would otherwise be unknown.

—John Calvin, commenting on Isaiah 11:3

senses (sight and hearing) and the "lower bodily senses" (taste and touch). The long-standing demotion of smell, taste, and touch became more pronounced around the sixteenth century: as people grew increasingly interested in pursuing refinement, emphasizing manners, politeness, and bodily elegance, the "lower" senses, especially smell, came to seem discomfiting and rude. Technology and philosophy also contributed to the marginalization of smell, as Enlightenment-era people became more and more invested in interpreting the data our senses perceived, and more and more intrigued by new inventions such as the microscope and the stethoscope (which sharpened certain senses but not others). This does not mean that smell was wholly ignored. Quite the contrary: under the ministrations of Freud, smell came to signify both eroticism and regression. Freud lauded vision's triumph over "intermittent olfactory stimuli," interpreting the centrality of the visual as a victory of human maturity, integration, and restraint over perversion

Smell may have been disparaged in much Western thought, but it often held the attention of biblical writers. The God of the Bible smells, in both senses of the term: God emits a fragrance, but more centrally in biblical texts, God inhales aromas and perceives scent. Specifically, God perceives the smell of sacrifices—this is mentioned some forty times in the Hebrew Bible. Smell first figures significantly in the scriptures in Genesis 8. This is the tail end of the story of Noah's ark. After the flood had receded, after the earth was dry and Noah and his wife and their sons and daughters-in-law left the ark, Noah made "burnt offerings" of animals and birds to the Lord. "And when the LORD smelled the pleasing odor," God pledged to never again destroy the earth. In addition to smelling Noah's "burnt offering," God also smells incense offerings: over and over in Exodus, Leviticus, and Numbers, we read of incense. It was lit twice daily, and on Yom Kippur (the Day of Atonement, the most sacred day of the year in the Hebrew calendar), the high priest brought incense into the Holy of Holies, where the Divine was especially present. When the Bible describes God's accepting one of these incense offerings, it speaks of a *reah nihoah,* a soothing odor. Human beings, in an effort to get God's attention or communicate with God, burned fragrant incense, and God found the incense to be a "soothing smell" and accepted the sacrifice.

This language has grabbed my attention and will not let go. Most of the time, the sacrificial system of the Bible feels alien to me; praying with words has, for my entire life, been the main thing I do to interact with God, and it is hard for me to wrap my head around the logic of sacrifices. But the language of God's accepting a soothing smell makes a certain sense to me—after all, I have experience with being soothed by scent. I have spritzed lavender on my pillowcases, and the scent has helped me fall asleep. I have walked into the kitchen after a maddening day at work and felt my whole body relax when I smell soup on the stove. I can imagine God being calmed in a similar way.

According to some scholars, the incense was a sort of aromatherapy for God. As Deborah Green puts it, the aroma of incense would "calm [God] and change his mood. Quite literally, incense is a 'soothing odor'—it has the power to lure and to calm and thereby to restrain or appease God's anger." Green goes on to explain that incense sacrifices, unlike other sacrifices performed by Israelite priests, did not "celebrate holiness, or rectify impurity. . . . The incense sacrifice is for God to smell and to enjoy just as humans smell and enjoy incense and perfume." The scent of incense is simply pleasing. It gets God's attention and calms God and thereby protects the priests "from God's holiness or wrath."* Indeed, the practice of lighting incense—the practice of offering God something pleasing to smell—is, in Green's assessment, "one of the primary modes of interaction and communication with God in the Hebrew Bible." The biblical portrait of God as one who smells may initially appear to be just a bit of quirky anthropomorphism, but it is in fact a ritual shorthand for God's intimate and close connection with us.

---

*In biblical Hebrew, the expression that means "to be angry" is literally "to have an inflamed nose." So when we read in our English Bibles that Job's friend Elihu "became angry," the Hebrew says Elihu's nose was inflamed. The idiom makes a certain kind of sense: picture a horse, snorting in anger, or consider whether you in fact flare your nostrils when ticked off. (I do.) So too with God; when God promises, through the prophet Jeremiah, to fight Zedekiah "in great wrath," the Hebrew says "with a nose snorting with rage." Conversely, a Hebrew idiom for patience is *erech apayim,* literally "long noses"—one who is patient has a long, or unscrunched, nonflared nose. That human beings should attempt to calm God's angry nose with soothing incense makes idiomatic and lexical sense.

To describe God as one who smells—as one who enjoyed the smell of all that incense—is to imply something about God's emotional life. It turns out that, of all of our sensory perceptions, smell is the most directly connected to the seat of our emotions. As cognitive neuroscientist Rachel Herz explains, "The neurological interconnection between the sense of smell (olfaction) and emotion is uniquely intimate. The areas of the brain that process smell and emotion are as intertwined and codependent as any two regions of the brain could possibly be." Both smell and emotion are located within the limbic system. The amygdala—"the brain's locus of emotion," without which we can neither remember nor express emotion—becomes activated when we perceive a scent. "No other sensory system has this kind

You called, You cried, You shattered my deafness.
You sparkled, You blazed, You drove away my blindness.
You shed Your fragrance, and I drew in my breath
and I pant for You.
I tasted and now I hunger and thirst.
You touched me, and now I burn with longing
for Your peace.

—Augustine

of privileged and direct access to the part of the brain that controls our emotions." Smells can trigger emotions. (So can the sudden absence of smell. People who, due to an accident or a virus, lose their sense of smell are often plunged into depression.) And, according to Herz's research, smells can also "*become* emotions. . . . [O]dors can literally be transformed into emotions through association and then act as proxies for emotions themselves, influencing how we feel, how we think, and how we act."

Scents can help calm people when they are separated. Psychologists call this "olfactory comfort." This is why women sometimes sleep in their beloved's clothing when the beloved is away. Smelling someone's scent can infuse you, the smeller, with a sense of security. (Having observed that a child feeling intense separation anxiety was reassured by a garment with his mother's smell, a nurse in Minnesota invented a soft shirt that could be easily converted into a blanket. The idea is that mom would wear the shirt next to her skin for a few hours before heading off to work or out on a date, and baby, now wrapped in her scent, will

"Smell"—as the matter emitted from a thing, its being sensed, and the sensory communion of smelling—links self and other, in such a way that the fragrant or odorous other gives of its essence and is taken into the body of the self.

—Anne F. Elvey

be less hysterical when she steps out the door.) Mothers whose children have left for college report going into their old bedrooms, closing the door, and inhaling the smell as a way of feeling close to their absent kids.

I like to think of God's inhaling all that incense in the context of this olfactory comfort. God has, since Eden, been inviting us into intimate communion with God's own self; God has been inviting us into divine life, drawing us into divine life, and we are participants in that divine life—yet we remain separated from God. The final book of the Bible tells us that the "prayers of the saints" are, in fact, incense carried in golden bowls. It is the smell of our prayers that connects us to God, and God finds the smell comforting.

S mells are hard to describe. How do you describe the smell of an orange (without reference to something very

Prayers when they reach heaven become fragrant roses, pouring out their holy perfume before God. As from gardens of flowers blooming on the earth, fragrance rises, sweetening all the air, so from homes and hearts of praying ones, God's children in this world, there rises continually to God holy incense, a pure offering, sweet fragrance. God smells a sweet savor when we pray believingly, sincerely, adoringly, with love.

—J. R. Miller

similar, like the smell of a tangerine)? I find this so challenging that I now give it as an exercise to my creative writing students: in a sentence, convey to someone with no sense of smell what cinnamon buns smell like; in a paragraph, capture the smell of lavender. Smells are almost always, writes Deborah Green, described by "simile, metaphor, or metonym."

As is God. Hence the very book you hold in your hands.

I devote hours each week—in the classroom, in the pulpit, at my computer—to the task of putting words to my experience, and the church's experience, of God. The whole archive of Judaism and Christianity represents forays into such description. All of these images for God, from vine to shepherd to rock, are attempts to say something about God and how we meet and are met by God. Sometimes the words seem apt. And sometimes they seem as limited and useless as my efforts to describe the smell of a cinnamon bun.

According to the New Testament, God, on the cross, emits fragrance.

Almost every time I have ever attended a celebration of the Holy Eucharist, the priest says these words as the offertory sentence, the sentence that precedes bringing the bread and wine to the altar: "Walk in love, as Christ loved us and gave himself for us, an offering and sacrifice to God." That sentence comes from the fifth chapter of Ephesians, but if you open your Bible and look at the text, you will notice that it says something a little different than the version that gets quoted at the Eucharist: "And walk in love, as also the Christ did love us, and did give himself for us, an offering and a sacrifice to God for an odour of a sweet smell," or, as the King James has it, "And walk in love, as Christ also hath loved us, and hath given himself for us an offering and a sacrifice to God for a sweet-smelling savour." When Jesus was on the cross, He smelled to his father like all that incense: a sweet-smelling savour.

On Sunday, I am celebrating Communion at the tiny church in Louisburg, North Carolina, where I lead worship about once a month. I boldly try out the longer formulation:

> Walk in love, as Christ loves us, and gave Himself
> for us, an offering and a sacrifice, a soothing aroma
> to God.

I wonder if anyone in the congregation will notice the added sensory words. I don't think much about them myself, until the service has ended and I am helping the Altar Guild put away the silver chalice and the linens. Then it occurs to me that I have thought, before, about how the Eucharist tastes, and how it feels in my mouth. I have not devoted much thought to its scent. How does this particular soothing aroma smell? The wine smells sharp. The wafers smell like playing cards. But the smell I most associate with this rite is the smell of the people. Lizzy's perfume. The blunt leather of Bob's jacket. The lotion, which smells so much like my grandmother's, as I bend to put the wafer in Miss Dottie's open hands. Later, when I am at home setting the table for dinner, I think: if I stay at this church for years and years, it will one day be the case that, for me, the smell of the Eucharist will be the smell of Miss Dottie's hand cream.

But as Pomanders and wood
       Still are good,
Yet being bruised and better scented;
God, to show how far his love
       Could improve,
Here, as broken, is presented.

—George Herbert

"He gave himself for us, an offering, and a sacrifice to God, for a sweet smelling savour." Not that God took any delight or content in the bitter sufferings of Christ, simply and in themselves considered; but with relation to the end for which he was offered, even our redemption and salvation.

—John Flavel

Christ is the flower of Mary, who sprouted forth from a virginal womb to spread the good odor of faith throughout the whole world, as he himself said: "I am the flower of the field, and the lily of the valley" (Song 2:1). The flower, even when cut, keeps its odor, and when bruised increases it, and when torn does not lose it; so, too, the Lord Jesus on that gibbet of the cross neither failed when bruised, nor fainted when torn; and when cut by the pricking of the lance, made more beautiful by the sacred color of the outpoured blood, He grew young again, Himself not knowing how to die and exhaling among the dead the gift of eternal life.

—Ambrose of Milan

The author of Ephesians was not the only person in the early church to suggest that Jesus emitted a fragrance. Ephrem of Syria called Jesus the Glorious Lily, and the Treasure of Perfume. Just as God's smelling our incense quickens the encounter between human and divine, so too does our inhaling the scent of Christ, the "Fragrance of Life." As historian Susan Ashbrook Harvey has explained in *Scenting Salvation,* people today tend to think of revelation as something experienced through hearing or seeing (hearing the revelation at Mount Sinai, seeing the burning bush or the Light of Christ), but writers in the early church understood smell as a carrier of revelation. The notion of seeing God or hearing God seemed to imply that human beings and the divine would interact "face to face as distinct realities." Early Christian writers found in olfaction a means by which the human and the divine could "intermingle . . . in a communion of being. . . . [T]o smell God was to know God as a transcendent yet transforming presence, a presence actively known through bodily experience." Because smell travels sometimes far from the object emitting smell, you could smell God even if God wasn't appearing right next to you in some sort of rare theophany. You could, for example, smell God by attending worship—inhaling the incense used at church, inhaling the fragrant scent of holy oil. While this was not exactly the same thing as smelling God, it was understood that "knowledge of God was instilled in the believer who inhaled the scent of worship." If, in the Hebrew Bible, incense conveyed something of people to God, in early Christian worship, incense "conveyed divine presence" to the people. Jesus breathed out the "fragrance of His life" upon the cross, and that fragrance was elusively present, reprised in the incense lit during the liturgy.

Paul spoke of another way that Christians might smell Jesus. In his second letter to the church at Corinth, Paul wrote, "We are the aroma of Christ to God among those who are being saved and among those who are perishing; to the one a fragrance from death to death, to the other a fragrance from life to life." After the cross, after the resurrection and ascension, Jesus still emits a smell, and we, it seems, are it. But while Jesus emits a distinct scent, that scent doesn't smell the same to all people—or, alternately, the same scent doesn't smell the same to the same person all the time. Those who are turned toward God will find the

And we, as often as we hear anything of good people, draw in as it were through our nostrils a breath of sweetness. And when Paul the Apostle said, "We are a good odor of Christ unto God," it is plainly given to him to be understood that he exhibited himself as a savor indeed to the present, but as an odor to the absent. We therefore, while we cannot be nourished by the savor of your presence, are so by the odor of your absence.

—Gregory the Great, writing to a friend he missed

smell of Jesus-in-us delightful; those who are turned away will find it noxious.

On one level, Paul seems to be saying, simply, that the baptized are agents of Jesus—we carry information about God with us everywhere we go. Paul could have, perhaps, written, "We are the light of Christ among those who are being saved and among those who are perishing" or "Our voices are the voice of Christ among those who are saved and those

A student of mine called me late one evening after worship. He was really excited on the other end, and I had to ask him to slow down. So, he says, "Mother Kim, this strange thing happened to me today. After worship tonight, I was riding the train back to my apartment, when this woman sat down next to me. I had my earbuds in, so I wasn't really paying her any attention, but she tapped me to get my attention. She said, 'Son, you smell like church. You smell like church.'"

Now the Apostle Paul tells us in his letter to the Corinthians that those who know Christ have a particular smell. When we come to know God—come to trust and believe in the power of God's love, there's an aroma, a fragrance that lingers in the room even after we leave. To borrow from the words of the woman on the train, when we encounter God, we begin to "smell like church." Or to borrow from Paul, "We smell like Christ."

. . . That evening on the phone with my student, I asked him what happened next. He said, "She started to cry. And she looked up at me and said, 'Thank you. I haven't been to church in a long time.'"

—Kimberly Jackson

who are perishing." But smell is an apt metaphor for Paul to use, precisely because smell can convey the presence of something that is far away. I smell bread baking the minute I walk through my front door, even though the source—the loaf in the oven—is in the kitchen; the smell tells me the loaf is there somewhere. So, too, the Source of whatever goodness the baptized do and are is far away—but the goodness insists the Source is there somewhere. My friend Sarah and her family provide a regular illustration of this. They keep open a Christ room in their home, and they always seem to be welcoming yet another woman, recently released from prison, to live with them for a few months. Their hospitality is much like smell: as the scent of bread testifies to its source (the bread in the oven), so Sarah's hospitality testifies to the hospitality's Source—which is not, finally, Sarah herself. Sarah is one of

The aroma of the knowledge of God comes from Christ and through Christ. The reason why Paul said "aroma" was this: Some things are recognized by their smell, even though they are invisible. God, who is invisible, wishes to be understood through Christ. The preaching of Christ reaches our ears just as an aroma reaches our nostrils, bringing God and his only-begotten Son right into the midst of his creation. A person who speaks the truth about Christ is just such a good aroma from God, worthy of praise from the one who believes. But one who makes erroneous assertions about Christ has a bad smell to believers and unbelievers alike.

—Ambrosiaster

the strongest people I know, but she is not strong enough to do all this welcoming of strangers on her own steam. Her capacity for such hospitality comes from, and points to, the God who welcomes us and bids us to welcome others. Sarah's hospitality becomes the aroma of Christ, and if I let it, it will direct my attention to its Source: to Jesus, the Fragrance of Life, the Treasure of Perfumes.

There is, of course, an underside to Paul's words. The aroma of Christ only smells sweet to "those being saved"—to those turning or turned toward God. To people who are turned away from God, Christ smells like death. When people attuned to Jesus see other people practicing love and mercy, they are pleased; when people not attuned to Jesus see goodness, they can be unnerved. What is lovely to those who appreciate the Lord is unlovely to those who don't. So the aroma of Christ is diagnostic: it will help me learn where my own attentions and affections are—Godward, or not.

In truth, all of us but the saints are sometimes turned toward God and sometimes turned away; or all of us but the saints are always partially turned toward God and partially curved in on ourselves. Observing (smelling) Sarah's hospitality doesn't always pleasingly put me in mind of Jesus; it doesn't always stretch me more toward goodness, or inflame my desire to be more like the Source. Because of my own curvature and deathly sin, the very same thing—Sarah's hospitality—can smell repugnant to me. On some days I encounter her hospitality and instead of feeling moved to God, I am provoked to endless self-flagellation about my own totally unhospitable life, and I think false and extreme things like "If I can't be Dorothy Day, I may as well just embrace my own selfishness and go to the mall." And then I come up with a list of things to criticize about Sarah (mostly the criticisms stay in my head), or I become consumed with envy, a distorted and distorting near lust for all of the virtues I imagine Sarah possesses (and that I imagine I lack). On those days, a picture (a smell) of a life animated by Christ does not draw me closer to God—it bends me farther into myself. *To the one a fragrance from life to life, to the other a fragrance death to death.*

It is Tuesday, and I am in my friend Maisie's bedroom. Her husband died last year. For months, she wore his button-down Oxford shirts, which he had worn every day to work. She wore them with jeans when she was running errands; she wore them tucked into wool trousers and hidden under a blazer on days when she was teaching; she slept in them. Today, about fourteen months after his death, we are sorting through his closet and dresser drawers, making piles: Goodwill, Maisie's nephews, Maisie's own closet. Maisie swears she can still smell Robert on the Oxford shirts, and she is keeping them.

Absence, it seems, haunts smell. The profound work smell does on and for us presumes absence. People separated by time and space—that baby longing for his mother, the mother pining for the children who have left her empty nest—are reconnected through smell. Smell keeps us close to one another in our absence.

Maybe Maisie is a picture of God. Maybe we should picture God as a widow: God's beloved spouse has been taken
away, and God mourns. The funeral happens on a Tuesday.
There are the casseroles and the sympathetic notes. God
receives a few visits and phone calls—from angels, perhaps, although some of the angels stay away because they
"don't want to impose." And then a few weeks pass, and
the angels forget and go back to their seraphic business, of
singing hymns and delivering messages and mending their
robes, and God is left alone in God's grief. God is beside
Herself with the separation. And God puts on the robe
God's beloved had always worn, and God's grief is eased, a
bit, by the smell.

Is this what our absence feels like to God? Is our absence, our being far off and ignoring God, our remaining at
a distance, our remaining so far away—is this absence not
philosophical and abstract, but grievously real and present to God? Is God undone by grief? Is that the context
in which God receives the scent of our prayers? Is that the
reason God needs to be soothed?

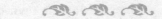

Paul is in an unidentified imperial city. He has been arrested on unspecified charges and sits in a prison, and there
he writes a letter to the church in Philippi. More than the
people to whom Paul writes in some of his other letters,
the people in Philippi seem to be his friends—not only people
he has guided spiritually, but people he feels deeply connected
to, people he genuinely misses. Fred Craddock summarizes

the thrust of the letter thus: "Paul was absent from the Philippians and he wanted to be present, but he was in prison." The letter itself is an effort to bridge the geographical gulf that separates Paul from his Philippian friends. In the body of the letter, Paul discusses love and imprisonment and religious presumption and Jesus's self-emptying obedience and prayer and the resurrection of the Philippians' bodies. Then, near the end of the letter, he thanks the Philippians for sending him a visitor (Epaphroditus) and a gift (probably money).

Scholars have noted that Paul's expression of thanks is a little tortured. Indeed, they have described his thanksgiving with adjectives like "tense, detached, awkward, distant and discourteous." To put it another way, Paul would not have measured up to my mother's standard for the thank-you note, a literary genre she elevated to an art form. First of all, Paul fails to specify what the gift was, and he never directly says "thank you." Then he explains how much he did not need the gift (not in the sense of "Thank you for sending me something I would never have bought myself but just love! You know, the best kind of gift is the one you never knew you needed and then it turns out to be indispensable"; more in the sense of "Thank you—although, as I have tried to tell you every Christmas for the last four years, I really do not need another Santa-shaped soup tureen"). Furthermore, he defers his thanks to the end of the letter, and for the most part, he casts his gratitude in a crass and alienating commercial metaphor: "Not that I seek the gift," ahem, "but I seek the profit that accumulates to your account. I have been paid in full and have more than enough." My mother would have judged Paul's idiom gauche.

But Paul's awkwardly expressed semi-thanks ends with the evocative language of scent: "I have received from Epaphroditus the gifts you sent, a fragrant offering, a sacrifice acceptable and pleasing to God." On one level, of course, this is just another deflection of the gift Paul has received; he is suggesting that the Philippians' gift was not really a gift to him, but to God. ("Dear Grandma, Thank you so much for the generous check you sent for my birthday. I know you wanted me to treat myself to a nice dinner, but I have instead donated the money to the Red Cross.") But Paul did not liken the Philippians' gift to a generic sacrifice to God. He specifically said that it was a fragrant offering, a pleasing aroma to God.

I read this letter, and I think about the women who live in the prison in Raleigh. I think about how often they have described the ways their friends and family members on the outside stay connected to them—sending them money, sending them books. I think about Kaye, who is a lifelong member of a Baptist church in Clayton. Every single week that Kaye has been in prison, a lady from her church has sent her the Sunday worship bulletin, annotated with notes she took during the pastor's sermon and with explanations of why this person or that person is on the prayer list. (Kaye's friend also includes subtly catty scribblings about who was absent from the pews.) I think about how the gift of these bulletins helps Kaye remain connected to the community she is physically separated from and dearly longs to rejoin. I think about how smell bridges absence, how smell can hold together people who love one another and are far apart. However distancing all the commercial language in

Paul's letter, the concluding aromatic language is intimate. More important to Paul than the financial need that this money would meet was its smell; more important than the financial need it would meet was the way it connected him to friends he was absent from, friends "he wanted to be present [with], but he was in prison."

What does it mean to say that my sensory life is entangled with my life with God? What does it mean to say that my olfactory practices—the way I smell scents, and the things I think about the scents I smell—might also be spiritual practices? What does it mean to say that I am to smell Jesus in and on other people?

I think it has to mean something more than squirting some calming lavender around the room or lighting my Servanthood candle before I sit down to pray.

Many years ago, I was volunteering at a food pantry. Most of the volunteers were kindly church ladies devoting a few hours a week to trying to fill the gaps in people's kitchens. It was a good service, a kind of taking literally Jesus's commandment to feed His sheep, and yet there was still a certain noblesse oblige about it all. One day, I overheard one of the older women I worked with say to another woman, "Whoo, there sure is some smell in here!" I couldn't see her, but I pictured her fanning her hand over her face. I knew what she meant: she meant that the people to whom we were handing bags of food stunk. Their clothes were unwashed; their bodies were unwashed. It was a mean and terrible comment, though the woman was not intending to be terrible and mean. I didn't say anything. I didn't whirl around and glare, or say, "Yeah, well, that's what happens when you live in a car and don't have access to a shower or a change of clothes." I don't know what I would say tomorrow if it happened. I hope I would say something, but maybe I would not.

A few months after I started volunteering at the food pantry, I read George Orwell's book about class and working conditions in early-twentieth-century England, *The Road to Wigan Pier*. The book's most famous passage considers smell:

> Here you come to the real secret of class distinctions in the West—the real reason why a European of bourgeois upbringing, even when he calls himself a Communist, cannot without a hard effort think of a working man as his equal. It is summed up in four frightful words which people nowadays are chary of uttering, but which were bandied about quite freely in my childhood. The words were: *The lower classes smell.* That was what we were taught—*the lower classes smell.* And here, obviously, you are at an impassable barrier. . . . It may not greatly matter if the average middle-class person is brought up to believe that the working classes are ignorant, lazy, drunken, boorish, and dishonest; it is when he is brought up to believe that they are dirty that the harm is done. And in my childhood we were brought up to believe that they were dirty. Very early in life you acquired the idea that there was something

subtly repulsive about a working-class body; you would not get nearer to it than you could help.

Orwell said bluntly what sociologists Gale Largey and Rod Watson would phrase more delicately decades later: "Odors, whether real or alleged, are often used as the basis for conferring a moral identity upon an individual or a group."

There is a long history to the conflation of smell and character. At the outset of Isaiah, God is furious at Israel, who is keeping company with idols and ignoring God's mandate to care for the poor and the friendless. Israel's faithlessness has transformed the divine sensorium—because of the people's terrible behavior, their incense no longer pleases God. Now it carries a stench. That is in the first chapter of Isaiah; by the penultimate chapter, it's not the people's incense that offends; it is the smell of the people themselves. They are, declares the Lord, "a stench in my nostrils, an acrid smell that never goes away." Bad people smell bad to (and are spurned by) God.

There is a pointed shock in God's finding Israel—partially because of Israel's failure to care for the poor—malodorous: most of the time, it is the poor who are castigated (by the elite and deodorized) as both putrid and, concomitantly, morally deficient. Still, even as Isaiah reveres the valence of virtue, the olfactory metaphor nonetheless connects scent and rectitude. I worry about Isaiah's suggesting a link between fragrance and virtue, and I worry about Christianity's role in further forging imagined connections between fragrance and probity, fragrance and holiness. In the early church and medieval church, saints were thought to have the smell of sanctity—they were so holy that their bodies, even their corpses, smelled like flowers. What did that imply about people whose bodies smelled like dirt and urine and sweat?

I recently read about a court case that began in Morristown, New Jersey, when a homeless man named Richard Kreimer was barred from his public library because other patrons complained that his smell was keeping them from the library. Kreimer sued. Initially, the courts found in his favor: "If we wish to shield our eyes and noses from the homeless, we should revoke their status, not their library cards," wrote the judge. But on appeal, the judge's ruling was reversed. The court found that Kreimer was exercising his first amendment right to information by using the library, but "since Kreimer's odor was so offensive" to other patrons that they could not use the library, the library's policy of barring Kreimer and his stench was permissible.

In that story, it seems to me, Jesus is Kreimer and Jesus is the first judge.

A few days after I first read about Richard Kreimer, I am in my red chair trying to pray. My mind keeps wandering to last spring, when I joined some friends who were attempting to persuade the Durham City Council to revoke recently adopted laws against panhandling. This mind-wandering, I think, can be a kind of prayer—prayer in which you replay scenes from your day, scenes from your year, and try to see God in them, or try to see them with God standing alongside you, looking too. So here I am, trying to look with God at my sporadic participation in this anti-anti-panhandling effort. What do I see when I try to look with God? Preeminently, the paucity of my fitful liberal do-gooding. I see my own posturing, and my pretense. (Is this prayer? Or just morose preoccupation with myself? Might God convert the second to the first?) But eventually I see Jesus—at the city council committee meeting, I think. And I see Richard Kreimer there, too. Of course, this isn't about seeing after all. It is about smelling, and allowing Jesus to shape the meaning of what I smell.

Perhaps if smelling is to be part of my relationship with God, I might start here: trying to unlearn whatever I have been taught about the relationship of smell to virtue, trying to notice how I let smell become a barrier between me and people who might be my friends. Olfactory practice as part of my spiritual life, olfactory practice as part of Christian discipleship, might start with hearing the judge's call to "revoke" homelessness as a call closely related to the call to follow Christ. The possibility of my being a sweet-scented offering may turn precisely on my remembering that Jesus, the Fragrance of Life, was a sometimes homeless man whose body was not always perfumed by women bearing nard. He surely sometimes stank.

Put an altar of incense in your innermost
heart. Be a sweet aroma of Christ.

—Origen

A PRAYER

What do I love when I love Thee? Not the beauty of body nor the gracefulness of temporal rhythm, not the brightness of light so friendly to the eyes, not the sweet and various melodies of songs, not the fragrance of flowers and ointments and spices, not manna and honey; not limbs receptive to fleshly embraces: I love not these when I love my God. And yet I do love a kind of light, melody, fragrance, food, embracement when I love my God; for He is the melody, the food, the embracement of my inner self: Where that light shines into my soul which no place can contain, and where that voice sounds which time does not take away, and where that fragrance smells which no wind scatters, and where there is that flavor which eating does not diminish, and where there is that clinging which no satiety will separate. This is what I love when I love my God.

—Augustine

Bread and Vine

You, eternal Trinity, are Table and Food and Waiter for us. You, eternal Father, are the Table that offers us food, the Lamb, your only-begotten Son. He is the most exquisite Food for us, both in his teaching, which nourishes us in your will, and in the sacraments that we receive in Holy Communion, which feeds and strengthens us while we are pilgrim travelers in this life. And the Holy Spirit is a Waiter for us, for he serves us this teaching by enlightening our mind's eye with it and inspiring us to follow it.

—CATHERINE OF SIENA

It would not be a gross exaggeration to say that the Bible is a culinary manual, concerned from start to finish about how to eat, what to eat, when to eat. Food is the first way the Bible shows that God intends to provide for humanity: all those seed-bearing plants and trees with fruit in the garden of Eden given to Adam and Eve to eat. And food is the shorthand for our disobedience, the shorthand for all the ways we have moved far away from God: Adam and Eve eat the wrong thing, in the wrong way. Thereafter, the biblical writers often discuss God's relationship with God's people in alimentary terms. The dietary codes show God's interest in the quotidian details of people's lives (and though many foods are flat-out off-limits to Israel, there's an abundance of food still left for people to eat—figs and apples and raisins and vinegar and cheese and wine). Food accompanies hospitality—in Genesis 18,

There is communion of more than our bodies when bread is broken and wine drunk.

—M. F. K. Fisher

Abraham tells Sarah to bake cakes for three visitors, who turn out to be angels there to announce a great miracle. Food carries memory and food becomes sacramental vessel: Jesus instructs his friends and followers to eat a ritual meal in his memory. And finally there is God's own self as food: "My flesh is real food and my blood is real drink," Jesus tells his baffled audience in the Gospel of John.

That description—flesh, blood, real food and drink—is startling and graphic. (In fact, in the first centuries following Jesus's death, pagans who overheard Christian worship and teaching accused Christians of cannibalism.) There is a decided strangeness about the metaphor—but at the same time, the pair of foods that God most preeminently *is* seems almost unremarkable. Wine and bread. The fruit of the vine; the staff of life.

In calling Himself "the bread of life"—and not, say, crème caramel or caviar—Jesus is identifying with basic food, with sustenance, with the food that, for centuries afterward, would figure in the protest efforts of poor and marginalized people. No one holds caviar riots; people riot

That *he is There* (oh heavenly theme!) is as certainly true as that Bread naturally taken removes my hunger—so this Bread of Angels removes my pain, my cares, warms, cheers, soothes, contents and renews my whole being.

—Elizabeth Seton

for bread. So to speak of God as bread is to speak of God's most elemental provision for us.

Especially for people who have lived with hunger, this is a powerful, palpable image. But I admit that it is a biblical metaphor at which I sometimes find myself staring blankly. I have never been hungry for more than thirty-five minutes, and, though I always need to be nourished, I rarely notice this need, and I rarely credit God with my nourishment (more often I either take my nourishment for granted or credit myself—my labors, which provide the money to buy the food; my hours, devoted to cooking; and so forth). So for me (and maybe for you), the image of bread as provision can be a bit of a corrective, showing me how insensible to my dependence on God I really am. But instructing me in my hunger is not all this image can do. Bread is basic food, but bread nonetheless contains meanings beyond sustenance.

I once asked a circle of people from church, if Jesus is the "bread of life," what kind of bread is He? Not a one of them said, "He's that small round wafer we use at Communion." I wrote down their answers. I think they make a good prayer:

a bagel

rye

toast with jam

morning glory muffins

chocolate tea bread

rosemary ciabatta

my grandmother's sourdough

my grandmother's challah

French toast

a crusty baguette

This gorgeous list expands our attention from the usual thought "if God is bread, then God meets my needs" to the category of delectation. If God is chocolate tea bread, God is not only panary provision—God is also about delight. It is one of the beauties of this metaphor that bread, like the One who made the hands that made the bread, contains both: enjoyment and necessity, sustenance and pleasure.

Some mornings, when I notice that I have yet again turned Jesus into an abstraction, I unpin the bread-list prayer from my bulletin board and sit down and really try to pray: I try to picture the toast with jam and the ciabatta and smell them. I picture my father's French toast and his wife's challah. I ask God to cultivate my yearning and to help make this day a day on which I will taste and see that the Lord is good, that the Lord is sweet.

Of course, Jesus didn't specifically identify himself with chocolate tea bread or morning glory muffins. He identified himself with manna:

So they said to him, "What sign are you going to give us then, so that we may see it and believe you? What work are you performing? Our ancestors ate the manna in the wilderness; as it is written, 'He gave them bread from heaven to eat.'" Then Jesus said to them, "Very truly, I tell you, it was not Moses who gave you the bread from heaven, but it is my Father who gives you the true bread from heaven. For the bread of God is that which comes down from heaven and gives life to the world." They said to him, "Sir, give us this bread always." Jesus said to them, "I am the bread of life. Whoever comes to me will never be hungry, and whoever believes in me will never be thirsty."

Medieval artists depicted this narrative as if the manna raining down from the clouds were round communion wafers. This iconographic tradition is not our style of ecclesiastical art—and for heaven's sake, can we finally be done with pre-packaged communion hosts that resemble nothing? The point is real bread. But I appreciate what the art was conveying: Christians attend to the stories of the Hebrew scriptures, John referring to Christ as the Bread that comes down from heaven, because the baptized community relies on Old Testament vocabulary to speak its metaphors. These are the best metaphors we have. So who is he? He is Manna, Bread graciously provided to us as we slog through our wilderness.

—Gail Ramshaw

Manna was the food God provided for Israel while they wandered in the desert. It was, says the Book of Exodus, "like coriander seed, white; and the taste of it was like wafers made with honey"; or, according to the Book of Numbers, it was like "cakes baked with oil."

The rabbis say that manna tasted like whatever the Israelites wanted it to taste like. If you were craving chocolate that day, your manna tasted like *pain au chocolat;* if your palate was set for savory, the manna tasted like broccoli quiche or mushroom crepes. (There were a few exceptions: as Rashi, the eleventh-century interpreter of scripture, noted, manna could not taste like leeks, onions, cucumbers, watermelons, or garlic, because those five foods might hurt nursing mothers.) It was not until I

Cinnamon has a naturally pleasing sweetness that delights the taste. At the same time, it also has a sharp strength that inflames the palate of the one who tastes it and that becomes more piquant and aromatic the more one chews it. Such is the Lord our God to us who always wait to see His desirable face. To us He is sweet beyond all things that can be tasted; nothing among other desirable things can be compared to His sweetness. It touches us with ineffable strength and penetrates us most intimately. It ignites and continually enflames us to love Him. And the more we feast on the taste of His sweetness, the more piquant and appetizing He is for us and the course of our desire for Him will have no end.

—Elisabeth of Schonau

was about twenty-five that I realized this teaching about manna's infinite toothsomeness was midrash, that it was not actually stated in the Book of Exodus. I now think it lurks underneath Jesus's identification with manna: Jesus does not just taste like honeyed wafers. Jesus tastes like morning glory muffins or chocolate tea bread—whatever you desire.

I n one of those endless imagery loops, God is the meal and God also provides the meal. Not just fruit and trees for Adam and Eve, and not just manna in the desert. God also spreads banquets (both temporal and eschatological banquets, it seems): "You prepare a table before me in the presence of my enemies," says the psalmist. "On this mountain the LORD Almighty will prepare a feast of rich food for all peoples, a banquet of aged wine—the best of meats and the finest of wines," says the prophet Isaiah. Jesus likewise describes God as one who throws a banquet, and Jesus tells us that God feeds even the ravens. Jesus Himself provides wedding guests with wine, feeds the five thousand, and, after the resurrection, gives His friends a beachside breakfast of fish and bread (it's really bruschetta, one book I read notes). Over and over, the scriptures show that God indeed is the one who fills the hungry with good things.

I wonder what it feels like to God, providing all those meals.

There is little I enjoy more than getting into the kitchen for a few hours in the late afternoon and cooking up a storm. I enjoy planning the menu, I enjoy chopping all the vegetables, I enjoy the chaotic whirl of a kitchen when you are trying to concoct three different courses at once. I enjoy the satisfaction of laying the table with china and silverware and platters heavy with food, especially if I am expecting two or four or five friends to drop by for the repast. Does God enjoy preparing banquets for us?

At the same time, weird things happen to me when I get into a kitchen—all sorts of complicated feelings around cooking for other people, providing food for them, creating meals for others to eat. I feel a deep delight when people seem grateful for the food and a prickly resentment when they do not. Also, I feel possessive—jealous of my own place in the kitchen and strangely threatened if, say, my husband tells me he wants to do some of the week's cooking. The rational part of my brain knows that this is egalitarian and great, and that in reality I don't have time to be in the kitchen two or three hours every night. But some less articulate, less rational, more 1950s part of my

You cause the grass to grow for the cattle,
and plants for people to use,
to bring forth food from the earth,
and wine to gladden the human heart,
oil to make the face shine,
and bread to strengthen the human heart.

—Psalm 104:14–15

brain rebels and wants to seize the whole cooking field for myself. Nourishment, delight, power, gratitude—all those things and more are whipping around the seemingly simple task of serving dinner.

Maybe God feeds us not just because that is what a god does—provide; maybe God gets something out of it. Maybe it makes God feel good to feed us. I wonder if God experiences feeding us as a really pleasurable thing, as a way of giving us not just something we need but something that delights us. I wonder if providing food makes God feel, as it makes me feel, needed and important. I wonder if God feels possessive of the kitchen, as I do. I wonder if God feels a sense of accomplishment, if God steps back from the table laden with food and takes deep satisfaction in all that finest wheat and honey and manna.

The poet Maxine Kumin wrote an essay about making blackberry jam. She says it is a lot of hard work, and that her property in Warner, New Hampshire, is so overrun with wild blackberries that in fact she is a little sick of them. Nonetheless, she writes, "making jam . . . is rich with gratifications. I get a lot of thinking done. I puff up with feelings of providence. Pretty soon I am flooded with memories." She remembers her mother, who used to visit during the canning and pickling and jamming season. Now her mother is dead, and Kumin finds herself talking to her mother as she stirs.

Kumin's mother would go home after her visits to New Hampshire with a package of jelly and pickles for fall eating. "When she died," writes Kumin, "there were several unopened jars in her cupboard. I took them back with me after her funeral. We ate them in her stead, as she would have wanted us to." There is something oddly Eucharistic about this jam.

I wonder if, while baking our manna and spreading our banquets and putting up preserves, God remembers. I wonder what memories flood the jam-making God. I wonder what beloved person, dead and gone, God talks to while sugaring the blackberries.

To say that God is bread is to say something about variety and delight. There are quick breads and slow double-rising breads. There is limpa bread, full of anise and orange peel, and there is French country bread. There is *pain de campagne* and Russian black bread and banana bread and cornbread and brioche. There is anadama bread and Irish soda bread. There is Amish friendship bread, which the bookkeeper at my new church made to welcome me. There is injera, oatmeal bread, gingerbread, panettone. There are biscuits and crumpets and scones.

At the altar, at the Eucharist, that profusion of bread shrinks. I have never seen morning glory muffins at the altar.

Sarah and I made chocolate zucchini bread last week; I've been using this recipe since college, but this was the first time I had grown the zucchini, which were the size of my husband's forearms. Sarah and I wondered aloud about celebrating a Eucharist with this bread, with our families or with friends from across the street, but it was a half-wondering, and in the end, we did not. Sarah sensed we would have to explain it—there was "regular" bread in her kitchen after all, so why opt for cocoa and zucchini? Jesus hadn't meant cocoa and zucchini, surely.

Many churches, including my own, use wafers instead of bread at Communion. Wafer bread or unleavened bread was first used in churches because people assumed that Jesus was using unleavened *matzah* at the Last Supper. In the last century, small manufactured wafers have come to owe their popularity more to tidiness; they are often used at churches where partakers of communion practice intinction, dipping the wafer into the cup rather than sipping from the cup directly. If all the communicants are dipping bread, the chalice fills up with soupy crumbs. Hence the ubiquity of wafers.

Some days I wish our Eucharistic meal in church were a bit more like a real meal, thick slices of focaccia and glasses of cabernet. But I have come to appreciate the small wafer, the small sip of wine. In the Holy Eucharist, we take a

I am going to learn to make bread to-morrow. So you may imagine me with my sleeves rolled up, mixing flour, milk, saleratus, etc., with a deal of grace. I advise you if you don't know how to make the staff of life to learn with dispatch.

—Emily Dickinson

miniature sip of wine and a small bite of wafer, and we call this God's abundance. I believe by regularly proclaiming that God's abundance can be found in something small, we are gradually retooling our understandings of what is truly necessary for life.

When real bread is used for Holy Communion, it seems usually to be some sort of nicely shaped white bread. I have never seen pumpernickel or rye; exactly once, for a potluck Eucharist at my home, I baked two loaves of whole wheat. At the chapel of the divinity school where I teach, we celebrate the Lord's Supper with commercially produced Kings Hawaiian Bread—our chaplain buys it at Harris Teeter, for $4.50 or $4.75 a loaf. "It tears well," Chaplain Bates notes, "right through the crust," and it is slightly sweet, refined in both senses—elegant, and made with refined flour. Some of the students refer to it as "sweet Jesus."

White bread has an interesting history. For centuries, people have been striving to produce ever whiter flour and ever whiter loaves. This is a story of cultural preference and symbolism, and it is also a story of technology. According to food activist and writer Michael Pollan, "The

When he said, "I am the bread of life," he must have meant he was scattering bits of himself like a trail of crumbs leading us to speak and act and scatter forgiveness in his name to the ends of the earth.

—Susan Springer, in a sermon for Ascension Day

prestige of white flour is ancient and has several sources, some practical, others sentimental. Whiteness has always symbolized cleanness, and . . . the whiteness of flour symbolized its purity." For centuries, white flour was hard to obtain; only the rich could afford white bread. But in the middle of the nineteenth century, roller milling—in which millstones were replaced with metal or porcelain drums that were arranged to grind the flour more finely—made white flour inexpensive, readily available, "and whiter than it had ever been." So even people of modest means began to buy porcelain-white flour and bake pretty white loaves in their ovens.

Within a few decades, further technological innovation—developments in "microbiology, cereal chemistry, climate control, and industrial design"—had again reshaped people's daily bread: in 1890, 90 percent of bread eaten in the United States was made by women at home; by 1930, 90 percent of America's bread "was baked outside the home by men in increasingly distant factories." In a study called *White*

Let the vineyards be fruitful, Lord, and fill to the brim our cup of blessing. Gather a harvest from the seeds that were sown, that we may be fed with the bread of life. Gather the hopes and dreams of all; unite them with the prayers we offer. Grace our table with Your presence, and give us a foretaste of the feast to come. Amen!

—A Lutheran prayer for Holy Communion

Bread: A Social History of the Store-Bought Loaf, Aaron Bobrow-Strain suggests that the appeal of "modern bread"—industrial white bread—went beyond convenience. People loved the "streamlined" look of company-baked bread. When the first automatically sliced bread was sold in the United States (in the summer of 1928, in Chillicothe, Missouri), a reporter wrote, "The housewife can well experience a thrill of pleasure when she first sees a loaf of this bread with each slice the exact counterpart of its fellows. So neat and precise are the slices, and so definitely better than anyone could possibly slice by hand with a bread knife

A loaf of bread is the bearer of at least four major narratives or histories; (1) a narrative of natural processes that yield diverse plant growth, yeast spores, salt, sugar, and water; (2) an agricultural narrative about the human domestication of plants, considerable experimentation with grains and heat, and the development of grain economies; (3) a moral/philosophical narrative about the transformation of humanity itself as people grow into the idea that they can control their habitats and relationships with each other in new and potentially hospitable ways; and (4) a theological narrative focused on Jesus as the "bread of life." This means that to consider fully what a loaf *is* requires us to move far beyond a particular slice to include the material, biological, social, and divine sources that feed into every bite. A "simple" food with this much ecological and cultural depth will, of necessity, presuppose many subplots that add significance to the overall meaning of bread.

—Norman Wirzba

that one realizes instantly that here is a refinement that will receive a hearty and permanent welcome." The guaranteed perfection of a store-bought loaf appealed to an America in love with science and captive to fantasies of scientific perfection. The *Ladies' Home Journal* wrote in 1923 that in contrast to the housewife who baked by guesswork and was likely to produce the occasionally underdone or misshapen loaf, "modern inventions have made an exact science of baking, and there is no reason whatever for failure."

Americans loved the bread's predictable uniformity, and they loved its *whiteness*. Echoing Pollan, Bobrow-Strain argues that white bread "had long stood as a symbol of wealth and status—and in America, racial purity," but in the early twentieth century, Americans' preference for white flour took on still new meanings. In an era obsessed with hygiene and sanitation, the color white came to represent "scientific control"—all those white lab coats, all those sparkling white kitchen appliances. Physicians took to the pages of national magazines to urge families, especially immigrant families and poor families, to whitewash their walls; dark walls would camouflage dirt, but on white walls dirt would, in the words of one pundit-physician, be "so conspicuous that shame" would "compel . . . the Polacks and Hungarians" to clean. The modern designer Le Corbusier was more succinct: "Whitewash," he wrote, "is extremely moral."

So, in short, the history of the lovely white loaf may be found in America's optimistic quest for scientific perfectibility and in America's history of shaming immigrants and shaming women.

It seems an odd genealogy for the bread that, week in and week out, Christians name as Jesus. Jesus, who consorted with shamed women. Jesus, who is neither orderly nor predictable. Jesus, who, with his parents, became a migrant to Egypt when his own country turned inhospitable to him. Jesus, who makes possible our immigration to the Kingdom of God. Jesus, whose skin was darker than the flour we prize.

Of course, it is easy to imagine the well-meaning pastor at all-white First Mainline Church preaching a chaotically horrible children's sermon about a pumpernickel loaf. May the good Lord spare me from ever preaching that sermon. Still: "Because there is one bread, we who are many are one body, for we all partake of the one bread," wrote Paul. My zucchini loaf is misshapen and a little burned around the edges. But maybe it comes closer to the loaf Paul meant than does the modern white loaf, with its perfection, its refinement, and its shame.

> Deep in our souls we know that *we* are the
> bread of life and that to become conscious of
> this and to live it makes all the difference.
>
> —Gunilla Norris

For some people—people who have tricked out their kitchens with top-notch speakers and who are usually drinking a glass of wine when they cook—the kitchen is leisure space. For other people, cooking dinner is work. If you have small children underfoot or arguing teenagers in the next room, if you are a harried single parent, if you cook night after night with no help and with an endless sense of obligation—then cooking might be more stressful than leisurely, more hectic than meditative.

I wonder: when is God's experience of providing us food leisurely and when does God find the kitchen a chore? Is Mary sitting companionably at the breakfast bar drinking a beer? Or are there angels standing in the corner, squabbling with their siblings? To borrow sociologist Michelle Szabo's terminology, does God find providing food for us to be "foodwork" or "foodplay"?

Standing in my own kitchen—which is filled with books by Alice Waters and Laurie Colwin, and which is awash in quinoa—I realize that I am at some risk of turning the God who provides food into a "foodie" for whom cooking the right food at the right time of year has become both a pleasure and a mark of status. Surely our image of God as provider of food might also include my mother, home from a long day at work and utterly without the energy to cook, microwaving a bag of popcorn for herself and opening a can of Chef Boyardee for me. *Wait*, one might object.

With all due respect to your mother, how can that picture have anything to do with the God who offers us flavor and nourishment, the God who created all those vegetables in Eden, the God who wants to provide for us abundantly?

My answer to that objection is this: God became incarnate, and God knew exhaustion and finitude, and God has a preference for those with no margins in their lives, and out of solidarity, God probably sometimes hands around a can of SpaghettiOs to the saints.

I do a lot of reading by the bookcase in my kitchen, seated in a brown leather chair, which some students once dropped off for temporary storage, and which I hope they never reclaim. Tonight, I am sitting in the chair reading a terrific monograph, Psyche A. Williams-Forson's *Building Houses Out of Chicken Legs: Black Women, Food, and Power.* It is about the many uses, from money making to self-expression, African American women have found for cooking chicken. I get this experience three times a year, if I'm lucky: a book I want to stay up all night reading, a book that excites me more

Bread of Heaven, Bread of Heaven
Feed me till I want no more.

—William Williams

than I can convey. Williams-Forson darts from antebellum
fiction to the beguiling silhouettes of twenty-first-century
artist Kara Walker, from black women's collaboration (and
sometimes competition) in church kitchens to discussions of
chicken in African American etiquette guides. (And yes, I
have made a note in my sermon notebook to return to this
book next time the lectionary comes around to the Jesus-as-
mother-hen passage; I am willing to bet that if I think about
Jesus alongside what Williams-Forson is teaching me about
chickens, I will have a different sermon than if I stick to my
tried-and-true commentaries on Luke.)

In chapter 4, which is about food and travel, Williams-
Forson recovers the history of black women packing up
shoe box lunches for family members who were setting off
on a trip. These box lunches allowed women who themselves might not be able to leave home to "vicariously"
travel, and helped African Americans navigate the hostile
landscape of the Jim Crow South, where few restaurants
would serve them. Williams-Forson illustrates this with
a quotation from a cookbook-memoir, *Spoonbread and
Strawberry Wine: Recipes and Reminiscences* by Norma
Jean Darden and Carole Darden. The Darden sisters recall
how exciting it was to stay up late the night before a trip
and help their mother pack the box lunches, which contained a bounty of goodies: fried chicken, peanut butter
and jelly, deviled eggs, chocolate layer cake, nuts, raisins,
and cheese. Except for the thermos of lemonade, "everything was neatly wrapped in wax paper" and tucked into
shoe boxes, "with the name of the passenger Scotch-taped

on so that special requests were not confused." Even as young girls, the Dardens knew these lunches were about traversing dangerous terrain:

> These trips took place during the fifties, and one never knew what dangers or insults would be encountered along the way. Racist policies loomed like unidentified monsters in our childish imagination and in reality. After the New Jersey Turnpike ended, we would have to be on the alert for the unexpected. So, as we approached that last Howard Johnson's before Delaware, our father would make his inevitable announcement that we had to get out, stretch our legs, and go to the bathroom, whether we wanted to or not. This was a ritualized part of the trip, for, although there would be many restaurants along the route, this was the last one that didn't offer segregated facilities. From this point on, we pulled out our trusty shoe box lunches.

Sitting in my kitchen in the borrowed chair, I think back to other books I've read about the era of Jim Crow, and I realize that what the Dardens recall was by no means unique (although, before reading Williams-Forson's analysis, I hadn't noticed it as a widespread cultural and political strategy). Other memoirs on my shelf discuss the same practice. For example, Gail Milissa Grant, who grew up in Saint Louis in the 1940s, recalls her mother doing something similar. Grant's parents often went to the Union Station not to pick up anyone but to feed their friends. My mother would prepare a meal and carefully select the menu for its shelf life since it might have to last for hours without spoiling. Negroes could not 'receive service' on trains until later in the 1950s, so they had to travel with their own food. The Negro Pullman porters couldn't even serve other Negroes. She usually included fried chicken, hard-boiled eggs, a few candy bars, and ice-cold sodas and placed them all in a shoe box or hatbox. Their friends would give Mommy plenty of notice, by telephone or telegram, of their itinerary before boarding the train, so she had time to cook. On long journeys, my mother's would be one in a string of meals, with other friends doing the same thing along the route.

Mrs. Darden and Mrs. Grant's food preparation is the best picture I have found for understanding God as a provider of food. Here is God preparing food for the Israelites journeying in the wilderness: God is not just abstractly raining coriander flakes down from the heavens. God is staying up late to prepare shoe box lunches for people on a perilous journey.

And this is the bread with which Jesus most explicitly identified—manna, journeying bread. Jesus as manna: fried chicken, peanut butter and jelly sandwiches, deviled eggs, chocolate layer cake, all carefully packed into a small box. Jesus, a traveler's lemonade in a thermos. Jesus as manna, the bread that sustains oppressed people on their journey through dangerous terrain.

From a study of women with eating disorders: two-thirds of the women who regularly participate in Eucharist report that they have decreased the frequency with which they receive Communion because they fear the calories in the wafer and the wine.

This seems sad, but it doesn't seem unintelligible. Although I have gotten through almost four decades in a fe-

What, for example, does it mean to celebrate the Eucharist as *food* (bread and wine) in a place where we are increasingly obsessed with and yet deeply afraid and ashamed of food, where we idolize *and* demonize food, where we are increasingly disconnected from the sensual pleasures of good food, and where we have gone a long way toward losing our sense of food as a blessing that ties us to life and others? Or what does it mean to celebrate the Eucharist as *body* of Christ when our diets seem to be waging a war against our bodies (particularly against the bodies of women), when the ways in which we eat do not honor our bodies, or when our eating patterns seem indifferent to the suffering bodies of all the Lazaruses gathered at the edges of our tables, as well as all the Marthas waiting on these tables?

—Patrick T. McCormick

male body without dancing too close to an eating disorder, the statistic makes sense to me.

Throughout this book I have been inviting us to consider what our day-to-day lives tell us about biblical metaphors. Just as men and women of the first century drew on what they knew about shepherding when they heard "feed my sheep," I have been inviting us to consider what we know from our own experiences of smell and clothing and friendship as we ponder the Bible's images of God.

Here is what I know about bread and wine: I know many women who don't eat bread, don't keep it in their homes, refuse the bread basket at restaurants. I know that I have bread around the house only because my husband insists, and he does have to insist. I often tell him about the glory days before we got married, when my kitchen was a breadless nirvana and I rarely ate sandwiches or toast. I know that every year, around February, I decide the most efficient way to lose the weight I gained in the deep-winter holiday

"Breaking bread" means eating. "Our daily bread" means food. It is also called the staff of life, which I like: bread there, all life leaning against it. Our lives don't lean against it anymore: we've decided that bread is bad for us. Our staff has broken, and that is part of why our diets seem so hard to get in balance.

—Tamar Adler

months would be to forswear alcohol and to stop eating foods whose primary ingredient is flour. (And doesn't it seem strange that so many of the weight-loss diets that are popular today take aim at staple foods, foods that are inexpensive and easy for the earth to yield? The instruction to lose weight by avoiding carbohydrates and eating more meat seems like an instruction to eat the food that is costliest for the planet to produce.) This is not so many steps from panicking about Communion bread. A few steps, but not many.

I can't imagine that this is what Jesus meant for us to think about when He called Himself bread and wine; I don't think He imagined twenty-first-century women whose visceral response to bread and wine was fear or a triggered self-disgust.

Or maybe He imagined just that. Maybe He sees it now, looking down from heaven with sorrow and understanding. Maybe one of the invitations He was making at the Last Supper was an invitation to anxious middle-class women two millennia in the future—the invitation to let His bread and His wine and His Eucharist reshape the way we hold and eat and sip and feel about all bread and wine.

In the Middle Ages, several female mystics compared the soul in union with God to bread that soaks up—and grows engorged with—honey or mead. This is a good image, especially so for a society in which women are told to make their bodies shrink or disappear. Jesus means for us to see bread as a metonym for Him, for His body, for His nearness. The mystics' prayers would suggest that our own bodies, too, are metonymed as bread, bread that expands with Jesus when we draw close to Him.

One of the women who used that image of bread and honey was a thirteenth-century Saxon mystic named Mechthild, who had two mellified visions. In the first vision, she saw Mary cradling the infant Jesus, and Jesus's own name was written across His chest in honey. In a later vision, Jesus asks Mechthild to place in His left hand all her "pains and adversities," so that they may be "sweetened" by union with Him, "just as a crumb of bread dipped in honey takes on the honey's fragrance."

This is a reverse Communion image. Usually, at Communion, we draw near to God by opening our hands to receive a crumb of bread. In Mechthild's vision, we draw near to God and find God's hand opened to us. I like picturing old woman Mechthild, and the ten-year-old girl down the block, and the man at my church whose brother just died, and Mrs. Darden and Mrs. Grant, and that journalist who reported on the first-ever mechanically sliced bread, and myself, all sidling up to Jesus, placing our crumbs of pain and adversity in His hands, knowing they will soak up His honey.

God comes near to us unendingly in the bread
of life, the food of resurrection. Everything
has to be built up round this seed of fire.

—Olivier Clément

"Dry is all food of the soul if it is not sprinkled with the oil of Christ," says another mystic, Bernard of Clairvaux. "When thou writest," he instructs, "promise me nothing, unless I read Jesus in it. When thou conversest with me on religious themes, promise me nothing if I hear not Jesus' voice. Jesus—melody to the ear, gladness to the soul, honey to the taste."

I like to picture the soul drawing closer to God; I like to picture this soul as bread that absorbs honey and finds its pain and adversity converted to the Lord's sweetness as it does.

W ho will enable me to find rest in you? Who will grant me that you come to my heart and intoxicate it, so that I forget my evils and embrace my one and only good, yourself?" So prayed Augustine at the beginning of his *Confessions*. His plea that God intoxicate his heart is a good reminder that our defining meal as Christians doesn't just include bread, but also wine, and Jesus identifies His father as a vineyard owner, Himself as the true vine, and His blood as wine itself. This vinous imagery was not original to Jesus. He was drawing on language that people had been using for centuries to describe life with God. The prophets of the Hebrew Bible envision Israel as a vine or a collection of vines. God has brought the vines out of Egypt, cleared the ground, planted the vines, and watched over them. But Israel is a vineyard that produces the wrong kind of fruit, the fruit of injustice and idolatry, so God destroys the vineyard. Isaiah 5

contains perhaps the most disconcerting of the biblical vineyard passages, in which God, with great devotion, clears a
hillside and plants the choicest vines—but finds they yield
"only bad fruit." "What more could have been done for my
vineyard than I have done for it?" asks God.

> When I looked for good grapes,
> why did it yield only bad?
> Now I will tell you
> what I am going to do to my vineyard:
> I will take away its hedge,
> and it will be destroyed;
> I will break down its wall,
> and it will be trampled.
> I will make it a wasteland,
> neither pruned nor cultivated,
> and briers and thorns will grow there.
> I will command the clouds
> not to rain on it.

In case there is any ambiguity, the prophet spells out that
the Lord droughted the vines to death because the Lord
had looked for "justice" and "righteousness" among those
vines and found none:

> The vineyard of the LORD Almighty
> is the nation of Israel,
> and the people of Judah
> are the vines he delighted in.

And he looked for justice, but saw bloodshed;
for righteousness, but heard cries of distress.

So there is love and care in biblical vineyards. To be a vineyard is to be lovingly planted by God and sometimes to flourish. But there is judgment in this imagery, too. Vines are fragile. Sometimes they wither. Sometimes God lets them go, or removes them if they are unproductive. Sometimes God destroys them.

This Old Testament imagery is the backdrop against which Jesus says, in the Gospel of John, "I am the true vine." Jesus's original audience would have known that when they heard a teacher talk about vines, they were hearing about themselves. They would have known Isaiah and Jeremiah and Hosea. They would have known that they were the vines, and God was the vinedresser who cleared the field and tended it. Jesus's audience was also aware of the risk. God might cease caring for them and give them up to destruction if they yielded wild grapes. To hear Jesus call

Good vines require cutting and more cutting. A mile of runners won't give you one more grape, so get rid of branches that do not bear fruit. Do you want to keep everything? Then expect nothing. Cut. And then cut some more.

—Sr. Judith Sutera, Benedictine nun and master vinedresser

Himself the vine, then, was to hear a metaphor of startling vulnerability: I, God, am one of you; I have come down from the manager's office to become, with you, part of the vineyard.

Usually we hear in Jesus's identification of Himself as vine a statement of our dependence on Him, and an instruction about what we need to thrive—if we abide in Jesus, we will have life; if we try to separate ourselves from Jesus, we will not. But perhaps Jesus the true vine tells us about something beyond our reliance on God. Perhaps the image also tells us about the perils of incarnation. It is as if Jesus studied the Hebrew scriptures and found the most precarious depiction of humanity He could, and said, "That is who I am: I am allying with humanity when it is most endangered." When I am producing bad fruit and farthest from God's pleasure, Jesus is already in that place. It is not alien to Him, and I am not alone.

Christmas is in a week, and I am setting out a few decorations at home: a tiny ceramic manger scene, three white angels that belonged to my mother, a neon pink tree. I also set out a goblet. It is a heavy pottery goblet, and on any given night in June or September or July, it can be found in my hand, full of something vermillion. I will leave it out at Christmas, next to the pink tinsel tree, to remind me that Jesus became not just "incarnate," but a vine and wine. I will leave it out at Christmas to remind me of the riskiness in incarnation.

There is indeed risk, for the destruction of Jesus the vine will come to pass. As Ephrem of Syria wrote in a hymn on the nativity:

> In Bethlehem the slayers mowed down the fair
> flowers so that with them
> would perish the fair Seed in which was hid the
> Living Bread.
> The Staff of Life had come so that it might come to
> the sheaf in the harvest.
> The Cluster that fled while young, gave Himself in
> the trampling
> to revive souls with His wine.

Later in Isaiah, there is another discussion of vineyards. In that discussion, the vineyard is an image of redemption, and God the vinedresser promises to care for the vineyard and shelter it from danger and drought:

> "Sing about a fruitful vineyard:
> I, the Lord, watch over it;
> I water it continually.
> I guard it day and night
> so that no one may harm it.

I am not angry.
If only there were briers and thorns confronting me!
    I would march against them in battle;
    I would set them all on fire.
Or else let them come to me for refuge;
    let them make peace with me,
    yes, let them make peace with me."
In days to come Jacob will take root,
    Israel will bud and blossom
    and fill all the world with fruit.

This passage, with its depiction of God as the guardian and caretaker of the vineyard, comes to mind while I am reading *Libation: A Bitter Alchemy*. The book is a memoir by a pastry chef and restaurant owner named Deirdre Heekin, who set aside her tart rings and whisk and taught herself to make herbal liquors and (although she lives in Vermont) wine. Making wine is a slow process. Many years will pass before Heekin gets to taste her wine—years of choosing varietals, tending grapes, picking the fruit and pressing it, fermenting it, aging it. She and her husband buy vines from a vineyard near Lake Champlain, and they till the ground and dig holes, and once the roots have been set down, they water and mulch. And all the while—every day, I imagine, though Heekin doesn't say that it's daily—they talk to the vines, "reminding them that they all can make a great wine."

I like to picture God the vintner talking in the same way to us.

Heekin has also experimented with making her own obscure liqueurs, mainly *amari*, herb- or fruit-based bitters made to be sipped after dinner. In Heekin's description, *amari* seem to be pure loveliness. "They have antique, floral sounding names," she writes, "which are pronounced with an almost religious fervor: Amaro Lucano, Ramazotti, Vecchio Amaro del Capo, Jannamaro." Maybe "religious fervor" is overstating it a bit, but *amari* were first concocted at monasteries, where monks steeped herbs in wine to preserve the herbs' medicinal properties.

The first *amaro* Heekin made was *rosolio*, a rose-based liqueur popular in nineteenth-century Italy. For the *rosolio*, Heekin grows her own roses—Seafoam roses, Mother's Day, Madame de Bourbon. Her recipe—from a book she found at a store in Naples, "where the cookbooks were sandwiched between Italian Victorian erotica and a stand of old . . . postcards"—tells her to pick her petals at high noon. Then she clips the white moons from the base of the petals, and pushes the petals and a vanilla bean down the neck of a bottle filled with grain alcohol. Two weeks later, in late August, she removes the bean and the petals, now "colorless [and] . . . fragile as moths' wings." Heekin adds simple syrup, and waits. In October, the drink is finally ready for tasting. After a lunch of leek soup and grilled cheese sandwiches, Heekin and her husband "pour ceremoniously" into Georgian sherry glasses. The taste is a complex blend of perfume and vanilla and sweetness, with "a fiery finish." Heekin thinks she might add a bit more simple syrup to cut the fire. She begins considering orange liqueur, and wonders if a bottle could be ready for Christmas, if she started it right away.

Heekin likes the ritual of this. She says she is making *amari* to interrupt and confuse her parents' and grandparents' ugly and decidedly unceremonious dance with liquor. To labor with such tenderness over this *amaro,* and then to share it with beloveds around the table, "creates a new experience of alcohol," she writes, one that might pacify the drunk demons in her family's history; the attention Heekin lavishes on her concoctions, the magic of it, might reset her experience with alcohol. This makes perfect sense to me, though perhaps it wouldn't to someone without alcoholic antecedents. I recognize a similar impulse in myself. Though I have only rarely made liqueur (and I'm not sure if infusing vodka with habaneros even counts), I derive endless delight from the objects of cocktail hour: the crystal decanters, the pale pink champagne flutes, the stack of 1950s bartending guides that sits in my butler's pantry. These objects represent a way of living with alcohol that is

Wine is God's special drink. The purpose of good wine is to inspire us to a livelier sense of gratitude to God.

—John Calvin

different from my mother's way, my mother with bottles of gin hidden inside the KitchenAid mixing bowl.

Heekin's *amari*, then, presume alcohol's danger. Rather than a pleasure and a means of enhancing other pleasures, alcohol can be a numbing means of escape. Alcohol can turn violent. Alcohol can carry a person farther and farther away from her loved ones, her duties, herself. In this light, scripture's identification of Jesus with alcohol can feel troubling, or at least complicated and strange.

Drink's danger is there in the Bible, of course. Noah gets drunk, and, as a colleague of mine once dryly said, things don't go as well as they might. God at times metes out drunkenness as punishment for idolatry and other sin: "I will make [Babylon's] officials and her sages drunk, also her governors, her deputies, and her warriors; they shall sleep a perpetual sleep and never wake, says the King, whose name is the LORD of hosts." Alcohol's dangers are also written all over our society—as seen, for example, in the ways that alcohol exacerbates domestic abuse.* And the danger is there in my own life—I could limn it with some sad vignette about my mother, or I could instead tell you about the disastrous things I have done when drunk, disastrous things that didn't come to disaster only through sheer luck.

But there are delightful stories to tell about drunkenness, too. There can be, in the right conditions (no car keys

---

*Alcohol doesn't cause intimate partner violence, of course, but there are strong correlations between alcohol use and the severity and frequency of physical abuse; a batterer who abuses alcohol is more likely to inflict serious injury than a batterer who doesn't.

around, for example; no untrusted or untrustworthy people around), a good way of being drunk—the alcohol opens up your capacity for modes of interaction that are normally beyond you. Things you are normally scared of no longer frighten; things you keep stitched up and closed most of the time show themselves. Although the biblical writers usually treat drunkenness with opprobrium, occasionally they encourage drunkenness of a sort. The lovers in the Song of Songs are enjoined to drink and get drunk on love, and the metaphor is apt: falling in love is indeed a kind of intoxication. Who doesn't know the consuming I-cannot-think-about-anything-else-and-am-obsessed superabundance of being drunk on a lover, or drunk with a lover on love? The Song's metaphor works because even this good drunkenness carries excess; even this good drunkenness carries a kind of danger—the love-drunkenness is wonderful, but it also makes it impossible to do any of the things you thought you were going to do that day (and sometimes it makes it impossible to do any of the things you thought you were going to do that year, or that lifetime). This is part of why Deirdre Heekin's beautiful, careful *rosolio* making appeals to me. She is not just creating new memories; she is trying to contain the alcohol—its danger, its excess—and make sure it doesn't carry her away.

The church has often read the Song allegorically: on one level, the poem is about a man and a woman, mere mortals, rapturously in love. At another level, the poem is about Jesus and the church, rapturously in love. When I think about the Song this way—when I consider that one of the protagonists is the Lord—the instruction to drink and get drunk on love is chastening. Is my church drunk on love for Jesus? Am I? Looking over my own life, I can conjure easily the fevered intoxication of human romance—I can conjure easily the ways I rearranged every single thing in my life, abandoned other responsibilities, renarrated my whole past and future because I was drunk-in-love with some man. It is harder to unearth my analogous intoxication with Jesus. It was a long time ago, and it was brief—I became a Christian because of it, and then, it seems, I went back to drinking wheatgrass juice and Perrier.

Perhaps, if I received Jesus as wine, I would know divine intoxication again. (Would that be bearable? Just as being drunk on a man seems to interfere with what I think I am supposed to do in a given day, or a given life, surely being intoxicated with Jesus would, too.) I get hints of divine intoxication now and again—quick flashes in prayer once or twice a year. Perhaps at the heavenly banquet, we will find good, true inebriation, excess that is somehow not unsafe. Or excess in a place where safety is no longer a concern; excess in a place where, since everything has been reordered for and by God, there is no other order, no other program, for divine intoxication to disrupt.

In the Bible, men and women observing others caught up in intense devotion to God tended to mistake those people, or gloss them, as drunk: Hannah was "pouring out [her] soul to the LORD," beseeching the Lord for a child, and a priest who happened upon her thought she was blotto; those observing the apostles, newly filled with the Holy Spirit at Pentecost, made the same charge. The metaphor doubles back on itself: it is not simply that people appear intoxicated when they are caught up in God. Rather, the presence of God—the God who identifies himself with both vine and wine—in fact makes us drunk. Erasmus, a Renaissance-era priest from Rotterdam, wrote at length about wine in the Bible. In addition to suggesting that the apostles were indeed drunk on the New Wine of the Holy Spirit, Erasmus was especially interested in the twenty-third psalm. In the translation of

But Not With Wine

"You are drunk, but not with wine."
—Isa. 51:21

O God of too much giving, whence is this
inebriation that possesses me,
that the staid road now wanders all amiss
and that the wind walks much too giddily,
clutching a bush for balance, or a tree?
How then can dignity and pride endure
with such inordinate mirth upon the land,
when steps and speech are somewhat insecure
and the light heart is wholly out of hand?

If there be indecorum in my songs,
fasten the blame where rightly it belongs:
on Him who offered me too many cups
of His most potent goodness—not on me,
a peasant who, because a King was host,
drank out of courtesy.

—Jessica Powers

the Bible Erasmus read—a Latin translation known as the Vulgate—the line most of us know as "my cup runneth over" reads *calix mens inebrians praeclarus est,* which in English is "My cup that makes me drunk, how delightful it is." The psalmist's cup, suggested Erasmus, was the one Jesus drank from after praying to his father, "Take this cup away from me." It is a cup we should approach, perhaps, with caution, for, in Erasmus's words, those who drink wine of the psalmist's cup will be made drunk to the point of utter indifference—indifference to "riches, family, stripes, stakes, racks, and life itself."

The mystics liked the metaphor of inebriation. Being drunk was a familiar experience that seemed to say something about their encounters with God. In the sixteenth century, for example, the Flemish monk Louis de Blois considered the question of being drunk on the Lord. He wrote that the inebriated soul will find—as all lovers do—that her thoughts are occupied utterly by her beloved, God. The lover's heart will detach from all things but God, and in that detachment the drunk lover will find a joyful peace that "surpasses all sense, and transcends all understanding," a peace "by which the mind is absorbed in the interior life, and, forgetful of all external things, reposes happily in the Lord!" The joy the lover feels defies speech—it cannot really be described. We can say only that the one thus in love with God is "filled with an incomprehensible and inestimable sweetness, and being filled she is inebriated, and being inebriated she is brought into the haven of holy security."

But this secure inebriation is short-lived, replaced by something like a hangover:

> Alas! while we bear about us a corruptible body, we
> cannot long enjoy this holy and secret union with
> God. For the Spouse approaches and withdraws;
> now He shows Himself, and again He hides Himself.
> O what distaste for present things, what groans,
> what sighs, invade the holy soul when it returns to
> itself from those raptures, when it falls back from
> such riches to such poverty, from such delights to
> such misery.

That is the danger of drinking God.

Another Flemish writer, Jan Ruusbroec—a priest and monk who, by my reading, delighted more than just about anyone in playing with figurative speech for the divine—took up the same topic. In *The Spiritual Espousals* (a long meditation on the verse "See the bridgegroom is coming; go out to meet him"), Ruusbroec speaks of "spiritual inebriation." This inebriation, says Ruusbroec, occurs when someone "receives more sensible joy and sweetness than his heart can either contain or desire." It may bring forth "many strange gestures." While inebriated, you might sob, or you might sing with joy. You might "run and jump and dance," or clap, or shout aloud. "Another cries out with a loud voice, and so shows forth the plenitude he feels within; another must be silent and melt away, because of the rapture which he feels in all his senses." Often, a person drunk on God "thinks that he never could, nor ever shall, lose this well-being." The drunk might assume that everyone in the world feels exactly as he does. At other times, "he wonders why all men do not become God-desiring." Sometimes, "the excess of joy becomes so great that the man thinks that his heart must break."

It sounds like the excess of falling in love with your college sweetheart, only more so, and, as in Song of Songs, inebriation seems the right metaphor—perhaps the only metaphor. This is why Jesus is hymned not as grape juice but as wine: because He is dangerous and excessive. He is more than you need, and He is more than pleasure, and if you attend to Him, you will find so much there that you will be derailed completely. And you will think your heart might break. And then, per Louis de Blois, He will withdraw and you will be miserable and sick until He returns.

TWO PRAYERS

Grant that my soul may hunger after Thee, the bread of angels, the refreshment of holy souls, our daily and supersubstantial bread, having all sweetness and savor and every delight of taste; let my heart ever hunger after and feed upon Thee, upon whom the angels desire to look, and may my inmost soul be filled with the sweetness of Thy savor.

—From the *Stimulis Amoris,* long attributed to Bonaventure, now thought to have been written by Jacopo da Milano

Blood of Christ, make me drunk.

—From the *Anima Christi*

Laboring Woman

The mother who bore me labored for perhaps a day to give me birth, or for a night, while you, lovely, sweet lord, suffered pain because of me not for a night or a day, but rather were in labor for more than thirty years. Ah, love, sweet lord how you must have suffered, your labor was so painful that your holy sweat was like drops of blood which run over your body and down to the ground.

—MARGUREITE D'OIGNT

I remember the first time I encountered the image of God as a laboring woman. I was reading Isaiah for an Old Testament class I took in seminary, and I was, it must be admitted, sort of skimming. Then I came to the middle of chapter 42 and I was stopped cold: "For a long time I have held my peace, I have kept still and restrained myself; now I will cry out like a woman in labor, I will gasp and pant."

What came to mind was a photograph I had once seen, an old, grainy, black-and-white photograph from the feminist 1970s (could it have been printed in *Our Bodies, Ourselves*?) of a woman in a hospital bed, her long blond hair tied back from her face, her right hand on her forehead, a nurse's hands on her engorged stomach, her face knotted in agony. Although it was just a photograph, you could practically hear the low, loud groan emerging from her throat.

So there I was sitting on my sofa, reading Isaiah and picturing that blond, anguished woman; God's face contorted in struggle; God groaning the way that laboring woman in the photograph groaned—I pictured all that, and I felt profoundly uncomfortable. I felt disturbed.

This turns out to be just one of three images of childbirth Isaiah uses to characterize God. In addition to depicting

God as a laboring woman, Isaiah also likens God to a midwife and a nursing mother. These images compel me, in part
because Isaiah is naming as the activity of God something
readily available to most of the world's women. (In our own
cultural moment, of course, an unprecedented number of
women are like me—that is, they have neither birthed nor
witnessed a birth—and an unprecedented number of men
have participated in births. This cluster of images, which
may have for much of history been primarily available to
women, is, by dint of fathers' moving into delivery rooms,
now more directly available to men.) And these birthing
images compel me because they bespeak God's intimate,
bodily involvement with our redemption. They compel me
in their suggestion of a divine body that suffers, changes,
swells, leaks. For me, a divine body that leaks is also a divine body that discomfits; Isaiah's pictures compel me precisely in their discomfiture.

The section of Isaiah in which the laboring woman appears (a section scholars call Deutero-Isaiah) was written
while a significant slice of the Judean population was living
in exile in Babylon. Jerusalem had been politically and mil-
itarily trounced, and both leaders and ordinary folks had
been forcibly removed from their homes and gardens and
soil, separated from friends and family, and made to live
somewhere else, in alien territory, with no realistic hope of
imminent return.

Deutero-Isaiah was written in the wake of this catastro-
phe, and the text aims to assure the exiled people that God
has not abandoned them: God is present; God is at work,
tending to God's people even now, even though the exiles

might have felt forgotten and renounced. Even though it looks like Babylonians are in charge, God is sovereign. Deutero-Isaiah includes some of the Old Testament passages most commonly read in church. At Christmas we read Isaiah's words about proclaiming peace and bringing good tidings, and on Good Friday, his description of a suffering servant being pierced for our transgressions. We do not often hear the passage that figures God as a woman in labor in church, however; if you attend a church that follows the lectionary, you will never hear that verse read on Sunday from the lectern, not once. Perhaps the lectionary crafters find the picture of God squatting and grunting in labor as disconcerting as I do.

Here is what is going on in Isaiah 42, in the verses just before the laboring woman image. God announces that old things are passing away, and that soon God will bring about something new. Then God pauses, and a narrator invites a large convocation to celebrate God and God's declaration by singing "a new song." The narrator, likening God to a soldier going forth into battle with a warrior's cry, affirms that the God of Israel will prevail over all opposition, and will indeed bring about what God has promised. Next, God begins to speak again, describing the new, redemptive action that God is about to undertake on behalf of God's people. The first thing God says is, "For a long time I have held my peace, I have kept still and restrained myself; now I will cry out like a woman in labor, I will gasp and pant."

I am not the first reader of Isaiah to linger over this provocative image. Readers of scripture have found a range of meanings in the picture of God as a laboring

Out of my womb before the morning star I bore you.

—Psalm 110:3

Let us then understand the Father saying unto the Son, "From my womb before the morning star I have brought thee forth."

—Augustine

One can learn that God the Father proclaims to the Word, born from out of himself, *From the womb, before the morning star, I have given birth to you.* That the birthing, so to speak, is authentic and the Son has been born from the same essence of the Father, the expression *from the womb* demonstrates this perfectly. It is a salient example, paradigmatic of our own life.

—Cyril of Alexandria

[The Gospel of John] says [the Only-Begotten] *is in the bosom of the Father* so that you may perceive him being in and of God as it is said in the Psalms, *From out of the womb, before the daystar, I gave birth to you.* . . . when the Evangelist say *in the bosom* he wishes to clearly signify nothing less than the Son being birthed from the womb of the Father. This is, as it were, by some divine shining forth and ineffable coming forth into his own Person, while containing him.

—Cyril of Alexandria

One must believe that the Son is begotten and born not from nothing, nor from some other substance, but from *the womb of the Father,* that is, from his substance.

—Council of Toledo, 675

woman. John Calvin suggests that Isaiah is trying to tell us something about the "astonishing warmth of love and tenderness of affection" that God has for us, "for he compares himself to a mother who singularly loves her child, though she brought him forth with extreme pain." The nineteenth-century Scottish pastor A. R. Fausset finds another meaning: the laboring woman's cry is an angry shout through which the Lord "will give full vent to His long pent-up wrath." Matthew Henry finds in the loud cries of God the volume that is required to "awaken a sleeping world" to the truth of itself. God's (idealized) maternal affection, God's anger, the toll of a bell sounding to wake slumbering humanity: those are some of the meanings that readers of the Bible have found in Isaiah's laboring God. These meanings, of course, are not exhaustive. Isaiah's metaphor derives its punch from real women groaning in labor, and when we pay attention to the choreography of labor and notice which aspects of labor Isaiah highlights, we uncover something beyond wrath and generic maternal love.

Isaiah's image is much more specific than "God is like a woman in labor." Isaiah focuses on God's breathing and the sound of that breathing: in this one verse, Isaiah uses three verbs that pertain to breath. Each verb means something slightly different, and none of them is merely a synonym for "breathing." The first word for God's breath, used just once in the whole Bible, is *pa'ah*, often translated as "cry out"—but "groan" or "bellow" is a better translation. I have often heard women describe the sounds they make in labor in animal terms. "Mooing was the only sort of deep moaning noise that made my whole body feel good." "Deep guttural, almost animal-noises came from within me. Loud noises. Noises I soon had no control over." This animal breathing, which a friend of a friend calls her "moose moments," are what we hear in Isaiah's first verb, *pa'ah*. (In Aramaic and Arabic, the cognates for *pa'ah* even more aptly capture sounds like those animal grunts. The Arabic means to "hiss," which recalls a sound used in the breathing techniques of the Bradley Method of childbirth—a hissing breath that comes from the back of the throat. The Aramaic cognate means to "bleat" or "bellow.") The next two breathing words in the verse continue to stress that God's breath is not at ease; it is, indeed, labored. God "gasps" (*nasham*) and "pants" (*sha'aph*). The work of bringing forth new life does not come without effort and cost on God's part.

Why, in depicting God as a woman in labor, does Isaiah focus so much attention on breathing, on the soundscape of God's labor? One answer may be found in an echo of earlier biblical breath. At the dawn of Creation, God breathed into Adam; so too, here in Isaiah's promise of

> Does the rain have a father?
> Or who begets the drops of dew?
> From whose womb comes ice?
> And who gives birth to the hoarfrost of heaven?
>
> —Job 38:28–29

new creation, God's breath is again the agent of life. For Christian readers of Isaiah, the image may also anticipate the church's efforts to speak about the third person of the Trinity, the Holy Spirit—the very word "spirit" is tied to breath, to aspiration (and the New Testament's word for "spirit," *pneuma,* is also the Greek term for breath). It is this Holy Spirit who, Paul tells us in Romans, prays for us with deep groans.

But I would suggest that more important for Isaiah's metaphor is the centrality of breathing to a woman's experience of labor. Panting and groaning are part of how women manage the pain of childbirth. "The key to the patient's ability to suppress pain lies in her . . . breathing," wrote Priscilla Richardson Ulin, a nurse, in 1963. "She is instructed to use this type of breathing in labor as soon as she feels a need for control." Yet it is a particular kind of "control"—the groans of labor signal the woman's active participation in the birthing process, a participation that does not fight the pain (fighting labor pain only makes the pain worse). Isaiah gives us this groaning woman as a picture of the sovereign God, the God who is in control of redemption: God chooses to participate in the work of new creation with bellowing and panting. God chooses a participation that does not fight the pain, but that works from inside the pain.

When discussing pain in childbirth, Christian readers have rarely turned to Isaiah. Far more often, the Christian tradition has focused on Genesis 3, where pain in childbirth is meted out to women as a punishment for Eve's eating from the tree of knowledge of good and evil: "To the

Now birds, by sitting on their eggs for an extended period of time transmit life to them, mediating their warmth at the disposition of the Creator. Similarly, our nature having been placed beneath the Law and the message of the Prophets for an extended period of time, was incubated by God the Father and the Son (who is referred to as our Bridegroom and Beloved), and was given birth to by the Mother of All, She who is his birther by nature, and ours by grace. This is why [the Bridegroom] uses the words *go into labor;* labor pertains to a *mother.* For this reason the Father is called Mother, Christ's mother and our mother as well. The Father, consequently, was in labor through the message of the Law and the Prophets. . . . Thus there is indeed only One Mother, our Birther—the Father Almighty.

—Gregory of Narek, commenting on Song of Songs 8:5

In Ecclesiasticus it says, *I shall irrigate the garden in my estate, and I shall abundantly water the fruit born to me.* Now the garden is the soul in which Christ as the gardener plants the sacrament by faith, he then waters the garden and makes it fruitful with the grace of compunction. With this in mind the text adds, *and I shall abundantly water the fruit born to me.* This means that our souls are like fruit born of the Lord, born of his pain. Like a woman in the labor of childbirth, he gave birth to our souls in the anguish of his Passion, as the Apostle remarks, *With a loud cry and abundant tears he made his offering.* And in Isaiah we read, *Shall not I myself, who cause others to give birth, give birth? declares the Lord.* God, therefore, abundantly waters the fruit born of him when he puts to death carnal pleasures by the myrrh and aloes of his Passion.

—Anthony of Padua

woman he said, 'I will greatly multiply your pangs in child-bearing; in pain you shall bring forth children." Throughout the history of the church, many Christian interpreters have thought labor to be practically unbearable—unbearable because of its physical pain, but also unbearably shameful because of its connection with the Fall. In this interpretation, pain at childbirth signals Eve's alienation (and that of any individual pregnant woman) from God and God's holiness.

Many theologians have sought to distance God from puerperal pain—to wit, patristic and medieval theologians' insistence that Mary's labor with Jesus was painless. But Isaiah seems to refute that distancing—God will be identified with humanity, utterly, even in those things that testify to our sin. As the laboring woman, God takes on the very punishment God assigned to us. God pointedly enters into the parts of our life that bespeak our finitude and "misdirected desire"—and Isaiah's metaphor converts the groans of childbirth from a sign of humanity's fallenness to a sign of God's intimate identification with us. Or rather, in Isaiah's metaphor, the groans of childbirth are both a sign of humanity's distance from God and a sign of God's nearness to us (they're the second exactly because they're also the first).

If God's groaning in labor claims laboring as a place where human beings are closely connected to God, *women's* groaning—as narrated by at least one voice from the recesses of the Christian tradition—expresses not just the pain of childbirth but also humanity's longing for salvation. A sixteenth-century devotional text called *The Monument of Matrones,* compiled by one Thomas Bentley, contains prayers to be used by pregnant women. Most of the book narrates pregnancy in a traditional key: the pregnant woman using the book is instructed to prayerfully attribute the labor pains she anticipates to the sin of "our grand mother Eve," and to acknowledge before God that she will "justlie" experience pain in childbirth because of "our sinfull transgression of thy commandments." The book includes prayers to be said by the woman during labor (or, more likely, read to her by an attendant). Like Isaiah, these prayers, which speak of the woman's "grievous groanes" and "deepe sighs," focus on sound and breath: "Thou seest, how I pant with paine, and groane through greife." Later, the echoes of Isaiah become even more explicit, describing, like Isaiah, two periods, a period in which the laboring woman kept silent, and a period in which she now groans: "I have a long time, O Lord, held my peace. . . . I have been quiet and still, and restrained my selfe . . . as much as I am able," but finally, "so intollerable is my graefe, so manie and vehement are my throwes," that the travailing woman "can not possiblie anie longer forbeare, but am forced through bodily paine, and inward greefe, to shrich and crie alowd unto thee."

Not all the prayers in *The Monument of Matrones* simply reiterate the cries of labor. One prayer turns the laboring woman's groans to metaphor. Make us pure and holy, begins the prayer, so that we might in the fullness of time "receive (of his gift) that which here with deepe sighes and groanes we greatlie long for"—our delivery by God, to God; that is, salvation. The laboring woman's "sighes and groanes" have ceased to be only, or even principally,

expressions of physical pain—they have become petitions
that express all humanity's longing for redemption and re-
union with God.

Today, women increasingly talk and write about groaning's being more than just an analgesic: groaning in
labor is a tool women use to bring new life into the world.
Groaning helps relax the woman's entire body, especially
the pelvic area, making it possible for the baby to make
her way out. Midwife Ina May Gaskin likes to say, "Open
mouth, open bottom." In other words, "A relaxed mouth
means a more elastic cervix." Gaskin encourages laboring
women to "make a sound pitched low enough to vibrate
your chest." It is by panting and groaning that a woman
relaxes her body so that her cervix can dilate and the baby
can be born. The woman's perineum also relaxes as she relaxes her mouth with low groans. This often speeds up the
baby's descent, and makes it less likely that a woman will
tear and need stitches.

Groans also communicate the woman's need for assistance: "Loud moaning may convey a beginning plea for
help." While it is the woman's labor that brings forth
new life, women do not go through delivery alone. First,
the baby has an active role in labor and delivery: it is the
baby who, a few days before labor, stimulates the estrogen
needed to soften the mother's cervix, so that it can dilate;
and it is the baby whose head, in early labor, will prod

the mother's cervix open. Second, the laboring woman is often assisted—by a spouse, a doula, a midwife, a doctor, a friend or relative serving as a birthing partner.

I suggest that we read in Isaiah 42 a suggestion that we—we who worship the God who has redeemed and is redeeming us—participate and play a role in the birthing process. Remember that the passage in which the laboring woman appears begins with the injunction to sing a new song to the Lord: "All who want to worship the Lord, come and sing a new song." Not "come and burn some incense"; not "come and recite a spoken prayer"; come and sing. The invitation to sing a new song to the Lord is not unique to Isaiah; the psalmist also enjoins, "Sing to the Lord a new song." What is the musical invitation doing in Isaiah, before the description of God groaning in labor? It is, I suggest, inviting the convocation, the potential singers, to help God during God's delivery.

Medical practitioners in fields as varied as dental work and oncology have integrated music, which is known to reduce pain, into their clinical practice, and many doulas and midwives encourage pregnant women to think about whether they want music playing while they labor. Studies of laboring women around the world, from Thailand to Ontario, show that women who listen to music during labor experience less pain and distress than women whose labors are nonmusical. (According to many of the scholarly articles, soft classical music is best, but my friend Juli says that her midwife told her to pick whatever music she could get into. "It doesn't have to be Mozart," said Juli's midwife, "just something you love." The midwife went on to share stories of women who played AC/DC during labor.) New mothers report that music helped them relax or withdraw themselves from the pain of labor, and that it sometimes helped them focus on the team supporting them (husband, doula, nurse, physician) and on the actual work of laboring (breathing, pushing). The music, said one mother, "helped me to breathe deeper." Another woman reported that she attempted to control her breathing before the music came on and found it significantly easier to do so once there was music. Even women having a C-section found that listening to music helped them relax and feel less pain. Indeed, for all this modern study, the insight that music aids labor is not new: in ancient Greece, birth attendants sometimes played the lute to soothe the pains of laboring women.

The next time you're belting out a hymn in church, consider that the hymn is the music that helps the laboring mother God focus on delivery. Perhaps our music, our new song, helps God in birthing the new creation. God is redeeming us, yet we are the singers encouraging God in the work of delivering a renewed creation. Thus the passage in Isaiah may suggest a sort of Mobius strip of redemption, in which God is redeeming, God is suffering the pains of redemption, and as we are being redeemed, the new song we sing helps—helps God breathe, helps God relax, helps God feel less pain, helps God deliver.

I n my efforts to understand Isaiah's image of God gasp-
ing and panting in labor, I have collected a lot of birth
stories, from books and from friends. As my friend Stina
Kielsmeier-Cook, a writer pregnant with her second child,
points out to me, there comes a point in nearly every birth
story when the woman does not believe she can keep going.
The laboring woman is no longer focused on meeting her
baby; she just wants the pain to stop, and she says to her
midwife or doula or husband, "I cannot do this anymore."

Stina says this reminds her of Jesus. We don't have to
brood uncertainly about whether God ever feels this way:
we know that, in the garden of Gethsemane, before the
labor of the cross, Jesus prays, "Please, Lord, take this cup
from me." For a moment—before Jesus faithfully intones,

[Christ] gives the analogy of bitter labor and says: "A woman
when she bears a child has anguish and sorrow" (John 16:21)
and He applies all of this to His suffering, in which He so hard
and bitterly bore us, nourished us and made us alive, gave us
to drink from His breast and side with water and blood, as a
mother nurses her child.

—Katharina Schutz Zell

"But not my will but thy will be done"—Jesus is the mother in labor saying, "I cannot do this anymore." Jesus knew that new life would be born out of His suffering on the cross, yet He still asked God to take away the cup.

Stina tells me that what is spoken to the mother in the moment when she feels she cannot continue is crucial. A good midwife or doula will look the woman in the eyes, remind her of her strength, and remind her of the baby she is about to meet. "It's a moment that stands still in most birthing mothers' memories," says Stina. Most women are "sure to remember exactly what the OB or nurse or midwife said—positive or negative."

I wonder what Jesus heard His father say in the garden. Whatever it was let Jesus go on.

Stina also muses about unproductive labor, which she experienced during her first birth. "Nonprogressing labor"; "failure to progress": these are phrases a laboring woman does not want to hear.

You've been in labor for hours, possibly days. Maybe your contractions, though they've moved from palpable to uncomfortable to painful, are too weak to move the birth along. Maybe the baby is breech. Whatever the case, you've been doing your job. You've been walking around, you've stimulated your nipples, you've drunk gallons of raspberry leaf tea, but the labor is stuck. You've been at five centimeters since morning. You are exhausted and discouraged.

There has been all this pain and effort, and it doesn't seem to be accomplishing anything.

Stina says she wonders if this is what God feels, looking around our world; at our wars; at our heedless destruction of the environment; at the violence behind closed doors in every one of our neighborhoods. Is this what God feels when God looks at our daily small dishonesties and our envy? Is this what God feels when God sees my routine unkindnesses, my fears, my selfishness, my own failure to progress? Is God bone-tired? Does God want a break from the pain? Does God wonder if the labor is working?

hen I think about the hard work of labor, I realize that my unreflective assumption is somehow that redemption is easy for God. Because God is all-powerful, I somehow imagine redemption being a snap of the divine fingers. But Isaiah's image tells us how hard God the laboring woman is working to bring forth redemption, a kind of hard work that many of us may be unaccustomed to in our

Suppose we admitted for the sake of argument
that motherhood was powerful.

—Laurel Thatcher Ulrich

technological, twenty-first-century world. Underpinning the hard work is the profound strength of laboring. "I felt so strong, primeval, and powerful. I experienced a trust in my own body that I'd never known before," recalls one mother. A midwife explains the strength of laboring in an even more explicitly political key: "We tap on inner strengths we may never have tapped before, and are amazed by what we are able to accomplish. Once we become aware of how powerful we can be in giving birth, we can call on this throughout all our lives, in all sorts of situations." Those two women are speaking about "natural birth," about unmedicated vaginal delivery. (Indeed, there is a polemics here—these women are adding their voices to a fraught conversation among middle-class American mothers about the ideal birth experience.) As someone who has never given birth, it looks to me like all kinds of birth experiences are strong; there is a strength in women who have C-sections and then care for newborns while also enduring a painful post-op recovery; there is a strength in departing from your birth plan and getting the

The mystery I wish to explore . . . is this: vulnerability as the condition, the enabling condition, for covenant relationship with God. . . . Vulnerability, the capacity to be wounded— what does that mean for us who claim to be the body of Christ in the world? . . . Calling vulnerability a capacity means that it is something more than a negative. . . . A capacity is a positive thing, a kind of strength.

—Ellen F. Davis

epidural you had hoped not to need; there is a strength in letting go of your expectations of what the birth should be like.

At the same time that laboring is an experience of strength and power, it is also an experience of bodily vulnerability. And that, I have come to realize, is the core of my discomfort with Isaiah's picture of God's groaning in labor: it makes me uncomfortable to think of God groaning in pain, God bleeding, God's body uncontrollably shaking, God exhausted.

The image of God as a laboring woman puts together strength and vulnerability in a way that tells us something about God and how God works. The point is not just that God is vulnerable, although that itself is startling. The point is that in the struggles of labor, we can learn what strength is. If our picture of strength is a laboring woman, then strength is not about refusing to cry or denying pain. Strength is not about being in charge, or being

But I also need to enter again into the womb of my Lord, and be reborn into life eternal, if I am to be amongst the members of the Church whose names are in the book of life. For the Church must return thither whence she came forth, and to enter into her reward must be born again of him who first gave her birth. . . . For this reason the days on which the saints departed from this world to go to Christ are called their birthdays.

—The Monk of Farne

independent, or being dignified. If our picture of strength is a laboring woman, then strength entails enduring, receiving help and support, being open to pain and risk. If our picture of strength is a laboring woman, strength entails entrusting yourself (to medicine, or to the wisdom of your own body, or to the guidance of someone who is there in the room with you). Strength even entails giving yourself over to the possibility of death.

Let us return to the context of Deutero-Isaiah. The people are in exile. Isaiah is writing to reassure them of God's abiding interest in them and to reassure them that God is sovereign. A woman in labor is a curious picture of sovereignty. A woman in labor cannot protect herself. She is dependent on others—and at the same time, she is exercising a profound power. She is receiving help—and at the same time, her body is strong and knows what to do to deliver. Hers is a sovereignty in which the best tool is not a scepter or a gun, but breath: panting, groaning, bellowing. In their darkest hour, the exiles wondered, "God, where are you?" In His final hour Jesus cried out, "My God, my God, why have you forsaken me?" In the image of the laboring woman we see that God does not respond with silence. God groans, gasps, and pants—making a new way for the exiles, breathing life into the whole of creation, offering God's own body to be broken open for the sake of the world God created. Of course, Christianity has always claimed that strength and power are something different than we had assumed they were. Christianity has usually told us to look at the cross to see how this is so, but maybe Isaiah is saying that we could just as well look at the birthing stool.

Still, thinking of God this way—the exposed female body, shaking and in pain—leaves me feeling unnerved and a touch frantic. Do I really want a God with a body? With this kind of body?

I walk around town pondering my unease with Isaiah's travailing God. Why does this image so unsettle me? Why does it make my shoulders tense?

It is the middle of Lent. I walk through the obstetrics unit at the hospital next door to my office. There—looking at the newborns and the new parents and new aunts and new first cousins; looking at the nurses, and a chaplain, and one very ebullient grandmother—I realize that my own discomfort must include not just theoretical worry about a god's vulnerability but fear of my own vulnerability. Isaiah's picture of God suggests that those moments when I stop fighting my own vulnerability are exactly the moments when I most participate in God's very nature, in God's very

We know that our mothers only bring us into the world to suffer and die, but our true mother, Jesus, he who is all love, bears us into joy and eternal life; blessed may he be! So he sustains us within himself in love and was in labour for the full time until he suffered the sharpest pangs and the most grievous sufferings that ever were or shall be, and at the last he died. And when it was finished and he had born us to bliss, even this could not fully satisfy his marvelous love.

—Julian of Norwich

life. (Do I really want a God with a body? Would I prefer a God who lives as I try to live—mostly in my head?)

We are moving toward Good Friday, the day on which we devote ourselves to recalling and praying about the Crucifixion. I am beginning to think that perhaps discomfort is a perfectly appropriate response to God's groaning labor. I am beginning to think that, indeed, maybe I should have exactly this reaction, this wild unease, not just when I ponder Isaiah 42, but when I ponder the cross. I should read about the Crucifixion and see there, too, God in bodily vulnerability—anguish, bleeding, the very opposite of control. Whatever I think or feel about God's body when I imagine God groaning and panting in labor, I should also think or feel when I remember God executed by a Roman prefect: if panic, then panic; if something high-minded and Pauline about strength in weakness, the same.

But I don't. I picture Jesus on the cross and I feel very little. The Crucifixion has become so sanitized in my mind, so normalized and familiar, that thinking of it does not shock me or disturb me or really produce much reaction at all, because I, along with much of the church, have turned a bloody state punishment into nothing more or less than tidy doctrine. Perhaps God as a woman in travail can remind me of God's vulnerability, and the centrality of that vulnerability for my relationship with that God. Perhaps Isaiah's image can show me (to borrow a phrase from theologian Beth Felker Jones) how "the body's availability is also its vulnerability."

Of course, God's vulnerability does not begin or end on the cross. God's election of a particular people makes God vulnerable to the people's refusal of life with God. The incarnation makes God vulnerable to all the ravages of human life. And the calling of the church—the naming of a collection of human beings as God's own body—makes God vulnerable to our continued failings, our continued rejections, our continued refusals to be God's body. "God is vulnerable because God loves," writes William Placher.

And that is the rub: right here, in the space of one paragraph, I have removed myself from the discomfort Isaiah provokes. In one short paragraph, I have carried myself from God panting and groaning on a delivery table, from God squatting in labor, from God with a baby's head threatening to tear at God's vaginal flesh. In one short paragraph, I have carried myself from that picture of God's vulnerability to something anesthetized and literally lovely, something polite and glassy and far away: just as the church so often turns the Crucifixion into the theological abstraction of "the cross," so here I have turned God's labored grunting neatly into "love." But the verse from Isaiah doesn't say

And in accepting our nature he gave us life, and in his
blessed dying on the Cross he bore us to endless life.

—Julian of Norwich

anything abstract or polite. The verse from Isaiah tells me
that God squats and pants and bellows like a moose.

Next year on Good Friday, I will read, as I always do,
the story of Jesus's arrest and execution. But in hopes that
I might hear that story for what it is—an account of God
given over to vulnerability for our sake—I will also read
Isaiah's depiction of God as a woman in travail:

> For a long time I have held my peace,
> I have kept still and restrained myself;
> now I will bellow like a woman in labor,
> I will gasp and pant.

Between 6 and 10 percent of women in American prisons are pregnant.

To put that differently, about forty thousand pregnant
women are incarcerated each year in the United States.

Most incarcerated women travel to hospitals to give
birth, though some birth in prison infirmaries. They are
usually shackled in transit. This transit happens only after
they manage to convince prison staff that they are really in
labor. A woman can labor for twelve hours in her prison
cell before she becomes convincing.

In some states, women are shackled during labor and delivery. By shackling, I mean placing "belly chains, leg irons,
belts, and handcuffs" around a woman's ankles, wrists,

or stomach. Eighteen states have laws that restrict the use of shackles on laboring women. Sometimes, as evidenced by subsequent lawsuits, women are shackled even in states where shackling is illegal.

Shackling is not only painful and degrading (and a violation of international human rights standards). It also reduces oxygen flow to the baby, who can thus sustain permanent damage.

Some hospitals practice "medicinal shackling"—giving an incarcerated patient an epidural so that she could not walk away even without cuffs on her legs.

Most incarcerated mothers are separated from their children within twenty-four hours of giving birth.

Arrest and imprisonment are central to the New Testament. Jesus is arrested and put through a show trial and then killed by the state, and Acts seems to suggest that being arrested, or visiting your friends who have been arrested, are key patterns of imitating Christ in the early church. (Incarceration is less ubiquitous in the Old Testament: Joseph was imprisoned in Egypt; Jeremiah was put under house arrest. But perhaps exile—forced separation from your family, forced relocation to a new place, no hope of return; the experience of the people to whom Isaiah was writing—offers a partial parallel to incarceration.)

For a moment, do not picture God as a generic laboring woman. Picture God—the very God who has a long history of identifying with people in the crevices and crannies of society—as an incarcerated woman laboring.

Remember Jesus, bound and led away to Annas, bound and led to Pilate—and picture Jesus as a woman in labor, bound.

What can I do to meet this God? How can I serve this God? How can I befriend this God?

My sweet Lord . . . are you not my mother and more than my mother? . . . For when the hour of your delivery came you were placed on the hard bed of the cross . . . and your nerves and all your veins were broken. And truly it is no surprise that your veins burst when in one day you gave birth to the whole world." So wrote Marguerite d'Oingt, a thirteenth-century French nun. "Ah! sweet Lord Jesus who ever saw a mother suffer such a birth?"

If this picture of God, embodied and laboring, is a Good Friday image, it also hints at Christmas. God not only births for our sake; God also submits to being born for our sake. Jesus in a manger is one of the most familiar Christian images of God there is. And yet, as with the cross, I tend to abstract the nativity into doctrine: Incarnation. If "the cross" can obscure the painful exposure of Jesus's death at the hands of the state, sometimes "the Incarnation" masks the granular bodiliness of childbirth. Usually, during Christmas, we skip quickly past Jesus's birth. We sing of a child laid to rest on Mary's lap sleeping, et cetera, and then we move straight into the rest of yuletide—into philosophical ruminating about God's having come to dwell among us, or into presents and figgy pudding. We skip the fetal Jesus's devoting most of the weeks before Christmas to sleeping, and to exercising his diaphragm muscles so he will be ready to breathe when he leaves the womb. We skip Jesus's pituitary gland, a few days before birth, sending some adrenocorticotropin to his adrenal glands, which then send cortisol to the placenta, at which point production of estrogen increases, production of progesterone decreases, and enzymes that can convert progesterone to estrogen are released. (Mary's cervix needs the estrogen so that it may soften and dilate, and Mary's blood needs the estrogen so that it will coagulate after delivery.) We skip the oxytocin, released by both Jesus's and Mary's pituitary glands, which ultimately gets Mary's contractions moving.

As the contractions pick up, Jesus would sense that he was being squeezed. His head helps stretch Mary's cervix open. This stimulates more oxytocin, which stimulates more contractions. Each contraction pushes Jesus farther down: Mary feels pain, but He feels pressure. As Mary's uterine muscles compress His head ever more forcefully, Jesus's body begins to release thyroid hormones and adrenaline, which will help Him adjust to the cooler temperatures He is about to encounter. He feels Mary's water break, He feels Himself still squeezed with pressure, pushed down the birth canal. The pressure lasts a long time. And then adult human hands—maybe Joseph catches Him; maybe Mary, squatting, catches Jesus herself.

We are accustomed, at Christmas, to singing generically about the miraculousness of Jesus's birth:

> How silently, how silently,
> The wondrous Gift is giv'n!

Part of the miracle that we don't often hymn is the fact that Jesus and his mother both got through the birth alive: in the centuries leading up to Jesus's birth, women often had four or five children, and usually one or two of them died in birth or infancy. Isaiah's laboring woman God is an image of vulnerability, not just because God endures a painful labor but because so many women and babies die during or shortly after labor. Mary could have died in childbirth. Jesus could have died in childbirth, and everything we know about vulnerability and power would have concentrated in that moment. The cross and the manger would have collapsed in on each other: vulnerability and power, kenosis and death and new life. Christmas and Good Friday would be one.

In the early church and the Middle Ages, people devoted a lot of time to pondering the nativity—they discussed it from the pulpit, performed it theatrically in nativity plays, and wrote evocative accounts of how, precisely, Jesus got born. In most of these accounts, Mary, unique among women, labored without pain. According to one text from antiquity, "It came about, when [Mary and Joseph] were alone, that Mary then looked with her eyes and saw a small infant and was astonished." In other words, the birth was so quick and painless that Mary didn't even know it was happening. More often, Mary did know that she was in labor, and Joseph was gotten off stage as quickly as possible. In some accounts, he goes to fetch midwives to help Mary, and in others he goes to fetch a candle. When he returns, midwives or candle in tow, Mary has already given birth. Joseph's absence comported with the medieval assumption that men didn't belong in birthing rooms, but his absence, and especially the midwives' absence, also testified to the miraculousness of this birth and the sanctity of this mother. No midwife was needed, because Mary did not exactly labor or travail; the birth was so easy that she didn't need any assistance.

[Joseph] went outside and brought to the Virgin a burning candle; having attached this to the wall he went outside so that he might not be present at the birth. . . . Suddenly in a moment she gave birth to her son, from whom radiated such an ineffable light and splendour, that the sun was not comparable to it, nor did the candle, that St. Joseph had put there, give any light at all, the divine light totally annihilating the material light of the candle.

—Birgitta of Sweden

But let us imagine an alternative: let us imagine that Joseph and the midwives' absence from the birth imply not that Mary had an effortless labor but rather that God—who is described in Isaiah as the one who opens the womb and delivers, and in Psalm 71 as the one who freed the psalmist from his mother's womb—midwifed the birth.

One Old Testament text that casts God as a midwife is Psalm 22. In that psalm, we petition the God who is holy, who is liberator, who is king, who is God of our ancestors, and who is midwife. The psalmist, writing in a place of deep despair, pleads for God to draw near:

> Yet it was you who took me from the womb;
> you kept me safe on my mother's breast.
> On you I was cast from my birth,
> and since my mother bore me you have been
>   my God.
> Do not be far from me,
> for trouble is near
> and there is no one to help.

Whenever we pray this psalm, we are calling the God who attended our birth to once again attend to us.

Biblical discussions of midwifery, coupled with other historical sources, shed light on the metaphor of God as midwife. Foremost, the midwifing God is a God who helps bring

about and sustain life—a midwife's skill could be the difference between a mother or a baby living or dying. The God
who midwifes us is the God who delivers us—in the sense
of a labor and delivery, but also a great political deliverance:
before Moses could act on God's behalf to deliver the children of Israel, the Hebrew midwives Shifra and Puah did,
delivering Hebrew babies and defying Pharoah's orders to
kill them. To think of God as a midwife is to identify God as
someone who comforts and encourages—in Genesis, when
Rachel laboring with Benjamin is in distress, it is her midwife who speaks words of reassurance to her. It also strikes
me, a woman who does not have children, that in the biblical basket of maternal imagery for the divine, the image
of midwife reaches out to draw into God's action childless
women—in ancient Israel, midwives were often either old
women, or women who were themselves barren; it was those
old or childless women who were free to get up in the middle
of the night and attend a laboring woman for hours or days.

Midwifery is foremost about life—about helping women
move from one life stage to another, and about helping to
bring new life into the world. But midwifery can involve
death: right after Rachel's midwife comforts her, Rachel
names her newborn son, and then she dies. There is a book
I have read annually since college. Written by historian
Laurel Thatcher Ulrich, *A Midwife's Tale* is a remarkable
re-creation of the life of Martha Ballard, who delivered
almost one thousand babies on the Maine frontier in the
late eighteenth and early nineteenth centuries. Most of the
mothers and children she delivered lived, but a few did not,
and Ballard typically recorded those deaths in her diary.

On August 16, 1787, Ballard delivered Susanna Clayton's child. Four days later, Ballard got word that Mrs. Clayton and the child were ill, and Ballard returned to their bedside, to help with care for mother and baby in the final hours before they died. Then, "I asisted to Lay her out, her infant Laid in her arms, the first such instance I ever saw & the first woman that died in Child bed which I delivered." To translate that into more modern idiom, Martha Ballard helped the other women in her community dress the corpses of the Claytons for burial, and once they were dressed, the midwife helped cradle the baby in its mother's arms. I like to think that this is the kind of midwife God is: the kind who delivers us, and the kind who attends our deaths, literal or figurative, with tenderness and dignity.

When I pray Psalm 22 or Psalm 71, I slow down and give thanks for Martha Ballard (and sometimes for her historian, Laurel Thatcher Ulrich). I give thanks for Rachel's unnamed midwife; for Shifra and Puah, without whom there would be no Jesus; and for the psalmist's imagination. I ask God to care for me as Mrs. Ballard cared for Susanna Clayton and her family.

Like newborn infants, long for the pure, spiritual milk,
so that by it you may grow into salvation—if indeed
you have tasted that the Lord is good.

—1 Peter 2:2–3

Stina says to me one day, maybe we can think of the Trinity as mother, baby, midwife.

Maybe we can. What if we do?*

God is a laboring woman. God is a midwife. Completing a troika of birthing images, Isaiah also compares God to a breast-feeding mother: "Can a woman forget her nursing child, or show no compassion for the child of her womb? Even these may forget, yet I will not forget you."

Today, this image of God has been ghettoized, dismissed as important only to those who are specifically interested in exploring "feminine" images of God. But in earlier moments in church history, God's nourishing us with mother's milk was a commonplace. Jesus was often likened to a

---

*There is much precedent in the Christian tradition for pondering the Trinity via metaphor, but it seems especially helpful to reply to Stina's suggestion with Augustine. In *De Trinitate,* Augustine argues that once the church has a formal understanding of the grammar of the Trinity, it then needs to develop what substantive understanding it can—since we can't love what we don't know, such an understanding will help the church love God better. Augustine suggests that Christians should look around the created order and find things that might help develop this understanding. Almost anything in creation, says Augustine, might help—so long as we understand how whatever triad-in-creation we are pondering is both like and unlike the triune Lord. Augustine rehearses many possibly helpful triads-in-nature, ultimately concluding that some of them are of very limited use (Lover, Beloved, Love; the thing we see, the act of seeing, and the attention of the mind on the thing seen), and that the one that works best (memory, reason, will) works only because it remains deeply inadequate. To Stina's suggestion, then, we might say—embrace the triadic metaphor of mother, baby, and midwife to the extent that we can discern how the metaphor is both like and unlike the Lord, and to the extent that it helps us think about and love the Lord.

mother giving suck; we, the church, drank mother's milk from His wounds. The metaphor of nursing captured how Jesus sustains the church with grace and love. As historian Caroline Walker Bynum explains, "What writers in the high Middle Ages wished to say about Christ the savior who feeds the individual soul with his blood was precisely and concisely said in the image of the nursing mother." The Holy Spirit was described as being "sent from heaven like milk poured out from Christ's own breasts," and prayerful Christians gazing at a crucifix in church were urged to realize that Jesus's "naked breasts will feed you with the milk of sweetness to console you." Clement of Alexandria, Aelred of Rievaulx, Ephrem of Syria, and many other theologians meditated on and preached about the image of the soul as a nursing child and Jesus as our lactating mother.

Most of the time, these saints of the tradition—few of whom, even the female saints, had themselves fed children at their breast—understood the picture of God or Jesus as nursing to be a reminder of our radical dependence on

When all is well with me, what am I but an infant
suckling your milk and feeding on you "the
food that is incorruptible" (John 6:27)?

—Augustine

He has given suck—life to the universe.

—Ephrem of Syria

God and, concomitantly, of God's power. To be sure, nursing *is* an image of power: "If someone were to ask me to describe my own breast-feeding experience in one word, I would have to choose either 'powerful' or 'empowering,'" writes twenty-first-century theologian (and mother of three) Elizabeth Gandolfo, in an essay on breast-feeding as contemplative practice. "There is something about the experience of successfully nursing an infant that can make a woman feel like she is the most powerful person on the face of the earth." This power is straightforward—your body has the power to keep someone else alive. And there are subtler powers in breast-feeding, too. As Gandolfo explains, "Like the power of a nursing mother, the power of divinity is the power to comfort. Babies who nurse often seek out their mothers' breast not only when they are hungry, but when they are tired, frightened, or distressed."

Yet just as the image of God as a woman in labor yokes power and vulnerability in ways we might not expect, to picture God as a nursing mother is to picture both our dependence on God and God's radical self-limitation for our sake. After all, in nursing, the mother gives herself over to her child and allows her life to be determined by the child's schedule and the child's demands. The breast-

Wee are thy infants, and suck thee.

—Henry Vaughan

feeding mother lives according to someone else's requirements. In this way, to speak of God's nursing is to speak in
synecdoche of all the ways God chooses to be confined by
our needs.

My friend Sarah Ruble writes perfect Christmas letters. She is a good writer of other things too—the historical monograph (*The Gospel of Freedom and Power:
Protestant Missionaries in American Culture after World
War II*), the solicitous friend-in-crisis text message. But I
think her crowning genre is the Christmas letter. This is, it
should be noted, a challenging form. Too often one has the
temptation to include everything beautiful (the ski trip and
the kayaking trip and the kids' Ivy League acceptances) and
omit everything else (the rehab, the fighting, the stultifying
boredom at work, the cancer scare). After my parents got
divorced, my mother didn't send Christmas letters for years
because she could not think of enough beautiful things to
say, and her friends' Christmas letters made her feel like a
toadstool. Sarah has turned the Christmas letter into lit-

Here below, He who has promised us heavenly food has nourished us on milk, having recourse to a mother's tenderness.
For just as a mother, suckling her infant, transfers from her
flesh the very same food which otherwise would be unsuited
to the babe . . . so our Lord, in order to convert His wisdom
into milk for our benefit, came to us clothed in flesh.

—Augustine

erature. Her letters are true, and funny, and a pleasure to read, and also theologically edifying. I think someone will collect them after she has died and publish them, a small December gift book for the ages.

Last year, when Sarah was adjusting to first-time motherhood and learning to care for her six-month-old son, she could have been forgiven for not getting out a letter at all, but it arrived right on time. "I have never thought much about the metaphor of God as nursing mother," Sarah's letter opened. "To the extent that I did, I thought of it as being about warmth, affection, and tenderness. That, after all, was how I thought about nursing. . . . I had seen mothers nursing children and it always looked peaceful, sweet and, quite frankly, easy. In my imaginings, nursing was an activity hazed in pastels and shot through with sweet whispers."

Through some secret aspirations the soul understands clearly that it is God who gives life to our soul. These aspirations come very, very often in such a living way that they can in no way be doubted. The soul feels them very clearly even though they are indescribable. But the feeling is so powerful that sometimes the soul cannot avoid the loving expressions they cause, such as: O Life of my life! Sustenance that sustains me! and things of this sort. For from those divine breasts where it seems God is always sustaining the soul there flow streams of milk bringing comfort to all the people of the castle.

—Teresa of Avila

Sarah wrote that she has now learned that babies eat more often than she thought they would, and not exactly on schedule, and that "having a baby reorients your entire life. . . . Time changes. Schedules once determined by the clock are now based on the hunger pains and circadian rhythms of a four-month-old." She no longer understands the God as nursing mother metaphor as primarily a picture of "tenderness and sweet cooings (although those have their place). Rather, it signals the orientation to another—an orientation that isn't merely about sentiment but is inscribed in our schedules, our bodies, our lives."

Can a woman forget her nursing child, or show no compassion for the child of her womb? Even these may forget, yet I will not forget you. It is hard to imagine that a woman nursing her child every two hours for six months could possibly forget him. But God will forget us even less than that. "This Christmas," wrote Sarah, "I am reminded that there is no greater sign of God's orientation for us, God binding God's self to us, than the Incarnation, the taking on of vulnerable human flesh. When we know, individually or corporately, that we have tested the patience of God with our unwillingness to be at peace and our insistence on our own way," God will remember and care for us even more ineluctably than a nursing mother will remember her child. "And this," concluded Sarah, "is good news indeed."

I n pursuing the Bible's images of God, I have discovered a lot about my own biases. When the scriptures depict

God doing something people do—such as nursing babies—I automatically go to an image of a middle-class white person's doing that same thing and reason backward from that picture to God. But I believe that God identifies foremost with the marginalized. The God of Israel commanded Israel to remember that they had been strangers in Egypt, and to look for their own flourishing in their welcoming of other strangers. The same God could have chosen to become incarnate as a rich person, but did not. Jesus could have told his friends, in Matthew 25, that they would find him whenever they patronized the craft cocktail bar in downtown Durham where I and my friends hang out. Instead Jesus told them He could be found when they fed hungry people or visited incarcerated people. All this suggests that if we are going to draw on our own daily experiences to help us interpret the Bible's metaphors for God, those of us who read the Bible, as I do, in well-appointed homes, with plenty of leisure time for this pondering, must make the effort to stretch our imaginations to include experiences beyond our own.

This is particularly tricky when it comes to nursing. Most of my friends with young children have nursed them, for periods ranging from four months to two years. What this tells you is that I have mostly middle-class friends, friends who can afford to take long periods off work or who work in professional settings where it is relatively easy for them to pump. (This is not to say that middle-class women do not take an economic hit for breast-feeding. As one woman reported to a sociologist studying motherhood, "The first time cost me $20,000 in savings to nurse her for six months. That's what I burned through by staying home! I couldn't afford to do that the second time. You think you're going to nurse for six months, but wait 'til you see what that costs when your salary isn't coming in." That woman, it should be noted, was speaking in the mid-1990s—adjust her $20,000 for inflation.)

Ours is a moment in which it is a cultural given that mother's "breast is best." This is a dramatic change from 175 years ago, when elite women handed off their babies to hired or enslaved African American or Irish wet nurses. And it is a dramatic change from sixty years ago, when many women were persuaded by physicians and manufacturers that scientifically engineered formula was more reliable than breast milk and would lead to smarter, healthier babies. Today, by contrast, medical wisdom holds that it is healthier for mother and child if the child nurses, and there is enormous pressure to breast-feed: the "good mother" is one who nurses.

But there are all kinds of women who cannot nurse or who choose not to nurse. There are women who can't nurse because their milk ducts are plugged, or because their babies are premature or ill or otherwise too weak to suck.

There are women who don't nurse because they have inverted nipples, or very small ones, or very large ones, or their baby has a cleft palate.

Some women don't breast-feed because they are HIV-positive.

Some women don't nurse because they are in prison.

Some women, despite their expectations that they will feel a sacrosanct closeness with their baby, hate nursing.

And there are women who cannot afford to nurse. In the United States, working-class women have a much harder

time nursing than women who can afford to delay their
return to work or women who work in white-collar jobs—
jobs that give women some control over their schedules,
jobs performed in offices with doors that close (so you can
pump with privacy). It is virtually impossible to nurse if, in
order to keep food on the table for yourself and the rest of
your children, you are back at work at a fast-food restaurant or a big-box store. So it is lovely that I have friends
who nurse for years and write Christmas letters about it;
what they have shared with me in their Christmas letters
is now part of my life with God. At the same time, I must
stretch beyond my own circle, and try to see what I might
see about God and nursing if I had any friends who were
different from me.

There is, it turns out, a biblical passage that helps me
to do just that—that helps me, when I think of God and
breast-feeding, to think of God not only as the mother
who has been given the social and economic support to
breast-feed, but also as the mother who has delegated the
feeding of her child to someone else. The passage comes in
Numbers 11. The people have their manna, but they are
complaining—they want quail, they want garlic, they want
the food they imagine they might be eating if they were
back in Egypt. Although God was providing this manna
for them every single night, although all they had to do
was gather it and cook it, the people are distraught, so distraught that they are actually weeping with complaint. God
hears their weeping and gets furious at them, and in turn
Moses becomes furious at God. In his cri de coeur, Moses
reminds God that God, not Moses, birthed this people and

God, not Moses, ultimately bears the responsibility for caring for the people: "Did I conceive all these people? Did I give them birth? Why do you tell me to carry them in my arms, as one who nurses carries an infant, to the land you promised on oath to their ancestors? Where can I get meat for all these people? They keep wailing to me, 'Give us meat to eat!' I cannot carry all these people by myself; the burden is too heavy for me." Then Moses tells God to just go ahead and kill him.

This passage implies nursing in two ways. First, most straightforwardly, Moses uses the idiom of birth and nursing. Second, the rabbis, reading Numbers in the early centuries of the Common Era, noted that we would do well to think of manna as breast milk: manna was nourishing, they wrote, not in the same way as cheese and crackers or grapes or steak. Rather, it nourished the way breast milk nourishes. So God is providing breast milk for the children of Israel, but God is not nursing Israel directly—God has hired Moses to do that. It is startling, in the context of ancient Israel, to think of God as a mother who has stopped nursing her own child and has given the child to someone else to feed. This happened very rarely in ancient Israel—in general, mothers nursed their own children, and only elite women and royal women hired wet nurses. In families of ordinary means, if the mother was not available to nurse (the principal reason being that she had died in childbirth), a lactating woman from the dead mother's circle of friends might feed the baby. But as Carol Meyers, the leading historian of women's lives in ancient Israel, underscores, "all too often these babies did not survive." In other words, for

Moses to paint God as a mother who has not nursed her own children is both to invoke God's royal status and to raise the specter that the child, Israel, might die.

In the biblical analogy, of course, Moses is not acting as a wet nurse—wet nurses produced the milk to feed other women's babies with their own bodies. In the biblical analogy, God provided the breast milk, the manna, and tasked Moses with—to borrow Winston Churchill's phrase—"putting milk into babies." God has expressed the milk or provided formula, and Moses is the overworked, overtired child-care worker. What is God's response? God tells Moses to appoint seventy wise elders to help him care for the Israelites. God, in other words, tells Moses to go get some help. God says, *Yes, there is too much going on here; here's some more child care.*

In real life, millennia after Moses, the child-minder is named Sharon. She lives down the street from you, and she provides day care, in her living room, for the children of eight different mothers, mothers who expressed their milk or prepared bottles with formula before going to the job that pays barely enough to cover day-care costs. Sharon is saying, "For the love of God, I cannot feed all these babies; I need another helper," but the children's parents don't earn enough money to pay for anyone to help Sharon. Or in real life, the woman caring for the children she did not birth is Mabel, the children's grandmother. Mabel is raising her daughter's three daughters, and she is sometimes overwhelmed by the work. Mabel cries out to God even as she keeps taking care of the kids. Seventy elders to help would be a happy addition.

In my experience, this chapter in Numbers 11 is read most often at ordinations. The sermon preached at these ordinations reminds the newly ordained minister that even Moses couldn't lead by himself, and your ministry will be a train wreck if you try to be a lone ranger pastor. You definitely need some support; you need your vestry or your board of deacons, your lay leaders, just as Moses needed his wise elders. This is a fine application, but Numbers 11 could be read just as easily as a parable about short-staffed day-care centers, about a society that does not allot adequate resources to caring for children, to supporting mothers or hired child-minders. It is striking to me that, in Numbers 11, God reaffirms the decision that God made when God called Moses to lead Israel out of bondage in the first place—the decision to place the children of Israel in someone else's care. God does not swoop in and do the work directly or send in a phalanx of angels. Perhaps this is another way that God puts God's own power at risk. This is not the groaning vulnerability of labor or the chosen self-limitation of nursing. It is a different kind of risk: putting work that is important to you—in this case, the work of redemption—in human hands.

A PRAYER

And you, Jesus, are you not also a mother?
Are you not the mother who, like a hen,
gathers her chickens under her wings?
Truly, Lord, you are a mother;

for both they who are in labour
and they who are brought forth
are accepted by you.
You have died more than they, that they may
  labour to bear.
It is by your death that they have been born,
for if you had not been in labour,
you could not have borne death;
and if you had not died, you would not have
  brought forth.
For, longing to bear sons into life,
you tasted of death,
and by dying you begot them. . . .
So you, Lord God, are the great mother.

. . . [Y]ou, my soul, dead in yourself,
run under the wings of Jesus your mother
and lament your griefs under his feathers.
Ask that your wounds may be healed
and that, comforted, you may live again.

Christ, my mother,
you gather your chickens under your wings;
this dead chicken of yours puts himself under
  those wings.
For by your gentleness the badly frightened are
  comforted,
by your sweet smell the despairing are revived,
your warmth gives life to the dead,
your touch justifies sinners.

Mother, know again your dead son,
both by the sign of your cross and the voice of
   his confession.
Warm your chicken, give life to your dead man,
   justify your sinner.
Let your terrified one be consoled by you;
despairing of himself, let him be comforted by you.
and in your whole and unceasing grace
let him be refashioned by you.
For from you flows consolation for sinners;
to you the blessing for ages and ages. Amen.

—Anselm of Canterbury

Laughter

There was the sound
of thunder, the loud uncontrollable laughter of
God, and in his side like an incurred stitch, Jesus.

—R. S. THOMAS

I am in class at the prison. This semester, Sarah and I are teaching "The History and Practice of Prayer," and we have all devoted a week to doodling prayer—which is just that, doodling one's intercessions to God, passing an hour with God just doodling. We ask the students what they imagine their relationship with God would look like if they adopted doodling prayer for five years, ten years. Most of the students say the same kind of self-serious thing that I myself would say: after ten years of doodling prayer, I think I would have a greater sense that intercession is nothing more and nothing less than holding people up to God's presence; after ten years of doodling prayer, I might be more comfortable just passing an hour in God's company. Then one student says this: "I think I would laugh with God more."

I am struck by her words. Have I ever laughed with God? Not often. I think about this all week. It sends me scurrying after what the Bible says about God's laughter: Does God laugh? Does God ever laugh with people? If I study the relevant biblical passages, will I learn how to laugh with God? (This is, of course, precisely why I don't: anyone who thinks study is the key to laughing more is starting with a handicap.)

What I learn is that God does indeed laugh, but it is not quite the carefree, throw-back-your-head-in-delight laughter I am hoping to share with God. Generally, when God laughs in the Bible, the laughter is derisive. God is laughing *at,* not with.

T he first laughter that sounds in the Bible is laughter God provokes. In Genesis 17 and 18, Abraham and Sarah laugh when God announces that they will have a child. First, God told Abraham that he and Sarah would have a son, and Abraham

> fell on his face and laughed, and said to himself, "Can a child be born to a man who is a hundred years old? Shall Sarah, who is ninety years old, bear a child?"

This translation, the New Revised Standard version, does a reasonably good job of suggesting the slapstick humor of the situation, the "mind-boggling, body-toppling laughter in the Hebrew text." (Not all translations manage even to gesture toward slapstick. For example, the Ronald Knox translation—"At this Abraham fell prostrate before him; but in his heart, he said laughing"—casts a rather different mood.) Upon hearing Abraham's laughter, God tells Abraham to name the child Isaac, or Let-Him-Laugh. Translator Mary Phil Korsak argues that this response is, in essence, God getting in on the joke: Genesis does not say directly that God actually laughed in response to Abraham's laughter, but in telling Abraham to name his son Let-Him-Laugh, God is joining in.

The story's next scene does something different with laughter. So far, only Abraham has been informed of Sarah's imminent pregnancy. Sarah gets the news in a roundabout way:

> The LORD appeared to Abraham by the oaks of Mamre, as he sat at the entrance of his tent in the heat of the day. He looked up and saw three men standing near him. When he saw them, he ran from the tent entrance to meet them, and bowed down to the ground. He said, "My lord, if I find favor with you, do not pass by your servant. Let a little water be brought, and wash your feet, and rest yourselves under the tree. Let me bring a little bread, that you may refresh yourselves, and after that you may pass on—since you have come to your servant." So they said, "Do as you have said." And Abraham hastened into the tent to Sarah, and said, "Make ready quickly three measures of choice flour, knead it, and make cakes." Abraham ran to the herd, and took a calf, tender and good, and gave it to the servant, who hastened to prepare it. Then he took curds and milk and the calf that he had prepared, and set it before them; and he stood by them under the tree while they ate. They said to him, "Where is your wife Sarah?" And he said, "There, in the tent." Then one said, "I will surely return to you in due season, and your wife

Sarah shall have a son." And Sarah was listening at
the tent entrance behind him.

The aim of this elaborate choreography—baking cakes,
ladling curds into a bowl, preparing a calf—is to get information to Sarah. (Abraham, after all, had just been told by
God that he and Sarah would have a child; he didn't need
reiteration from a trio of guests.) But just as it is elaborate,
the communication to Sarah is indirect—the annunciatory
visitor speaks to Abraham, and Sarah merely overhears, separated from the conversation by a tent flap. It is as though
in the Gospel of Luke, Gabriel had told Joseph, rather than
Mary, that Mary would unexpectedly find herself pregnant.

After overhearing the guest's prediction, Sarah laughs,
because she finds the idea of conceiving so many years
after menopause absurd. She laughs *bekirbah,* "inwardly."
Rashi, the great eleventh-century biblical interpreter, said
that Sarah's laughter was "inward" in two ways—she was
laughing to herself, but she was also laughing at herself, at
her dried-up inner parts. Sarah had just performed dazzling
hospitality, whipping up cakes for three visitors she hadn't
been expecting, but her womb, she thought, was inhospitable, and she laughed at it, scornfully.

God, who had seemed delighted with Abraham's laughter, responds differently to Sarah's laughing. Rather than
joining in with Sarah, God once more talks to her husband:

> The LORD said to Abraham, "Why did Sarah laugh,
> and say, 'Shall I indeed bear a child, now that I am
> old?' Is anything too wonderful for the LORD? At

the set time I will return to you, in due season, and
Sarah shall have a son."

Striking, again, is the indirection—God speaks to Abraham,
not Sarah, about Sarah's laughter. (There is, perhaps, an echo
of Genesis 2 and 3: there, too, only the man had the necessary information directly from God—in that case, the information was that a certain tree was off-limits. And there, too,
when God wants to respond, critically, to behavior, God
speaks first to the man, not to the man and woman who
were jointly culpable.) Sarah (presumably again overhearing?) responds to the Lord's rebuke with a disavowal: "But
Sarah denied, saying, 'I did not laugh.'" And only then
does God speak directly to her: "Oh yes, you did laugh,"
says God.

What is wrong, to God's ears, with Sarah's laughter? And
what is right about Abraham's laughter? Rashi says the problem lies in a distinction between two kinds of laughter—his
is joyful, and hers is scornful. Or (following the interpretation given by Nachmanides, who is glossing Rashi), Abraham draws someone else into the laughter (that someone else
is God), and Sarah keeps her laughter to herself.

Sarah will laugh again later, once Isaac is born. This second laughter is joyful and expands to include multitudes:

Now Sarah said, "God has brought laughter for me;
everyone who hears will laugh with me."

And then Sarah says something else:

"Who would ever have said to Abraham that Sarah would nurse children? Yet I have borne him a son in his old age."

This comment is usually taken to mean simply that Sarah is reveling in the surprise of it all, that she is eloquently and fluently declaiming the triumphant miracle of Isaac's birth. But I suspect Sarah is also taking a jab at God, for God's choosing to talk directly to Abraham, and only when forced by her denial of her own laughter, to her: *Who would have ever thought to tell Abraham about my pregnancy, my giving birth, my nursing? How ridiculous to tell him. Surely the proper person to tell would have been me.*

Typically, the three episodes of laughter in the story of Isaac's conception and birth are assessed as good and faithful (Abraham's laughter, in which God joins, and Sarah's final laughter, into which every subsequent reader of scripture is drawn) or bad, untrusting, and shamefully doubtful (Sarah's initial laughter, upon overhearing her guest's prediction). But when we think about God's own laughter in the scriptures, our assessment might change. God will never again laugh the way Abraham laughs—joyful and mirth-filled hilarity. Instead, God will laugh derisively and scornfully at God's enemies. If derision directed at God's enemy is the paradigm for divine laughter, it seems that it is Sarah, not Abraham, who is laughing like God. Put starkly, she is laughing scornfully at something that (she thinks) will interfere with God's program—her own womb. Without quite understanding what she is doing (and therefore unable to give a correct account of it when asked), she is laughing at the limitations she perceives in herself; at what she thinks she knows about her own body; at the self she thinks is not fit for God's designs. Yet through the laughing, she is transformed—it is Sarah's scornful laughter (and her denial thereof) that brings about God's direct communication with her and that opens her up to participation in God's admittedly risible plan.

I have the practice of praying the Psalter each month. Or, to put it more accurately, I have the practice of reading a few psalms aloud each day, such that I read through the Psalter monthly, a handful of psalms each morning and each evening, starting over again with Psalm 1 at the beginning of the next month. Some days, I know this to be prayer. Other days, I am not sure that my frazzled inattention even constitutes reading.

The Psalter offers scripture's most sustained account of God's laughter. In the Psalms, God laughs three times at evildoers and plotters of injustice. God is laughing because God knows the right ordering of the cosmos, the final ordering: God knows that ultimately the unjust will not triumph. In Psalm 37,

> The wicked plot against the righteous,
> and gnash their teeth at them;
> but the Lord laughs at the wicked,
> for he sees that their day is coming.

In Psalm 59, the enemies of the psalmist are crowding around yelling violent things, and God meets them with a mouth full of scathing laughter:

> They return at evening,
> snarling like dogs,
> and prowl about the city.
> See what they spew from their mouths—
> the words from their lips are sharp as swords,
> and they think, "Who can hear us?"
> But you laugh at them, Lord;
> you scoff at all those nations.

And in Psalm 2, "the kings of the earth rise up in revolt, and the princes plot together, against the LORD and against his Anointed," and the Lord responds with laughter:

> He whose throne is in heaven is laughing;
> The Lord has them in derision.

Now that I have noticed the laughing psalms, I find them hard to pray, because prayer breeds intimacy, and intimacy with the God of this menacing laugh is not something I want. In the schedule laid out in my prayer book, Psalm 2 falls on the first day of the month, Psalm 37 on the seventh day of the month, and Psalm 59 on the eleventh. For a few months I read them, sort of. I try to remember that in Genesis, Sarah's scornful laughter destroyed things that were good to destroy (her misconceptions about herself; perhaps her distance from a God who wouldn't communicate with her directly) and ultimately brought about life. Nonetheless, these psalms feel harsh and hard to me, and I dislike it when they show up in the calendar of daily prayer. I wish instead for a psalm that depicted God laughing with the psalmist over dinner and then declaring something like "Happy is the one who knows he is the laughter in God's heart." In November and December, I try out new translations, but the new translations do not turn the Psalter into *opera buffa*. God still laughs caustically. God still bares teeth like a dog and foams rabidly at the mouth.

It is the canine psalm, Psalm 59, that most repels me. There, the psalmist's enemy is described as a pack of wild dogs roaming the city at night, and the psalmist calls upon God to act like a pack of wild dogs in response. As Brian Doyle explains, the psalmist specifically enjoins God not to kill his enemy "as a human hunter would with bow and arrow," but to draw out the chase, "scattering and isolating the prey before bringing it to the ground and devouring it . . . very much as a pack of dogs might." The laughing God stalks and traps the psalmist's enemies, and then eats them alive.

And then it is January, and on the first and seventh and eleventh days of this month, instead of wondering how I would rewrite these prayers if I were a psalmist, I decide to go to a place of wickedness to pray. I drive to the house in which my friend P. used to live. She doesn't live there anymore; when she did, she was beaten nearly to death by her husband. I hope the house has been redeemed, that whoever lives there now has cleansed and blessed and hallowed it, but to me it is a place of great evil. I sit in my car and read Psalm 37. I cannot imagine laughing at the violence that was done here, but I try to imagine that there is something meet and right about God's laughing—not at the pain my friend endured, but at the man who brought it upon her.

At home, I read the psalms again, and I slow down and picture God laughing in the face of my friend's once-husband, and, slowly, it becomes consoling. It becomes consoling to picture God laughing in the face of those who oppose God's justice and God's peace. I picture God weeping with P.'s weeping, and raging for her, and laughing at the man who battered her. This picturing begins to feel like prayer.

The psalmist's notion that God laughs at those who want to thwart God's aims is consistent with that most striking biblical proclamation about laughter: those who weep now will laugh later, Jesus says in his sermon on the plain, and those who laugh now will weep later. Those words have been understood by many Christian interpreters as suggesting that devout Christians should, in fact, eschew laughter. The interpretation offered by Jerome, a fourth- and fifth-century theologian and priest, is illustrative: "As long as we are in the vale of tears we may not laugh, but must weep. So the Lord also says, 'Blessed are those who weep, for they shall laugh.' We are in the vale of tears and this age is one of tears," and Christians should not laugh until the Second Coming. Or, even more starkly, the Carolingian reformer Benedict of Aniane: "Since the

Lord condemns those who laugh now, it is clear that there is never a time for laughter for the faithful soul."

In the context of God's own laughter, there is another way to think about Jesus's proclamation: the laughter of God is inseparable from God's justice. In the here and now, the kind of laughter that friends of God pursue is laughter that is proleptic—laughter that hints at, or partakes of, the world to come. The best laughter now is laughter that bespeaks a heaven in which those who have been made to weep by earthly rulers will, in the fullness of time, heartily laugh. In other words, laughter is political. Laughter arranges power, and God provokes us to laugh as testimony—testimony to our belief in a God who is ruling over a calamitous or oppressive situation, despite all signs to the contrary.

God is, of course, not the only One to laugh in the face of injustice (though God is the only One who can be rightly certain that things the laugher judges to be unjust in fact are at odds with God's justice).

The annals of political protest are littered with instances of activists using laughter—to ridicule their enemies, to sustain their own spirits. My favorite examples of this come from the women's suffrage movement. Looking back on her years of suffrage work, English activist Annie Kenney recalled that suffragettes "were taught never to lose our tempers; always to get the best of a joke, and to join in the laughter with the audience even if the joke was against us.

This training made most of the Suffragettes quick witted, good at repartee. . . . [T]he speakers that an audience took a delight in listening to, even though they did not agree with them, were those able to make them laugh." The suffragettes learned that when they were being heckled or even attacked, they could make lighthearted jokes that would provoke the crowd's laughter: Mary Gawthorpe was holding a political meeting when a group of men began hurling hard peppermint candy at her; "Sweets to the sweet!" she declared with a smile. On another occasion, a man threw a cabbage at her, and Gawthorpe "laughingly remarked that she had been afraid that the gentleman would lose his head at some point."

In recent years, clowning has played a particularly prominent role in political demonstrations. In Charlotte, North Carolina, representatives of the local Latin American Coalition and other concerned citizens turned up at a KKK gathering dressed as clowns. While members of the Klan, in their uniforms of white robes, chanted, "White power," the clowns chanted, "White flour" and "Wife power." The clowns outnumbered the Klan members five to one, and their message, in the words of the youth coordinator for the Latin American Coalition, was, "You look silly. We're dressed like clowns and you're the ones who look silly." Groups like the Clandestine Insurgent Rebel Clown Army see clowning as a provocative way to protest consumerism and war: "Nothing undermines authority like holding it up to ridicule," says one of the Clown Army's manifestos. Clowns are not just funny—they try to jolt observers out of their unreflected assumptions and habits. Because clowns mock the order of things, they can prompt the rest of us to consider whether a reordering might be possible.

Scholars who study the role of laughter in protest say laughing serves several ends. Laughter binds together oppressed people and expresses criticism of dominant institutions. Laughter alleviates the stress and tension of political organizing and protest, and can "defuse threatening situations." Costumes and funny songs also command observers' attention (and garner media coverage), perhaps more than a humorless rally with only serious signs and ponderous speakers. As one Australian activist noted, you might forget what was said in the speeches, but you remember the dramatic spectacles—the larger-than-life puppets, the clowns, the costumes.

When read through a biblical scrim, laughing during a political protest seems to do something even greater than what the sociologists and humorologists enumerate. Laughter indeed relieves stress and forges bonds. But it is also a sign of defiance, a sign that the ruler who rules unjustly is not ultimately in control. Because it is hard to laugh when you are terrified or furious, laughter fosters (and proclaims) confidence. If those who laugh now will weep later, and those who weep now will laugh later, then saying that God laughs and provokes laughter is synonymous with saying that God overturns the hierarchies of the world. That overturning will make you laugh or cry, depending on where you sit.

I think about all this during the protests—the Moral Monday protests, as the NAACP has christened them—that grip downtown Raleigh all summer. The state legislature wants to cut funding for education, roll back a six-year moratorium on the death penalty, restrict early voting. Those of us at these weekly protests think, to put it mildly, that this is the wrong direction for our state. On some Mondays, it seems there are people here from every part of my life: women from my church; my bishop; my dance teacher; friends of my sister, of my aunt; colleagues from work; a waitress from my neighborhood sandwich shop; a reporter I know, who seems to be here as a citizen, not a journalist. I can't imagine that any of us think demonstrations at the statehouse will actually persuade the legislators to vote differently. I am here because being here for a few hours offers a brief, vivifying antidote to the political despair I have been feeling. In the coming months, when I do things that might have more of an actual impact—registering people to vote, working for a candidate I'd like to see elected—the energy to do it will come in part from these summer rallies. As a friend of mine said to me, "What these protests do is prevent the legislature's current behavior from becoming

It is of course difficult to laugh in the face of danger. When hundreds of police and military personnel are lined up in their riot gear with weapons aimed at you, it is difficult to dance or sing. The natural human reaction of those oppressed by what they consider to be unjust forces of order is to fight back: after all, that is what justice is all about. Or is it?

—M. Lane Bruner

normalized. These protests prevent us from thinking, 'Oh, of course this is happening; this is inevitable.'"

One of the senators whose proposed legislation is being protested at Moral Mondays has come out swinging against the demonstrations. "The circus came to the State Capitol this week, complete with clowns, a carnival barker and a sideshow," he wrote in an op-ed. In fact, the senator may be more right than he knew. A few people at Moral Mondays, motivated by their quite grave political concerns, are, like the suffragettes of old, protesting by poking fun. My friend Amy Laura has come decked out in a vintage yellow tea dress and proper white gloves. She holds a banner proclaiming, in purple letters, "Ladies for Justice"; the words are flanked by a red high heel and a silhouette of a fancy lady wearing pearls. She is politely mocking the grumpy legislators who have claimed that the protests are uncivilized, disrespectful, and unladylike.

Also in attendance is a klatch of Raging Grannies. The Grannies first got together in the 1980s, to protest the nuclear arms race. As far as I can tell, the only requirements to join are that you have to be old enough to be a grandmother, you have to wear clothes that mock stereotypes of dried-up old women, and you have to lustily sing protest songs. At the Moral Mondays, their songs include these lyrics, sung to the tune of "My Bonnie Lies over the Ocean": "Arrest us and throw us in prison, if that's what it takes to be heard. But you can't keep us quiet forever. The people will have the last word."

I want to be like these women when I grow up.

At Moral Mondays, I find myself smiling at the Grannies, and smiling and then chuckling at Amy Laura's banner. I turn to my pastor. "These ladies give a new twist to the Proverbs 31 woman," I say. "'She is clothed with strength and dignity; she can laugh at the days to come.'" I think the Grannies' and Amy Laura's laughter is the kind God wants God's people to laugh.

Of course, the politics on display at these Monday rallies aligns more or less neatly with my own political certainties, some of which I am very certain about indeed. I am, for example, certain that to work to end the death penalty is to participate in God's justice. I am certain that to change the laws that penalize battered women who respond to their abusers with violence in self-defense would be to participate in God's justice. I believe, unswervingly, that to welcome the stranger, to follow Jesus to prison, to imagine the abolition of the penal system—I believe that all of this participates in God's justice. I cannot imagine otherwise.

What a beautiful sight it is for God when a Christian mocks . . . the clatter of the tools of death and the horror of the executioner; when he defends and upholds his liberty in the face of kings and princes, obeying God alone to whom he belongs. Among us, boys and women laugh to scorn torture and the gallows cross, the wild beasts and all the other horrors of execution.

—Minucius Felix

And yet: humming through all my certainty is the dim awareness of my own dogmatism. My sense of what is just and unjust, my sense of what to laugh at and what to rage against—some of this certainty must be mistaken. Some of my confidence that I know the precise objects of God's derision must be misplaced. Humming through all my sure convictions is the suspicion that that my need to craft political certainties of a kind that aren't, finally, available is also, in a sense, laughable.

When he was in his early thirties, the French painter Georges Rouault was walking through town and passed a circus caravan. An "old clown sitting in a corner of his caravan in the process of mending his sparkling and gaudy costume" caught his attention. Gazing at the clown, Rouault began to think about the contrast between the clown's eye-catching costume and props, "made to amuse," and the clown's own marginal place in society: the man dressed as a clown was, underneath the costume, a poor, itinerant wayfarer. "I saw quite clearly that the 'Clown' was me, was us, nearly all of us," wrote Rouault in a letter to a friend. "This rich and glittering costume, it is given to us by life itself, we are all more or less clowns, we all wear a glittering costume." Having seen his own existential condition reflected thus, Rouault began to paint clowns—yellow clowns, wounded clowns, a clown with a drum, young clowns and old clowns. Rouault's contemporaries noticed resonances between his paintings of clowns and his paintings of Jesus, between pieces like *Head of a Tragic Clown* (1904–1905) and *Head of Christ* (1905); Rouault's depictions of costumed harlequins and of the savior of the world had begun to resemble one another. Rouault's "clowns have the faces of Christ ravaged and sublime," wrote novelist Francois Mauriac.

Rouault was taking up a long-standing, if quiet, tradition in the church: the idea of Jesus as clown. Arguably, that tradition goes all the way back to Paul, who reminded the Corinthians that the world deemed "foolish" the things of Christ and that disciples were to indeed be "fools" for Christ. In those verses, Christians have discerned a suggestion that Jesus Himself is a holy fool or a trickster. Rouault's clowning Christs expressed at least two true things about Jesus: Jesus is the marginal wayfarer, and Jesus specializes, as clowns do, in interruptions, in behavior that violates etiquette and social norms, in impropriety, surprises, and mockery of convention.

Jesus interrupts the normal order of things before He is even born—what is the Virgin Birth if not a transgression of the normal order? Throughout His life, in His teaching and preaching and friendships, Jesus shows up where He is least expected and does unexpected things once He gets there; He

One who is slapped.

—John Chrysostom's definition of "fool"

is rude at dinner parties; He speaks in riddles. And at the end of His life, He is the protagonist in a drama that is both parodic and ironic: the Crucifixion. Crucifixions generally, not just Jesus's, were understood by contemporaries as ironic punishments—a sort of contrapasso in which those who had gotten above their raising were literally raised up in torture and death. As Joel Marcus explains,

> This strangely "exalting" mode of execution was designed to mimic, parody, and puncture the pretensions of insubordinate transgressors by displaying a deliberately horrible mirror of their self-elevation. For it is revealing that the criminals so punished were often precisely people who had, in the view of their judges, gotten "above" themselves—rebellious slaves, for example, or slaves who had insulted their masters, or people of any class who had not shown proper deference to the emperor, not to mention those who had revolted against him or who had, through brigandage or piracy, demonstrated disdain for imperial rule. Crucifixion was intended to unmask, in a deliberately grotesque manner, the pretension and arrogance of those who had exalted themselves beyond their station.

Jesus's crucifixion was layered with many more layers of irony—calling Him king, clothing Him in mock-royal garb. But if Jesus's elevation was mocked by the Roman punishment, that very mocking was in turn undone by the resurrection. It was not the Romans who had the last laugh.

I am in Ashe County, at my aunt's mountain house. I have come here to be alone with my computer and my library books; there is a sermon to write and a lecture to write. I have come for the solitude and quiet. I have come away from a household where, at the moment, I don't feel at home. I am praying the psalms. And as I pray, I think I can hear God laughing at me. It is not acidic—it is gentle; but it is very much a laughing at, not a laughing with. It is a touch rueful, as though God appreciates that I cannot do any better but wishes that I could. As though God is numbering the many times I have run away from a home I have not liked, a home where I have found it hard to be loving. As though God wishes that I would become a little bit more transformed, and sees that I have not. I hear the faintest, briefest chuckle escape from my own lips, also rueful, a laughing at myself, a laughing with God laughing at me.

Some months later, I will read a commentary on Ecclesiastes: "Laughter makes it possible for us to make a negative judgment while yet remaining open to the other person, or even to parts of ourselves that we find inadequate or embarrassing." I will think back to the morning in Ashe County when I heard God laughing at me. I will think: *God has made a negative judgment; God is still open to me. I am still open to myself, even to my small, sinful, curdling parts. I will welcome them with laughter.*

There is a rabbinic tradition that Proverbs 31—the woman of valor hymn—was a eulogy for Sarah. It was Sarah who planted vineyards and fed the poor and spun purple wool and spoke with wisdom, and it was Sarah who will, as Proverbs 31:25 has it, laugh until the end of days. How does Sarah laugh, in the World to Come? Is she laughing derisively? Or is she laughing her postpartum laughter—joyful and generative and inclusive of everyone who hears?

Biblical laughter is not only about God's justice—it is also strongly eschatological; it is about redemption and restoration. Or, perhaps put more accurately, it is the first because it is the second; because biblical laughter is eschatological, because it is about God's redemption and God's final ordering of things, it is definitionally about justice, and about mercy, too.

Who will be laughing and who will be weeping in the World to Come? And what kind of laughter will heaven's laughter be?

When hell is finally harrowed, when God's program has been consummated and all God's creation redeemed, there will be no one to weep but also no one to occasion the laughter of derision. Perhaps now, in this in-between time, Sarah's laughter alternates between the laughter she laughed behind the tent flap and the laughter she laughed after giving birth. Perhaps we can hear them both—her practiced cackle, aimed just so; and her relaxed, delighted mirth, which she is practicing for the time when there are no more enemies to scorn.

A year has elapsed since that class on doodling prayer at the prison. This semester, Sarah and I are teaching a new class, one on reading the Bible through the lens of incarceration: what do prisons have to teach us about the Bible, and what can the Bible teach us about prison? I am trying to cram what feels like a lifetime of reading about the American prison system into this one semester, so that I can have informed things to say in class about solitary confinement, the death penalty, convict labor.

This week, I am reading an article by sociologist Kimberly Greer about incarcerated women's emotional lives. Greer notes that "the ability to laugh was viewed as an invaluable asset within the prison walls." One of the incarcerated women Greer writes about, identified in the article only as Vanessa, describes her efforts to keep her friends in good

The mouth filled with real laughter . . . is an image representing the end of days, the overcoming of separateness and closure. In this world, it remains a mere possibility that constantly destroys itself.

—Avivah Gottlieb Zornberg

spirits: "I try to give a pep talk you know . . . and I'll get them laughing . . . a lot of my good friends . . . every time they got depressed, the other ones would come and get me to talk to them and I'd cheer them up. Like they'd be crying and I would have them laughing."

This seems to me a small glimpse of the world that Jesus promises, a small glimpse of the comedy that God is writing. In that comedy, of course, there will be no prisons, and all the women who used to be locked up crying will be free and will laugh.

A PRAYER

Lord, to laugh in the midst of trial and to rejoice in the darkest valley is another way of saying, "Our hope is in you." Fill us with laughter and joy while we work for peace and strive for justice. . . .

Help us to live so foolishly for you that we draw onlookers and those who would deride us. And while they watch and mock, change all our hearts that we might learn to laugh at the foolishness this world calls normal and run away with the circus that is real life. Amen.

—Prayers for December 21 and January 27,
Common Prayer: A Liturgy for Ordinary Radicals

Flame

God tastes like fire.

—HANS HUT

I t is one of those passages that the scholarly commentaries say is obscure: Jesus, in the Gospel of Luke, is recounting the division He will bring, the ways He will separate parents from children, the sword that He is: "I came to bring fire to the earth, and how I wish it were already kindled!"

What, the commentaries on my shelf all ask, does Jesus mean? What is that fire? It's hard to say, the commentaries say. The fire is opaque.

I ask my friend Alex what Jesus is talking about, and he says the fire is Jesus's Crucifixion, the suffering that must precede the final redemption of Creation—Jesus wishes, says my friend, that this suffering were already over and the redemption already brought about. Alex sometimes has a way of speaking that implies any right-thinking, nonconfused person will naturally arrive at the judgments Alex himself has made, and that is how he sounds now, naming this fire as Jesus's suffering and death. (It turns out there is a precedent for Alex's view: Cyril of Alexandria also thought that by fire, Jesus meant His Crucifixion.)

I am taken aback by Alex's reading, because I imagine Jesus is saying something entirely different: *I have come to set alight your ardor for Me and for all things good and lovely, and I wish that fire were already lit.* The fire that will burn in the disciples' hearts after Emmaus, I think—that is what Jesus means, surely. (There's a precedent for this, too. Ambrose, the fourth-century bishop of Milan: "With its fire, love makes whatever it has touched better. The Lord Jesus sent this fire on earth. Faith shined brightly. Devotion was enkindled. Love was illuminated. Justice was resplendent. With this fire, he inflamed the heart of his apostles, as Cleophas bears witness, saying, 'Was not our heart burning within us while he was explaining the scriptures?'")

The disagreement that Alex and I are having, I think, points not only to the opacity of the verse in Luke. It also points to fire's paradox, its contradiction and doubleness:

I, the highest and fiery power, have kindled every spark of life. . . . I, the fiery life of divine essence, am aflame beyond the beauty of the meadows, I gleam in the waters, and I burn in the sun, moon, and stars. With every breeze, as with invisible life that contains everything, I awaken everything to life. The air lives by turning green and being in bloom. The waters flow as if they were alive. The sun lives in its light, and the moon is enkindled, after its disappearance, once again by the light of the sun so that the moon is again revived. . . . And thus I remain hidden in every kind of reality as a fiery power. Everything burns because of me in the way our breath constantly moves us, like the wind-tossed flame in a fire.

—Hildegard of Bingen

fire warms us, and gives us light, and makes it possible for us to cook and to read late into the night and to keep warm in winter. But fire can also destroy: fire can engulf bodies, devour towns, annihilate whole cities. Fire is essential for life and civilization, and fire is a threat to both. Fire warms but can blister; fire heats but can consume.

Jesus, somehow, is all of that. Jesus brings the fire, and the fire He brings is Himself. Jesus the Fiery One (as the ancient Syriac hymns name Him); the Burning Fire Whom Mary suckles and the Flame she embraces in her arms, the Burning Flame.

Yes, I too wish for that flame to be kindled.

The house I live in, which was built in 1921, has four fireplaces, though one is currently behind a wall. When my husband and I moved in, we outfitted the three available fireplaces with electric faux fires. I felt some ambivalence about this: aesthetically, I'd rather pass an evening in front of the crackle and snap of real logs, but in reality, I'd light an actual fire about twice a year. With these electric fauxnesses, almost every morning, from October to April, I flip a switch and have fire immediately, and for not a moment more than I wish—the twenty-first-century simulacrum warming me in my very own dining room, as domesticated as possible.

Do I even know what fire is? If you ask me for a definition, I come up with something inaccurate, tautological, and lame: an orange flame that is warm; something that burns. Hazel Rossotti, a chemistry professor at Oxford, writes this: "We can define fire as a self-sustaining, high-temperature oxidation reaction which releases heat and light; and which usually needs a small input of heat to get it going; but we may feel that this pedestrian statement denies fire its true nature by excluding any aesthetic considerations." I have to look up "oxidation reaction" (basically, oxygen atoms are caused to combine with other atoms, and this attaching of atoms to each other, making

Now an angel of the Lord appeared to Moses
in a blazing fire—
a fire that devours fire;
a fire that burns in things dry and moist;
a fire that glows amid snow and ice;
a fire that is like a crouching lion;
a fire that reveals itself in many forms;
a fire that is, and never expires;
a fire that shines and roars;
a fire that blazes and sparkles;
a fire that flies in a storm wind;
a fire that burns without wood;
a fire that renews itself every day;
a fire that is not fanned by fire;
a fire that billows like palm branches;
a fire whose sparks are flashes of lightning;
a fire black as a raven;
a fire, curled, like the colours of the rainbows!

—Eleazar Ben Kaller

new molecules, tends to give off heat), but then, thinking about God, I go back to Rossotti's definition, and what leaps out at me is "self-sustaining." God is, and I am not.

In Rossotti's book I underline statements about ignition: fires can be hard to get started when you want them and impossible to control when you are trying to stamp them out. We could say the same of life with God—we cannot always summon a sense of God's presence, even when we do the things we were taught in Sunday school would work; in other seasons, God roars into our lives in ways we wish we could avoid, tamp down, put out entirely. "By far the simplest way to supply heat to kindling is to light it from some fire which already exists," Rossotti explains, and my mind goes immediately to those women, themselves close friends of God, who first sparked my curiosity about the life of faith.

Rossotti describes the clever methods early fire users devised to harness and sustain fire: "Considerable skill must have been needed to prevent the combustible material either from burning too fast, or from cooling and 'going out.'" The same danger seems to obtain in my friendship with

Lie down in the fire and see and taste the flowing Godhead in your being. Feel the Holy Spirit move in you, compelling you to love God, His fire, and His flowing in many different ways.

—Mechthild of Magdeburg

Jesus, that my ardor might burn up too fast, or cool down and flicker out; in either case, the flame is ultimately extinguished. There are indeed habits and learnings—praying, attending church, practicing patience, practicing penance, practicing generosity—that can help keep the flame of God's presence near, neither burning up too quickly nor simply fading out into coolness. Still, sometimes the flames leap and dance, not because of anything you did. Sometimes the flame dies, despite everything you did. We may develop considerable skill, yet the spirit bloweth where it listeth.

Bernard of Clairvaux wrote that the Word "opens up what was closed and sets fire to what was frigid." There is a violent eros in that image, and it allures—God might enflame a frigid soul. But the fire of God can also leave: when the Word disappears, says Bernard, it is like a boiling pot being removed from the flame. God's flame can enliven us, and God's flame can die down.

Maybe what I need to learn is how to bank a fire.

God appears as flame again and again in scripture. God reveals God's self to Moses in the burning bush, and then, centuries later, at the first Pentecost after Jesus's death, the Holy Spirit comes upon the disciples as flame. Those two episodes might be the most familiar flames in scripture, but there are many other instances of God drawing near to people as or in fire: God's presence as a "flaming torch" in the covenant of Genesis 15; the pillar of fire that leads the Israelites through the wilderness, and God's glory "like a consuming fire" on Sinai.

Fire means love, and fire means suffering. Fire holds the things we need for survival and flourishing, and the promise of destruction.

What might all these flames mean for our friendship with God?

Often, in scripture, especially in the prophets, fire seems to stand principally for God's anger, God's jealousy. But some Christian readers suggest that God's fire carries a doubleness even there. Turn-of-the-century English evangelist F. B. Meyer made the point thus: "When, therefore, our God is compared to fire, is it only because of the more terrible aspects of his nature, which are to be dreaded by transgressors? Is there not also, and perhaps more largely, a suggestion of those beneficent qualities which are needed for our purity and comfort?" Is it not also true, wrote Meyer, that fire is light and warmth? "We talk of ardent desire, warm emotion, enthusiasm's glow and fire; and when we speak of God's being within us as fire, we mean that he will produce in us a strong and constant affection to himself."

The danger of conflagration should not be minimized (I am sure that had I ever lost anything to fire, I would approach the flaming God differently). But it is worth noting that fire's very destructiveness is sometimes regenerative. Fires can clear weaker trees from a forest and therefore allow the healthier, larger trees to flourish. Soil nourished by burned vegetation becomes more nutritious for the trees that remain. Some trees require fire to survive: many "fire-dependent" firs need fire because the pinecones that contain their seeds can only open and let the seeds out if exposed to intense heat. The seeds then find a congenial place to germinate in the beds of ash left after the fires have died down.

Could the Bible's fiery imagery suggest that God's destruction is regenerative? That God destroys not me but my sin, my hardness of heart, my fear, precisely so that I might be renewed? English mystic Walter Hilton, commenting on Hebrews 12 ("Our God is wasting fire"), proposes this: "God is not elementary fire, that heateth and burneth a body, but God is love and charity. For as fire wasteth all bodily things, that can be wasted, even so the love of God burneth and wasteth all sin out of the soul and maketh it clean, as fire cleanseth all manner of metals."

Maybe, if God is fire, we are a grove of ponderosa pines. Without the heat and burn of God's flame, our pinecones would remain closed tight around the seeds that are needed for our thriving and growth and new life.

There is labour and great struggle for the impious who are converted to God, but after that comes inexpressible joy. A man who wants to light a fire first is plagued by smoke, and the smoke drives him to tears, yet finally he gets the fire that he wants. So also it is written: Our God is a consuming fire. Hence we ought to light the divine fire in ourselves with labour and with tears.

—Amma Syncletica

In the church, Pentecost is the season of fire. In honor of the Holy Spirit's appearance as "cloven tongues like as of fire," priests began in the Middle Ages to wear red vestments on Pentecost. In Italy, the custom of throwing rose petals from the church ceilings—again in commemoration of the tongues of flame—became so widespread that the day was sometimes called *Pascha Rosatum*.

There is a fair amount of fire during Lent, too. We begin the forty-day penitential season by marking our faces with crosses of ash and reading from the prophet Joel. The day of God's judgment is near, says Joel. A great army of judgment is coming off the hill:

> Before them fire devours,
> behind them a flame blazes.

This is the fire of God's wrath; it is the fire of Sherman's March to the Sea, the thoroughness of God's judgment, a fire that will leave nothing green. So God's flame is not

Barn's burnt down—Now I can see the moon.

—Masahide

all cozy warmth from my fireplace. God's flame doesn't always not consume. "For now is the axe put unto the root of the trees, so that every tree that bringeth not forth good fruit is hewn down, and cast into the fire," says one Ash Wednesday liturgy, echoing the Gospels of Matthew and Luke.

This Lent, there are wildfires in the West, again. We are making the earth pay for our sins, and I keep noticing the wrathful fire of God in the scripture passages appointed for daily reading during the weeks after Ash Wednesday. In Jeremiah, the Lord is fed up with the people's idolatrous ways, their worshipping other gods, their setting up altars to other gods in every available glade. God tells Jeremiah that She is finally going to enact some punishments, and that Jeremiah is not even to bother praying on behalf of the people. The people "have kindled a fire in mine anger, which shall burn for ever." "The LORD once called you, 'A green olive tree, fair with goodly fruit'; but with the roar of a great tempest he will set fire to it, and its branches will be consumed." The same images recur in the psalms appointed for Lent: "Our God comes and does not keep silence, before him is a devouring fire." "As wax melts before the fire, let the wicked perish before God."

Come, Holy Ghost, all-quick'ning fire.

—Charles Wesley

"Remember not, Lord, our offences . . . neither take thou vengeance of our sins," we pray. "From lightning and tempest; from earthquake, fire, and flood; from plague, pestilence, and famine; from battle and murder, and from sudden death, *good Lord, deliver us*." Fire is God's wrath and God's judgment. We are asking, during Lent, for God to spare us from the fire.

On the third Sunday of Lent, we read, in church, the story of the burning bush. The rabbis note that it takes some time—five minutes, seven minutes, ten minutes—for a bush to burn and that the miracle of the story of the burning bush is not the burning-but-not-consumed shrubbery. The miracle is that Moses paid attention long enough to notice that the shrubbery was not being consumed. Only after God saw that Moses had stood still long enough to notice the bush in its unconsuming fire did God call out to him. As Ellen F. Davis has put it, "Evidently it was Moses' conscious resolve . . . to turn away from the task at hand"—tending his father-in-law's flock—"and investigate 'this great sight' that prompts God to speak to him for the first time." Attentiveness, apparently, was the key attribute God needed in his chief prophet, deliverer, and friend. God needed a prophet and friend who could stop and stay still and look with focus and concentration; God needed a prophet and friend who could really see. God could have called to Moses in the form of a fellow shepherd, or in the form of a rock, or in the form of a breeze. Instead, God arrested the attention of Moses as flame.

Fire entrances. If I sit at a museum and look at a painting, I am twitchy after about two minutes, but if I am at home staring at a lit candle, I can gaze for an hour. In the winter, I sometimes sit on my sofa and stare into my (faux) fireplace for almost a whole evening. (Only occasionally do I have to shush the voice of my dead mother urging me to get up and do something more productive.) Fire captivates. To encounter the blazing God is to encounter the God who can hold, and wants to hold, our gaze.

For several years, I read the burning bush as an apt twenty-first-century cultural critique: we are all so busy and so distracted, rushing so hurriedly through the day that we barely notice our friends or ourselves, let alone the Lord. In a sermon I preached on the burning bush, I said that had I been Moses, I would never have looked at the bush long enough to notice that it wasn't consumed—I'd have been too busy sending text messages. This is, I suppose, a fair enough point—but it rather reduces the ignic God to a curmudgeonly op-ed writer fretting about the fragmenting pace of modern life.

The God who wants to hold our gaze is not that. The God who wants to hold our gaze—the God who wants to fix our attention and say, *Here, look here, look at Me, don't look away*—that God is a lover. That's what lovers do, after all. They gaze at each other utterly not distracted, utterly focused in their longing and their delight. Perhaps it is for this reason that Christian mystics so often turn to the language of fire to capture the love they feel for and from the Lord (so pervasive in mystical accounts is the notion of burning with love for God that it almost seems a cliché). Catherine of Siena wrote of her soul being set afire in the furnace of divine love. Gertrude the Great cried out, "Lord, how I want my soul to burn with such fire that it would melt and become a liquid so it could be poured—all of it—into You!" Teresa of Avila described God's igniting a "fire in the heart" and in the "very fundament of the body," whereby God "comes to the soul so that the soul, its flesh opened to God, can come to dwell, to dance, in the life of the Triune mystery." The God who is fire wants to hold our gaze—and indeed, our bodies—as a lover does.

The fiery God is a lover, and (to borrow a term from Hazel Rossotti) the fiery God is also a sleuth. Fire can tell the truth about an object's composition. Since antiquity, ore has been "tried" by fire; the fire revealed which precious metals, if any, the ore contained. The biblical prophets like the metaphor of trying ore—Isaiah, for example, uses metallurgical imagery to say something about what Israel has become, now that it has abandoned God's justice, failed to defend the cause of the orphan, and turned a deaf ear to the widow: "Your silver has turned to slag"—slag, the stony refuse you get during the smelting process. Jeremiah uses the metaphor at greater length, to characterize Israel and to name his own vocation as one who tests metal to determine its content:

The bellows blow fiercely,
the lead is consumed by the fire;
in vain the refining goes on,
for the wicked are not removed.
They are called "rejected silver,"
for the LORD has rejected them.

In our current era, as Rossotti explains, a chemist can tell
what elements are present in a solution by the color flame
it produces: sodium produces a yellow flame, potassium a
lilac flame, lithium a lovely crimson, and barium an apple
green.

So the God who is fire could sift and sort through my
properties; my true elements, the things I keep hidden even
from myself, could be revealed.

Do I want this for myself? Do I want to know the truth
of what I comprise?

Catherine of Siena wrote of dwelling in the cell or cave
of self-knowledge; she urged people to "hide in the cave
of knowledge of themselves and of God." (Idiomatically,
she was echoing the desert fathers, who characteristically
said, "Go sit in your cave" and "Go and sit in your cell and
your cell will teach you everything.") Catherine said this
self-knowledge was necessary for everything else—it was
essential. The self-knowledge she meant was neither individ-
ualistic nor separate from God. Instead, it was knowledge
of the self as the self stands before God and knowledge of
the self that is attentive to the neighbor. As Susan W. Rakoczy put it, "When self-knowledge is rooted in the depths
of divine love, one can face one's limitations and admit to

complicity in sin." That kind of self-knowledge beckons, and I hide from it. I long for it, and it terrifies me. What color flame do I produce when lit afire? Do I want to know?

In order to stack the deck in favor of self-knowledge and against my own terror, I have tried to find a cave. I once went on a three-night backpacking trip so that I could sit in an actual cave and see what it was like. I lasted one night and then, remembering that one of the desert mothers, Amma Syncletica, preferred to speak of the cave as a nest, I went home.

My cave is now a falling-apart tiny brick building in the backyard. It was once a greenhouse but somewhere along the way it lost all its glass. Since the day I first laid eyes on it, this greenhouse has looked to me like a chapel—so now the windows have been replaced, and a few wooden shelves hung up, and there is a chair and a lime tree, and sometimes I go there and sit.

Sometimes, when you go to the cave, your monsters will come out of their closets. Sometimes, as soon as you are approaching stillness, the monsters come out. My monsters

To contemplate is to look intently at reality, and to begin to see it as it is. Contemplation begins with a sharp perception of our rock-bottom poverty and powerlessness . . . in the sense of an individual self exposed finally without props and pretention.

—James W. Douglass

are purple with lots of eyes. They seem to have springs in their legs; they jump around and twirl and taunt me. My monsters tell different stories depending on the year. This year, the monsters are on a jag about money and security; they tell me I will never have enough savings, that I will never be secure, and that I will die cold and alone with no one to take care of me. Next year, they'll get on to some other theme—next year it will be relentless, self-defeating comparisons to my perfect sister, or unremitting self-flagellation about my petty dishonesties and sloth, or possibly next year the monsters will review every major decision I have ever made and show me clearly that each one of them was a mistake—but money and security and aloneness is their theme for the present, and I get to my cave and they come out and dance.

Usually, after they dance for a while, the monsters get tired or bored, and they head out for a hike, and then I have some quiet, I with the lime tree.

In the quiet, I might ask God to show me what is true and what is not true.

What is true?

What is true?

I do not know. I have built elegant mazes and follies so that I do not have to see myself too clearly.

What is true?

That I cling fiercely to the story that I alone have always taken care of myself, that no one else ever has or will, that I must. This story holds me like a pair of stays, keeps me upright like stays.

In the greenhouse, I think about all the painstaking choreography we develop from earliest childhood to keep from knowing the truth about ourselves.

There are some afternoons, occasional afternoons, on which I would like to welcome myself in from the maze.

For the last few weeks, I have been taking a volume of Catherine of Siena's letters to the greenhouse. It seems fitting to read her letters here. More and more I feel that it is Catherine who is giving me a grammar for articulating self-attentiveness as part of my friendship with God.

Today I am reading a letter she wrote in September 1377 to Trincio dei Trinci and his brother Corrado. In the letter, she praises their service to the Church, but urges them to a deeper appreciation of God, the God who lowered Himself that we might elevate ourselves, and made Himself visible so that even the blindest among us might see. In the midst of

For no one can lay any foundation other than the one that has been laid; that foundation is Jesus Christ. Now if anyone builds on the foundation with gold, silver, precious stones, wood, hay, straw—the work of each builder will become visible, for the Day will disclose it, because it will be revealed with fire, and the fire will test what sort of work each has done.

—1 Corinthians 3:11–13

this lovely ode, I find a remarkable thing: Catherine names Jesus's body as a cave. "The cavern of your body is open through the heat of the fire of your love for our salvation."

The cave of self-knowledge is really Jesus's body pushed open by the flames of God's love for us, the flames of God's longing to save us.

I came to bring fire to the earth, and how I wish it were already kindled.

It is Holy Thursday, near the end of Lent, the day we remember Jesus's Last Supper. Jesus took a towel and a basin and washed His disciples' feet, and He told them to love one another. After supper, He went into the garden of Gethsemane and prayed.

My friend Isaac and I are driving, as we do every year, to a small, ineffectual protest at an immigration detention center in Cary, North Carolina. Every year, a stalwart band of Holy Week pilgrims gathers in a grocery store parking lot in Cary, and we process to the immigration detention center and set up two chairs. One chair is occupied by whoever is having her feet washed, and the other is left empty, as a reminder of the people who are absent from us—from our families and our churches—because of current immigration law. I attend this foot washing because I think it is good to put myself near a space of arrest and incarceration on the days when we commemorate Jesus's arrest and incarceration. I attend as a tiny witness to my belief that regardless of national policy, Christians are called to welcome the stranger in our midst. I attend because a few years ago, in a season of my life when I felt very far away from God, the foot-washing service outside the detention center called me back into something like recognition of God's nearness and God's majesty. Also, I attend this service every year because it is one of the few times I get to see Isaac. He lives a mile away from me and we ride over to Cary together, and I may not see him for five or six more months, but I know we will have this one car ride to catch up on our lives.

On this Holy Thursday, I am thinking about Jesus, and I am also thinking about Nhat Chi Mai. She was the Buddhist nun who, on May 16, 1967, went to the Tu Nghiem temple in Saigon and sat down with a basin. Her friends assumed she was there for the traditional washing of the Buddha, but her basin was full of gasoline, not water. Nhat Chi Mai poured the gasoline over herself and lit herself on fire. She sat in the lotus position while she burned, and she prayed, and she died. "I offer my body as a torch to dissipate the dark to waken love among men to give peace to Vietnam the one who burns herself for peace," she had written to the

You, God, light coals on fire with the love
that eventually melts hatred and bitterness from the hearts
and minds of those who are full of anger. It will even turn
their hatred into tenderness.

—Catherine of Siena

American government. "I AM BURNING MYSELF," she had written. "I pray that the flame that is consuming my body will burn away all ambition and hatred which have been pushing many of us into the Hell of the soul and creating so much suffering among human beings. I pray that the human race will be able to inherit Buddha's Compassion, Jesus' love, and the legacy of man's humaneness."

During the Vietnam War, at least six other Buddhists in Vietnam burned themselves to death in protest, and at least eight Americans self-immolated, perhaps most famously Norman Morrison, a devout Quaker who burned himself in a garden outside the Pentagon on November 2, 1965, and whose death, it is thought by journalists, catalyzed Robert McNamara's turn against the war. But it is Nhat Chi Mai that I am thinking about on Holy Thursday.

Or maybe it is not really accurate to say that I am thinking about her, for I don't know what to think. It is a venerated thing in the Christian tradition to imitate Christ even to the point of death, but I wish it were not so venerated. I wonder what kind of faith one would have to have—in the resurrection, in the resurrected body, in setting your treasure by in heaven—in order to burn yourself to death in protest. I am not alone in not knowing what to think: even Buddhists and Christians in Vietnam in the 1960s did not know what to think about self-immolation. Was this truly a nonviolent protest? Was it worship or suicide? How can something be nonviolent when it does violence to the self? So I am not so much thinking about Nhat Chi Mai today as holding my imagined picture of her burning body in my mind. Our basins, unlike Nhat Chi Mai's, hold water.

At the detention center, Isaac leads us in a liturgy, as he does every year, and he offers a short sermon, as he does every year. He says he is tired of coming here. He is tired of it because nothing ever changes. Protest, like prayer, can become tedious. While Isaac is talking, my mind flashes forward forty years to him and me in our seventies, still making this pointless annual drive to Cary. It is both a deeply depressing thought and a hopeful thought. Part of the hope is this: if we are still coming here, that means we are still praying. This is Isaac's point, I think. Protest ultimately *is* prayer, in part because in protest you are ultimately protesting against God. Why has God not kept God's promises? Perhaps a life of contemplation is the most profound resistance there is—certainly it is more profound than my annual appearance at this foot washing.

There is some relationship that I can't quite pin down between Nhat Chi Mai's body and the burning bush. Her body's being consumed and the bush's refusal to be consumed—both command attention.

It is not just attention to the truth about ourselves that God's flame can direct. God's flame also wants to focus our attention on the world. If you wish to do politics, you have to be capable of paying attention to the world. You have to pay enough attention to notice that there is anything you might want to do politics about. You have to pay attention long enough to notice the harsh way that power is arranged, and long enough to see the suffering. Before you can act, first you have to see. (This is even true even of God. "I have seen the misery of my people in Egypt," God says to Moses from the burning bush. "I have seen their suffering, and I have come down to deliver them." God, too, has stopped to gaze. God has gazed at the Israelites in slavery, and seeing their suffering, God determined that it would be impossible to remain up in heaven or up on Mount Olympus or wherever it was God was before taking to that bush. God determined that it would be unbearable to stay so far away from the suffering of the Israelites, and God came down to deliver the people. You have to see before you can act.)

I do not want to instrumentalize prayer. Prayer, finally, is not productive, and it is not a means to an end. And yet, I know from my own halting two decades of prayer—of on-again, off-again prayer, of prayer that is consistent and prayer that is sporadic—that it is precisely contemplation that is turning me into a person with the capacity to attend to God and to God's world. How can I become a person who pays enough attention that I might notice something and then act in response? Prayer, *lectio divina,* reading the same passage of the Bible again and again and trying to notice what God has for me to notice; sitting in silence; walking in silence; repeating the psalms over and over— these habits might teach me how to pay attention. As I pay attention, this Holy Thursday, to the ignic witness of Nhat Chi Mai, with her basin of gasoline.

Abba Lot went to see Abba Joseph and said to him, "Abba, as far as I can, I say my little rule of prayer, I fast a little, I pray and meditate. I live in peace, and as far as I can, I purify my thoughts. What else can I do?" Then the old man stood up and stretched his hands toward heaven. His fingers became like ten lamps of fire, and he said to him, "If you will, you can become all flame."

A PRAYER

finally I say

all right, it is improbable, all right, there
is no God. And then as if I'm focusing
a magnifying glass on dry leaves, God blazes up.
It's the attention, maybe, to what isn't

there that makes the notion flare like
a forest fire until I have to spend the afternoon
dragging the hose to put it out. . . .

Oh, we have only so many words to think with.
Say God's not fire, say anything, say God's
a phone, maybe. You know you didn't order a phone,
but there it is. It rings. You don't know who it
    could be.

You don't want to talk, so you pull out
the plug. It rings. You smash it with a hammer
till it bleeds springs and coils and clobbered up
metal bits. It rings again. You pick it up

and a voice you love whispers hello.

—Jeanne Murray Walker

In This Poverty of Expression, Thou Findest That He Is All

To whom then will you compare me,
or who is my equal? says the Holy One.

—ISAIAH 40:25

The Bible and the church are abundant with speech about God: so many ways of describing God, so many words fragile people offer as we attempt to say something about the infinite, about our encounters with the Holy One—language about God, language for God, language to God; language to petition, to remind, to describe, to announce.

But in the Christian tradition there is also a worry about this very abundance, a worry that, since God is infinite and we and our tongues are finite, perhaps we should not—indeed, cannot—say anything about God. God is boundless and perfect; human language is precarious and contingent and decidedly small. Perhaps, say some philosophers, the only true things you can say about God are what God is not—God is not unjust, God is not finite—because to say anything positive is to limit a limitless God. To speak about this boundless being with our pockmarked words might be insulting, or deceiving, or just plain false. Maybe we would come closer to telling the truth if we said very little, or nothing at all.

There is no clear biblical mandate against speaking about God. There are, however, biblical passages that mystics and theologians have turned to when considering speech about God. Chief among these biblical texts is the discussion in Exodus of Moses's encounter with God on Mount Sinai. Readers in the early church were interested in Moses's encountering God in "a dark cloud." This dark cloud, a cloud of unknowing, is taken as negating all sense, all categories, all material analogies that we use to speak about God. The cloud has taken on great significance in Christian theology and Christian devotional life. It serves as a bit of punctuation, a semicolon or at times a period, giving pause in people's speech about the divine.

This way of organizing one's thinking about God is sometimes called "apophatic theology" ("apophatic" comes from the Greek for "negative" and "to speak away from"). To invoke apophatic theology is to imply that God is ultimately unknowable, so we can say very little about God, or, alternately, we can say things about God but we cannot really know what the many things we do in fact say actually mean. One of the earliest followers of Jesus to articulate these apophatic concerns was a fifth- or sixth-century writer known as Pseudo-Dionysius. A prayer he wrote gives a hint about his approach to God:

> Lead us up beyond knowing and light,
> Up to the farthest, highest peak
> Of mystic scripture
> Where the mysteries of God's word
> Lie simple, absolute, unchangeable
> In the brilliant darkness of hidden silence.

God's darkness is brilliant, and God's word speaks in "hidden silence." Later in the same text, Pseudo-Dionysius says, "Darkness and light . . . [God] is none of those." Dark and light, but neither dark nor light; brilliant darkness, but also not. Theologian Denys Turner says this kind of speech is "self-subverting"—it "first says something" about God, "and then, in the same image, unsays it." Maybe that is the best way to speak about God—to say and then unsay whatever we say.

Elsewhere, Pseudo-Dionysus explains that since God is the Cause of all, we can image God with reference to the things God summoned into being. But to image God with reference to only one or two or twenty of the things God caused would be to stumble back into the problem of shrinking, even falsifying God. As Denys Turner explains in his reading of Pseudo-Dionysus, if we are going to follow the logic of describing God with reference to that which God has caused, then

> to name God adequately, we not only may, but
> must, name God by all the names of creatures:
> only the "sum total of creation" adequately reflects
> the superabundant variety of God. Theological
> adequacy therefore requires the maximization of our
> discourses about God—and, whatever constraints an
> apophatic theology may impose, they cannot justify
> the restrictions of theological language to just a few,

favoured, respectful, "pious," names. . . . In a pious vocabulary of unshocking, "appropriate" names, lies the danger of . . . being all the more tempted to suppose that our language about God has succeeded in capturing the divine reality in some ultimately adequate way.

Setting aside a quibble about diction (what God speaks from the burning bush is God's name; Jesus is also God's name—the maximal vocabulary called for here cannot really be about names for God, but rather about figurative speech for God), we hear from Turner's analysis of Pseudo-Dionysus that it is inadequate to say anything about God, and it is inadequate to "arbitrarily restrict" the words we use when describing God. Silence is required, and the multiplication of our words is required. This is where all our speech about God is poised, and perhaps all our prayer, too—between a prolix alphabet of images and no words at all.

If we attend to the Greek etymology of the word theology, then a curious state of linguistic affairs results from its combination with the word apophatic. For theology means "discourse about God" . . . so the expression "apophatic theology" ought to mean something like: "that speech about God which is the failure of speech."

—Denys Turner

The insight that human language is tarnished, even fallen, and that when applied to God, it can distort—the "astringent" suggestion that God's unknowability demands we say nothing of God at all—threads through the centuries of Christian prayer and writing. In the fourteenth-century mystical text *The Cloud of Unknowing*, the author (appropriately enough, we do not know his name) instructs monastic novices in the life of faith. The author is very worried about language. He devotes one whole chapter to explaining how the novice might be led astray by the word "up." (When they hear someone say, "Lift your hearts up to God," "right away they look up to the stars as if they wish to travel beyond the moon and cock their ears in that direction, as if they could hear the angels singing in heaven. Sometimes they decide to use their clever imaginations to penetrate the mysteries of the planets and make a hole in the firmament to

There is a sense in which *any* writing or speaking about God can only be an edging close and then a veering off again, a fumbling after hints, shadows, and guesses, a groping in the dark. Christian tradition has at times seemed far too certain of itself and of its affirmation of the names and nature of God. Yet Christianity has also hallowed the apophatic way, the way of silence, negation and paradox, in which we can only stutter 'Not this, not this' and every positive image must be canceled out by its opposite.

—Nicola Slee

look through.") In prayer, the *Cloud* author writes, use only one word, only one syllable. Indeed, the only two words you need are "sin," which represents all that is bad, and "God," which represents all that is good. The woman caught in a burning house only needs a few small words—"help!" or "fire!"—and that is all we need, too.

It is six o'clock in the morning. I am sitting at my dining room table. A fire is humming in the fireplace; it is not yet light. I am wearing a blue bathrobe, and open in front of me is a prayer book.

> Know this: The Lord himself is God;
> he himself has made us, and we are his;
> we are his people and the sheep of his pasture.

> I will sing to the Lord, for he is lofty and uplifted;
> the horse and its rider has he hurled into the sea.
> The Lord is my strength and my refuge;
> the Lord has become my Savior.

> Give peace, O Lord, in all the world;
> For only in you can we live in safety.

God as refuge, God as giver of peace and all good things. Sometimes I imagine that I know what these words mean, and sometimes I imagine I do not. Sometimes I grow tired of these words, and I set them aside, for days or weeks at a time. On this morning, it is dark outside, and the fire hums, and I have not set aside the words but have taken them up in the hopes that they will deliver me to God, that they will carry me into God's own prayer.

What God reminds me on this particular morning of prayer is that it is only through prayer that I become able to speak about God at all; it is only in speaking *to* God that I can say anything *about* God. I remember this morning how prayer is first and finally a confession of dependence on God, and it is that confession alone that drains my speech of the power and argument and self-assertion that speech usually implies. It is that confession that orients me, that places me in a posture wherefrom I might, this morning, risk saying something about God—the risk always haunted by the awareness that it could be nothing more than my own will I am speaking, my will iced and decorated with a lofty spirituality and an earnest mien. With that haint stalking my words, I begin.

The point is not that our language is limited; the point (to borrow Benjamin Myers's paraphrase of Rowan Williams) is that God is "too much." God's utter difference from the world is too much to describe, and God's nearest intimacy with the world is too near to name. We cannot really say that nearness; we can only gesture toward it and surround the gesture with the knowledge that what we have said is inadequate; and then sometimes stop altogether, and put away all the gestures and all the description and all the speech. I cannot describe God in the same way that I cannot describe a picture I am holding millimeters from my eyes—the picture is made strange and unknowable not because it is distant but because it is so close. Or, to return to an analogy we considered in the first pages of this book, I cannot describe God in the same way that I cannot describe the collections of the Metropolitan Museum of Art: there is too much there for me to describe. To come out of the museum and describe the one blue bowl I looked at for an hour does not tell you about the museum. That is the hush of negation: the interrupting reminder that you can't hazard a statement about, let alone a description of, the museum, because there is always so much more to be seen. There is too much to speak of. God is nearer and more than I can say.

Of course, even these analogies fail the test of apophasis, for God's refusal to be described is, in some essential way, unlike the limits of description posed by the museum gallery or the picture I am looking at too hard. There is excess in the museum, as there is excess in each one of us—could I ever exhaustively describe you, or myself? God resists description because God is the One who is what God has, and the One in whom and from whom all beings have what they are—which is not true of the museum.

"In spite of everything," wrote Rowan Williams, "we go on saying 'God.'"

This dance between saying and unsaying is the way we know it is God about whom we long to speak.

One of my favorite biblical images for God is lodged in the middle of Isaiah 45, a robust litany about God's freedom to use Cyrus, the Persian king, for God's own purposes, even though "you do not know me." And then, writes the prophet, "Truly, you are a God who hides himself, O God of Israel, the Savior." The key phrase—*El mistater* in the Hebrew—has been translated many different ways: the God who hides Himself; the self-hiding God; in the Vulgate, the fourth-century translation of the Bible into Latin, the verse runs, *Vere tu es Deus absconditus Deus Israhel salvator,* and that is how you will hear scholars refer to this hiding God, as the *Deus absconditus.*

I love this image. Sometimes God hides. Sometimes what I might first name as God's absence is in fact God's hiding. In a sense, God hides amid all the many divine metaphors and similes that litter the scriptures. This is a God who conceals and reveals, who gives and takes away—for our edification? For our growth? For God's own whimsical pleasure?

In a 1987 article about the self-hiding God of Isaiah 45, the theologian Belden Lane wrote that we might think of God as one who plays hide-and-seek. When playing the game, the children who are hiding almost always give themselves away by laughing or giggling. Our job, as friends and disciples and reverencers and lovers of the Lord, says Lane, is to listen for God's laughter. The self-hiding God, in this formulation, is not one whose end is to stay hidden. The self-hiding God is also, at the same moment, the God who self-discloses, so that God might be found, by us.

Another thing that is true about kids who play hide-and-seek is that they usually hide in the same places over and over again, and so the parent or friend tasked with looking might reasonably know, even without the sound of laughter, where she is likely to find the one hiding. This is true of God, too. God has a habit of hiding in the same places; thus, we know where to look, and indeed the Bible spells out where many of these places are (we have explored some of them in this book): God hides in bread and wine, in silence, in gardens, in cities, in prisons, in hunger and privation and poverty, in song. The self-hiding God seems to be the God who wills Her own disclosure.

Says the prophet Jeremiah, "When you search for me, you will find me; if you seek me with all your heart."

Augustine wrote:

> God becomes all to thee; for He is to thee the whole of these things which thou lovest. If thou regardest things visible, neither is God bread, nor is God water, nor is God this light, nor is He garment nor house. For all these are things visible, and single separate things. What bread is, water is not; and what a garment is, a house is not; and what these things are, God is not, for they are visible things. God is all this

to thee: if thou hungerest, He is bread to thee; if thou thirstest, He is water to thee; if thou art in darkness, He is light to thee: for He remains incorruptible. If thou art naked, He is a garment of immortality to thee, when this corruptible shall put on incorruption, and this mortal shall put on immortality. All things can be said of God, and nothing is worthily said of God. Nothing is wider than this poverty of expression. Thou seekest a fitting name for Him, thou canst not find it; thou seekest to speak of Him in any way soever, thou findest that He is all.

The philosophers who pioneered apophatic rumination were not, I suspect, aiming to comfort. Probably they were aiming to unsettle. But there is a comfort here nonetheless. The philosopher's hesitation about language is a chastening reminder that we ought not place too much faith in whatever our religious construct is. When the construct fails us, as it surely will, we will remember that there was presumption in giving our heart so wholly to whatever it was we had said about God anyway. And when the construct fails us, maybe we will glimpse the God beneath the picture we had faithfully, longingly, lovingly made.

Hush.

In this poverty of expression, thou findest that He is all.

A PRAYER OF THE APOSTLE PAUL

O the depth of the riches both of the wisdom and knowledge of God! how unsearchable are his judgments, and his ways past finding out!

For who hath known the mind of the Lord? or who hath been his counsellor?

Or who hath first given to him, and it shall be recompensed unto him again?

For of him, and through him, and to him, are all things: to whom be glory for ever. Amen.

—The Epistle to the Romans

A Short Note from the Women's Prison

There is a chapter missing from this book.

The images I have considered in *Wearing God* are, of course, incomprehensive. They are the images that caught my attention during a season of becoming reacquainted with God. One way to describe the past eight or so years of my spiritual life is this: for a long time, I could see only God's hiddenness (and even that I didn't see clearly; I didn't see it for what it was). And then things shifted, as they will, and it seems I had attention for something else: clothing, bread, laughter, and the ways those things could help a person draw near to God. Each of the images I have considered here is, in some way, connected to everyday life—connected, that is, to *my* everyday life. I have written about images that are mundane: as mundane as a neon running shirt or a glass of wine.

It tells us something about God that God's self-revelation in the scriptures draws all of these mundane objects— clothes, bread, fire—into depictions of divine life. God's choice to reveal God's self through such ordinary things partakes of the same logic of—is perhaps a small expression of—the God who took our flesh in order to live with us. If God wants to communicate with us about God's goodness, then using the good things that God created and put in our lives, the good things that are right at hand, is precisely the strategy God would use to become intimately related and unified to us: because God loves us as the creatures we are, God must love not only us, but what's lovely to and good for us.

There are, of course, other images of God in the Bible, images that I do not discuss in *Wearing God*. I have not discussed God the soldier, for example. I have not written about Isaiah's strange and mercenary depiction of God as a beekeeper.

The image whose absence is (to me) most conspicuous is the image of God as an abusive husband, battering and raping Israel, God's wife. This image haunts Isaiah and Jeremiah and Lamentations. It arguably structures the entire book of Hosea. To my eye the most sickening example of the trope is Ezekiel 16:36–42, which imagines God as a husband who strips his wife, and then invites other people to gang-rape her.

The chapter on God the batterer is the missing chapter. I chose not to include that image in *Wearing God,* and I worry about that decision.

I am writing this final note from the women's prison. A staggering number of incarcerated women—over 90 percent, according to some studies—have been physically or sexually abused (or both), and many are in prison because of something they did, like kill their abusers or use drugs, which are in fact perfectly reasonable responses to abuse.

During the four years I have worked on this book, the women's prison has asked me a question each week: given the ubiquity of abuse, could I really omit the texts that describe God as a batterer from a book about the biblical images of God that we encounter in our daily lives? To be sure, God as battering husband has little to do with my daily life: I have never been hit. But for many, battery is routine.

In the end, I omitted these violent images of God from the book precisely to make a claim about their commonplaceness: although battering (and war) are the daily reality of many people, they should not be. I omitted Ezekiel 16 precisely because the needful response to pervasiveness of domestic abuse is lament.

Lament, of course, is one way to seek and find God with all your heart. You might open your Bible to Hosea 1 and 2. You might read with the memory that one in four American women has experienced or will experience domestic abuse. You might tell God that you are furious about this epidemic. You might pray a prayer of confession for the church's complicity in intimate partner violence. You might pray a prayer of lament and, in that lament, listen for God.

After you have lamented, when you are looking for a different kind of encouragement than the encouragement lament provides, you might turn in your Bible to a passage Sarah called our attention to recently at the prison: the second chapter of Malachi. Malachi is railing against Judean men who have fallen for and run off with foreign women. God is so furious at the men who are doing this—"breaking faith" with "the wives of their youth"—that God refuses the men's offerings (and their lachrymose petitions):

> You flood the LORD's altar with tears. You weep and wail because he no longer looks with favor on your offerings or accepts them with pleasure from your hands. You ask, "Why?" The LORD is acting as the witness between you and the wife of your youth, because you have broken faith with her, though she is your partner, the wife of your marriage covenant. Has not the LORD made them one? In flesh and spirit they are his. And why one? Because he was seeking godly offspring. So guard yourself in your spirit, and do not break faith with the wife of your youth.

In many English translations, the next verse is a little confusing, because the Hebrew idiom is odd. The verse is a declaration about the things the Lord hates. Here is how Sarah translates it—at the prison, she invites us to write this translation right into our Bibles:

> "I hate divorce," says the Lord God Almighty. "But I also hate a man covering his wife with violence as with a garment."

Listening to Sarah, I am struck by the sartorial idiom: the Lord speaks of intimate partner violence in terms of clothing. The man who beats his wife, clothing her in violence, has divested himself of the love and mercy in which God had dressed him.

It is just one verse, stacked up against whole biblical chapters that depict God as a wife-batterer and rapist. But it is a powerful one verse. It is the Lord telling us what He hates: violence against wives and the husbands who commit it.

"I hate divorce," says the Lord God Almighty. "But I also hate a man covering his wife with violence as with a garment."

Here, too, is an image of God: God as fierce advocate for abused wives. God as the friend who helps you pack up your car and leave. God as the person who helps you put together a safety plan. God as the voice at the other end of the phone when you call the crisis hotline. God as a battered women's shelter. God as protector of women.

I recently learned that the passage I so recoil from in Ezekiel is intentionally omitted from Jewish public liturgy, and has been since a rabbinic decree in the first centuries of the Common Era. During the course of a year, Jews will read through many sections of the prophets in Saturday morning worship. But Ezekiel 16 is omitted from this cycle of readings.

The rabbis omitted Ezekiel 16 for reasons unrelated to domestic violence: what disturbed the rabbis was the chapter's depiction of Jerusalem as a faithless whore, not that the text thus underwrites spousal abuse. Still, the rabbis' decision to omit the chapter from their community's lectionary is instructive.

We cannot, of course, finally omit Ezekiel 16, or any of the other passages that depict God as a batterer, from the scriptures. Those passages are there, in the scriptures, and as Sarah often says, since this is the Word of God, we are committed to wrestling with it, in the belief that it will eventually bless us, even if we come away from the wrestling limping, like Jacob. But we can choose, as Jewish communities ordering their public reading of scripture have chosen, to make some texts more central than others to our proclamation. Indeed, every church makes that choice every week, when it chooses what texts to read from the pulpit on Sunday, and what texts to study in Bible study. Churches make that choice, too, whenever they interpret whichever scripture they are studying. Churches, and individual readers, make that choice precisely because they read some scriptures through the lens of other scriptures. Some passages of scripture, in other words, become primary interpreters of other passages of scripture. One of my primary interpreters is John 6:56. Another of my primary interpreters is Romans 11:1. Another is Psalm 145:9. What are yours?

I want to make the second chapter of Malachi one of those interpreters; I want to see what the other prophetic texts, studded as they are with God's violence, look like when read through Malachi. I want to see what Judges 11 looks like. I want to see what all those texts about clothing—Galatians 3 and Genesis 3 and Matthew 25—look like when read alongside Malachi 2. I want to pursue my friendship there, with the God who hates it when women are covered with violence like a garment.

A PRAYER

Almighty God, we pray for all victims of abuse. We ask You to surround them with Your care and protect them by Your loving might and permit them to enjoy health and healing, wholeness and strength, calmness and peace and love. We confess that, even in this faith community, many women, children and some men are . . . abused. . . . [W]e pledge our faith community to be a safe haven for those who are battered, a support for abusers sincerely seeking help and an advocate for non-violence in the world. Help us to be signs of Your unconditional love in the world. We ask for your perfect peace. Amen.

—Stitched together from two prayers, from the Community of Our Lady for Perpetual Help, Salem, Virginia, and from the Metropolitan New York Synod Domestic Violence Awareness Task Force

A Bookshelf to Quicken
Your Scriptural Imagination

Here are a few of the books I most loved reading as I was writing *Wearing God*.

If you want to read more about the place of metaphor in the spiritual life, read:

The Kindness of God: Metaphor, Gender and Religious Language by Janet Martin Soskice

> Twenty-three years after her first book, *Metaphor and Religious Language* (which still defines academic conversation about the topic), Soskice collected a dazzling set of essays on God and metaphor, all of which touch on her proposal that the Bible's central metaphors for our relationship with God are familial. "It is on the face of it preposterous that we, creatures, should be the kin of God," she writes. "Yet there is a sense in which both Old and New Testaments point to nothing less."

Seeing the Psalms: A Theology of Metaphor by William P. Brown

> Brown considers not just metaphors for God but the "bewildering array" of metaphors found in the Psalter, such as "pathway" and "cup." We miss the theology of the psalms, says Brown, if we don't attend to the imagery.

God the What? What Our Metaphors for God Reveal About Our Beliefs in God by Carolyn Jane Bohler

> Bohler, a Methodist pastor, encourages readers to think deeply about the metaphors they may unconsciously hold for God, and to investigate

metaphors like the God who knits (see Psalm 139) and the God who is a jazz band leader.

If you want to read imaginative considerations of specific scripture passages, to help you remember how rich an experience engaging the Bible can be, consider:

Like a Tree Planted: An Exploration of Psalms and Parables Through Metaphor by Barbara Green

> This book brilliantly pairs psalms with passages from the Gospel of Luke, starting with a wonderful reading of Psalm 1 and Luke 13.

Getting Involved with God: Rediscovering the Old Testament by Ellen F. Davis

> If you are not sure what to make of the Old Testament—if it feels alien, or confusing, or dull, or too long, or if you are always starting out with good intentions but getting bogged down somewhere in Leviticus—read this book. It is the single best book I know for Christians entering the Old Testament. Davis goes many places in this book, but she always circles back to the theme that her title suggests: the Old Testament is the lively record of Israel's efforts to get involved, and stay involved, with God.

Consider the Birds: A Provocative Guide to the Birds of the Bible by Debbie Blue

> I myself am not interested in birds, but pastor Debbie Blue shows that birds are fascinating, and that the birds of scripture say a lot about God. Blue is a consistently illuminating reader of the Bible.

Home by Another Way by Barbara Brown Taylor

> If you want to feel like you have visited a biblical story—really visited it— dip into this collection of sermons. Each sermon creates a whole biblical world.

Creating with God: The Holy Confusing Blessedness of Pregnancy by Sarah Jobe

> This book, which argues that pregnant women bear the image of God, contains some of the most compelling readings of scripture, from Genesis 4 to John 6, that I have ever encountered.

If you want to explore different ways of engaging the scriptures in prayer, pick up:

The Word Is Very Near You: A Guide to Praying with Scripture by Martin Smith

> Smith offers an excellent overview of the Christian tradition's many fecund ways of praying with the Bible.

Praying in Color: Drawing a New Path to God by Sybil MacBeth

> One day, community college math professor Sybil MacBeth was sitting on her porch doodling. She looked down at her doodles and realized she had in fact been deep in intercessory prayer—and a new prayer discipline, praying in color (in my discussion of laughter, I call it doodling prayer), was born.

Water, Wind, Earth, and Fire: The Christian Practice of Praying with the Elements by Christine Valters Paintner

> I discovered this book only recently. I wish I'd known about it forever. It is a treasury of some of the ways Christians over the centuries have faithfully and engaged God in the company of the natural elements.

Notes

The God Who Runs after Your Friendship

"Turn it and turn it": Ben Bag Bag, quoted in Jonathan Rosen, *The Talmud and the Internet: A Journey Between Worlds* (New York: Picador, 2000), 7.

"There are many metaphorical names for God": Janet Martin Soskice, *The Kindness of God: Metaphor, Gender, and Religious Language* (New York: Oxford University Press, 2007), 1.

correlations between the ways a person imagines God . . . "changes t-cells in randomized trials": F. Carson Mencken, Christopher Bader, and Elizabeth Embry, "In God We Trust: Images of God and Trust in the United States among the Highly Religious," *Sociological Perspectives* 52, no. 1 (2009): 23–38; Elizabeth Mary Marcellino, "Internalized Homonegativity, Self-Concept, and Images of God in Gay and Lesbian Individuals" (dissertation, Boston University, 1996); Gail S. Harber, "God Image, Self-Image, and Length of Abstinence among Active Members of Alcoholics Anonymous" (dissertation, Capella University, 2005); Cara E. Wheeler, "Eating Disorders and God Image: Relationships Between Eating Disorders, Attachment, and God Image" (dissertation, Regent University, 2008); Mary Lynne Mack, "The Relationships Between Images of God, Self-Esteem, and Spiritual Well-Being: A Case Study of Roman Catholic Women" (dissertation, Boston University, 2003); Jeanette Anderson Good, "Shame, Images of God, and the Cycle of Violence in Adults Who Experienced Childhood Corporal Punishment" (dissertation, Boston University, 1999); Matt Bradshaw, Christopher G. Ellison, and Kevin J. Flannelly, "Prayer, God Imagery, and Symptoms of Psychopathology," *Journal for the Scientific Study of Religion* 47, no. 4 (2008): 644–59; John Francis Robison, "Images of God, Parents, and Self in Substance Abuse Recovery" (dissertation, University of California, Los Angeles, 1996); Matt Bradshaw, Christopher G. Ellison, and Kevin J. Flannelly, "Prayer, God Imagery, and Symptoms of Psychopathology," *Journal for the Scientific Study of Religion* 47, no. 4 (2008): 644–59; Thomas G. Plante, "Mind and

Body Interact in Surprising and Remarkable Ways," *Psychology Today,* April 23, 2012, http://www.psychologytoday.com/blog/do-the-right-thing/201204/mind-and-body-interact-in-surprising-and-remarkable-ways.

the characteristics we attribute to God will always be those characteristics we value most highly in our own society: Mary Daly, *Beyond God the Father: Toward a Philosophy of Women's Liberation* (Boston: Beacon Press, 1973), 19; Judith Plaskow, *Standing Again at Sinai: Judaism from a Feminist Perspective* (New York: HarperCollins, 1990), 121–28.

"Both paternal and maternal imagery are given in quick succession": Soskice, *The Kindness of God,* 79.

"God is too full, too communicative, too bright and piercing" . . . There is "too much" there to describe: Benjamin Myers, *Christ the Stranger: The Theology of Rowan Williams* (New York: Continuum, 2012), 103–4.

One of my favorite sermons . . . "would have us come home anyway": Margaret Moers Wenig, "God Is a Woman, and She Is Growing Older," in Rifat Sonsio, ed., *The Many Faces of God: A Reader of Modern Jewish Theologies* (New York: URJ Press, 2004), 241–48.

"All images are necessarily partial": Marcia Falk, "Notes on Composing New Blessings toward a Feminist-Jewish Reconstruction of Prayer," *Journal of Feminist Studies in Religion* 3, no. 1 (04/1987): 41.

"Every meaningful metaphor implies": Carolyn Jane Bohler, *God the What? What Our Metaphors for God Reveal about Our Beliefs in God* (Woodstock, VT: SkyLight Paths Publishing, 2008), 5.

"No one image or model, however elusive or rich": Nicola Slee, *Praying Like a Woman* (London: SPCK, 2004), 12.

images and metaphors that can be found in my daily life: Throughout this book, I will claim that I am describing the Bible's "metaphors" for and "images" of God, but strictly speaking, this book considers no "images" (since I am describing arrangements of words, not visual depictions), and only some metaphors ("I am the bread of life"). It also examines some similes, metonymies, and anthropomorphisms. It might be more accurate to say the book is about the Bible's figurative language for God, and about the Bible's divine tropes (a term that appears only rarely in the text of the book, because I couldn't bring myself to write "trope" over and over again). More than these competing formal terms, two phrases taken up by Rowan Williams (he is borrowing from linguist Margaret Masterman) may be a helpful way to frame the various instances of figurative language this book explores: Williams writes of "extreme" language, or "language under pressure." " 'Extremity' in language," writes Williams, "works by pushing habitual or conventional speech out of shape—by insisting on developing certain sorts of pattern (rhyme, assonance, metre), by coupling what is not normally coupled (metaphor, paradox), by undermining surface meanings (irony) or by forcing us to relearn speaking of perceiving (fractured and chaotic language, alienating or puzzling description)." To use "language under pressure" can be a "means of exploration, invoking associations which may be random in one way, yet generate a steady level of unsettling alternative or supplementary meanings in the margin of simple lexical sense." This is a helpful way of thinking about what the biblical writers are doing when they write of God—they are deploying extreme language (most of the examples considered in this book fall under Williams's category of language that couples that which is not usually coupled—God, and anything else). There is, it may be argued, really no other way to make language speak about (toward) God: only *in extremis;* definitionally under pressure. See Rowan Williams, *The Edge of Words: God and the Habits of Language* (London: Bloomsbury, 2014), especially 133, 150.

"We should exercise that far higher privilege": Christina Rossetti, *Letter and Spirit: Notes on the Commandments,* in Rossetti, *Poems and Prose,* ed. Simon Humphries (New York: Oxford University Press, 2008), 334–35.

This metaphor comes from the writers of: See Exod. 33:11, 2 Chron. 20:7, Isa. 41:8, John 15:15, and James 2:23.

"The child became a man and the man became a preacher": Barbara Brown Taylor, "Preaching the Body," in Gail R. O'Day and Thomas G. Long, eds., *Listening to the Word: Studies in Honor of Fred B. Craddock* (Nashville: Abingdon Press, 1993), 211–12.

people's friendship with God: Samuel Wells, *God's Companions: Reimagining Christian Ethics* (Oxford: Wiley-Blackwell, 2006), 1, 9–10, 42–43, 104–11, 207–10; Samuel Wells, "I Call You Friends" (sermon, Duke University Chapel, May 17, 2009), http://chapel-archives.oit.duke.edu/documents/sermons/May17ICallyouFriends.pdf.

friendship with God is the entire goal of the Christian life: Roberta Bondi, *To Pray and to Love: Conversations on Prayer with the Early Church* (Minneapolis: Fortress, 1991), 123.

"God is friendship": Aelred of Rievaulx, quoted in Mary Margaret Keaton, "Friendship as Communion with God," *Catechist* 35, no. 5 (Feb. 2002): 28.

"Jesus makes it so": Mindy G. Makant, "The Pursuit of Happiness: The Virtue of Consumption and the Consumption of Virtue," *Dialog* 49, no. 4 (2010): 291–99.

The fourth-century preacher John Chrysostom . . . "I ran after your friendship": Michael Sherwin, OP, "Friendship with God and the Transformation of Patronage in the Thought of John Chrysostom," *New Blackfriars* 85, no. 998 (2004): 387–98.

"One of the aims of prayer is to grow in friendship with God": "Learning to Pray: An Interview with Roberta Bondi," *The Christian Century* 113, no. 10 (March 20–27, 1996): 327.

A Short Note on Gender and Language for God

father: Throughout *Wearing God,* I capitalize "Father" when the word is used as an invocation or when the word is used as the name of a person directly addressed; I do not capitalize it when it appears as an epithet.

60 percent of church attendees on any given American Sunday: I am grateful to my colleague Mark Chaves for this figure, which he derived from the General Social Survey and the National Congregations Study. In the GSS, about 60 percent of people who say that they attend religious services at least weekly are female, and that figure has been more or less the same since 1972. In the NCS, informants (mainly senior clergy) are asked what percent of regular adult participants in their congregation are female. In NCS surveys from 1998, 2006, and 2012, the mean response is 60 percent.

"in the deity there is no sex": Eugene F. Rogers, *After the Spirit: A Constructive Pneumatology from Resources Outside the Modern West* (Grand Rapids, MI: William B. Eerdmans, 2005), 21, note 9; Susan Ashbrook Harvey, "Feminine Imagery for the Divine: The Holy Spirit, the Odes of Solomon, and Early Syriac Tradition," *St. Vladimir's Seminary Quarterly* 37 (1993): 121.

liturgy from the Book of Common Prayer: "Let us give thanks . . ." is from "Holy Eucharist II," *The Book of Common Prayer* (New York: Seabury Press, 1979), 361. "Happy are they . . ." is from Psalm 1:1–2, *The Book of Common Prayer,* 585.

"All Creatures of Our God and King": Francis of Assisi, "All Creatures of Our God and King" (no. 527), in *Lutheran Book of Worship* (Minneapolis, MN: Augsburg Publishing House, 1978).

"It is particularly important to use female language": Janet Morley, "I Desire Her with My Whole Heart," in Ann Loades, *Feminist Theology: A Reader* (Louisville, KY: Westminster John Knox, 1990), 161–62.

Clothing

"The LORD *God made garments of skin for Adam and his wife and clothed them"*: Gen. 3:21.

not "a separate piece of clothing to be put on like a jacket but as human flesh itself": Gary Anderson, *The Genesis of Perfection: Adam and Eve in Jewish and Christian Imagination* (Louisville, KY: Westminster John Knox Press, 2001), 124–25. Anderson explains that the reading opens up a problem: "If this understanding makes sense of Genesis 3:21, it certainly wreaks havoc on the earlier narrative. If Adam and Eve put on human skin before leaving the Garden, what sort of 'skin' do they discover after they eat of the fruit (Gen. 3:7)? To answer this problem, another wrinkle must be explored. According to Rabbi Meir, there was a copy of the Bible that had a different reading for Genesis 3:21 (Genesis Rabbah 20:12). Instead of saying that God dressed Adam and Eve in 'garments of skin,' it said that God had dressed them in 'garments of light.' This interpretation was derived from a wordplay in the Hebrew. The words for 'skin' and 'light' sound exactly alike to a Hebrew speaker, so Rabbi Meir believed that God had vested Adam with a 'garment of light.' Adam and Eve, in this line of thinking, sinned, and only then put on mortal flesh." In other words, Adam and Eve are originally clothed with garments of light or glory—because they are made in the image of God. After they eat of the fruit of the tree, they are stripped of the garments of light and clothed with garments of skin.

at least two different ways of reading what is happening: Theodore of Mopsuestia offers a third interpretation: God clothed Adam and Eve with clothes of tree bark. Sebastian Brock, "Clothing Metaphors as a Means of Theological Expression in Syriac Tradition," in *Typus, Symbol, Allegorie bei den östlichen Vätern und ihren Parallelen im Mittelalter,* ed. M. Schmidt with C. F. Geyer (Regensburg: Pustet, 1982), 17.

Adam and Eve become fully human only upon leaving the garden: Anderson, *The Genesis of Perfection,* 124–25.

"The expulsion was indeed the finishing touch": Lawrence Kushner, *God Was in This Place & I, i Did Not Know: Finding Self, Spirituality and Ultimate Meaning* (Woodstock, VT: Gemstone Press, 1993), 74–75.

"All these changes did the Merciful One effect": Ephrem of Syria, "Hymn 23 on the Nativity," *Ephrem the Syrian, Hymns,* trans. Kathryn McVey (Mahwah, NJ: Paulist Press, 1989), 190.

"As many of you as were baptized into Christ have clothed yourselves with Christ": Gal. 3:27.

"For our salvation, He put on a man and dwelt in him": Theodore of Mopsuestia, "Catechetical Homilies, III.5," quoted in Brock, "Clothing Metaphors," 17.

"rhetoric of being clothed with a person": Roy R. Jeal, "Clothes Make the (Wo)man," *Scriptura* 90 (2005): 688.

"It takes a lifetime to fathom Jesus": Alexander MacLaren, *St. Paul's Epistle to the Romans* (New York: A. C. Armstrong and Son, 1909), 322.

"Our body became your Garment; Your spirit became our robe": Ephrem of Syria, "Hymn 22 on the Nativity," *Ephrem the Syrian, Hymns,* 185.

"If you see acquaintances of yours in deepest mourning": Emily Post, *Etiquette in Society, in Business, in Politics, and at Home* (New York: Funk & Wagnalls, 1922), 399.

"A man elbowed me aside": Meghan O'Rourke, *The Long Goodbye: A Memoir* (New York: Riverhead Trade, 2012), 157.

"For thousands of years human beings have communicated": Alison Lurie, *The Language of Clothes* (New York: Random House, 1981), 3.

"Through their wearing apparel, people can say": Linda Baumgarten, *What Clothes Reveal: The Language of Clothing in Colonial and Federal America: The Colonial Williamsburg Collection* (Williamsburg, VA: Colonial Williamsburg Foundation, 2002), 56.

"In every culture, clothing not only is utilitarian but also symbolizes a person's or group's identity": Sarah A. Chase, *Perfectly Prep: Gender Extremes at a New England Prep School* (New York: Oxford University Press, 2008), 94–95.

only the wealthy could wear clothes with lace or gold thread: Dorothy A. Mays, *Women in Early America: Struggle, Survival, and Freedom in a New World* (Santa Barbara, CA: ABC-CLIO, 2004), 383.

school uniforms "serve as a social and economic equalizer": Kathleen Wade and Mary Stafford, "Public School Uniforms: Effect on Perceptions of Gang Presence, School Climate, and Student Self-Perceptions," *Education and Urban Society* 35, no. 4 (August 2003): 399–420; Kerry White, "Do School Uniforms Fit?" *School Administrator* 57, no. 2 (February 2000): 36–40.

a garment called a stola: Bruce W. Winter, *Roman Wives, Roman Widows: The Appearance of New Women and the Pauline Communities* (Grand Rapids, MI: William B. Eerdmans, 2003), 99.

"There is neither Jew nor Greek": Gal. 3:28 (ESV). On the importance of rendering the verse "there is no male and female," N. T. Wright notes, "Many Bible versions actually mistranslate this verse to read 'neither Jew nor Greek, neither slave nor free, neither male nor female.' That is precisely what Paul does *not* say; and as it's what we expect he's going to say, we should note quite carefully what he has said instead, since he presumably means to make a point by doing so, a point which is missed when the translation is flattened out as in that version. What he says is that there is neither Jew nor Greek, neither slave nor free, *no male and female*. I think the reason he says 'no male and female' rather than 'neither male nor female' is that he is actually quoting Genesis 1:27." N. T. Wright, "The Biblical Basis for Women's Service in the Church," *Priscilla Papers*, vol. 20, no. 4 (Autumn 2006): 5–6.

as the Fourth Lateran Council of 1215 declared: Fourth Lateran Council, Article 68, in Norman P. Tanner, ed., *Decrees of the Ecumenical Councils*, vol. 1 (London / Washington, DC: Sheed and Ward / Georgetown University Press, 1990), 266.

lawmakers tried to distinguish enslaved women: Sandra R. Joshel, *Slavery in the Roman World* (New York: Cambridge University Press, 2010), 132.

it was typical for planters to order the linen: Thomas M. Truxes, *Irish-American Trade, 1660–1783* (New York: Cambridge University Press, 1988), 187.

"How do we tell ourselves apart from what we wear": Daneen Wardrop, *Emily Dickinson and the Labor of Clothing* (Durham: University of New Hampshire Press, 2009), 203–4.

Perhaps the most famous proposal of the movement: Sylvia D. Hoffert, *When Hens Crow: The Woman's Rights Movement in Antebellum America* (Bloomington: Indiana University Press, 1995), 22–26.

"the body interacts and changes places": Wardrop, *Emily Dickinson and the Labor of Clothing*, 204.

"The Lord Jesus Christ himself . . . is said to be the clothing of the saints": Origen of Alexandria, Gerald L. Bray, and Thomas C. Oden, eds., *Romans* (Downers Grove, IL: InterVarsity Press, 1998), 323.

"See the day-spring from afar": Charles Wesley, "A Morning Hymn," in Charles Wesley and John Wesley, eds., *Sacred Poems* (London: Strahan, 1739), 178–79.

"What good is it . . . if you say you have faith but do not have works?": James 2:14–17.

"Then the King will say to those on his right": Matt. 25:34–35.

"Several years ago, having miscarried a cherished pregnancy on the day after Christmas": Stephanie Paulsell, "Body Language," *The Christian Century* 119, no. 2 (Jan. 16–23, 2002): 22–23.

"the long struggle to be at home in the body": Jane Kenyon, "Cages," *Collected Poems* (St. Paul, MN: Graywolf Press, 2005), 40.

"You are always in God's sight comely": Charles Spurgeon, "None But Jesus," *Sermons*, vol. 7 (New York: Funk & Wagnalls, 1861). Full text available at http://m.ccel.org/ccel/spurgeon/sermons07.txt.

"Clothing is our most intimate environment": Susan M. Watkins, *Clothing: The Portable Environment* (London: The Hogarth Press, 1930), 83.

"Awake, I beseech thee, O my soul, and let the fire of a heavenly love": Saint Anselm, *The Devotions of Saint Anselm*, ed., Clement C. J. Webb (London: Methuen and Co., 1903), 63–64.

Smell

an Illinois-based company called His Essence: http://www.hisessence.com.

Senses and sensory perception pervade the Bible: On sense perception in the Bible, see Roger Ferlo, *Sensing God: Reading Scripture with All Our Senses* (Cambridge: Cowley Publications, 2002); and Yael Avrahami, *The Senses of Scripture: Sensory Perception in the Hebrew Bible* (New York: T&T Clark, 2012). A terrific guide for drawing sensory perception into your spiritual life in J. Brent Bill and Beth Booram, *Awaken Your Senses:*

Exercise for Exploring the Wonder of God (Downers Grove: InterVarsity Press, 2011).

People praying the psalms can taste the Lord's sweetness: The germane verse from the psalms (34:8) is usually rendered "taste and see that the Lord is good." On translating the verse as "sweet," see Rachel Fulton, " 'Taste and See That the Lord is *Sweet*' (Ps. 33:9): The Flavor of God in the Monastic West," *Journal of Religion* 86, no. 2 (2006): 169–204.

"He that planted the ear, shall he not hear?": Ps. 94:9 (KJV).

In contrast to idols who "have ears, but do not hear; noses, but do not smell": Ps. 115:6–7. See also Jer. 10:5.

God "looks on the earth and it trembles": Ps. 104:32.

"When a man's senses are perfectly united to God": John Climacus, quoted in Sarah Coakley and Paul L. Gavrilyuk, "Introduction," in Coakley and Gavrilyuk, eds., *The Spiritual Senses: Perceiving God in Western Christianity* (New York: Cambridge University Press, 2012), 1.

God's eyes are upon the righteous and God's ears are attentive to their cry: Ps. 34:15.

Six people get the name Elishama . . . appears over and over: Avrahami, *Senses of Scripture,* 69–73.

Aristotle ranked the senses: Matthew Milner, *The Senses and the English Reformation* (Burlington, VT: Ashgate, 2011), 31.

"And by his smelling in awe of the Lord": Isa. 11:3 as it appears in Deborah A. Green, *The Aroma of Righteousness: Scent and Seduction in Rabbinic Life and Literature* (University Park: Pennsylvania State University Press, 2011), 113.

Ibn Ezra's and Calvin's commentaries on Isa. 11:3: Constance Classen, "The Breath of God: Sacred Histories of Scent," in Jim Drobnick, ed., *The Smell Culture Reader* (New York: Berg, 2006), 388.

Enlightenment-era people became more and more invested in interpreting the data our senses perceived: Mark Smith, *Sensing the Past: Seeing, Hearing, Smelling, Tasting, and Touching in History* (Berkeley: University of California Press, 2007), 33–34; and Leigh Schmidt, *Hearing Things: Religion, Illusion, and the American Enlightenment* (Cambridge, MA: Harvard University Press, 2000).

under the ministrations of Freud . . . restraint over perversion: Susan Stewart, *Poetry and the Fate of the Senses* (Chicago: University of Chicago Press, 2002), 21; and Carol Mavor, "Odor di Femina: Though You May Not See Her, You Can Certainly Smell Her," in Drobnick, ed., *The Smell Culture Reader,* 281–82.

God perceives the smell of sacrifices: "Smell, Scent," in *Dictionary of Biblical Imagery* (Downers Grove, IL: InterVarsity Press, 1998), 801.

reah nihoah: Green, *Aroma of Righteousness,* 68.

"calm [God] and change his mood" . . . *"one of the primary modes of interaction and communication with God in the Hebrew Bible"*: Green, *Aroma of Righteousness,* 75–76, 4.

In biblical Hebrew, the expression that means "to be angry": Silvia Schroer and Thomas Staubli, *Body Symbolism in the Bible,* trans. Linda M. Maloney (Collegeville, MN: Liturgical Press, 2001), 94–96; and Rami Shapiro, *Amazing Chesed: Living a Grace-Filled Judaism* (Woodstock, VT: Jewish Lights Publishing, 2013), 10.

As cognitive neuroscientist Rachel Herz explains . . . smells can also "become emotions": Rachel Herz, *The Scent of Desire: Discovering Our Enigmatic Sense of Smell* (New York: William Morrow, 2007), 3–4, 8–15.

You called, You cried: Augustine, *The Confessions,* X.xxvii.38, translation found in Rowan Williams, *The Wound of Knowledge* (London: Darton, Longman and Todd, Ltd., 1990), 73.

"olfactory comfort" . . . *when the beloved is away*: Donald H. McBurney, Melanie L. Shoup, and Sybil A. Streeter, "Olfactory Comfort: Smelling a Partner's Clothing During Periods of Separation," *Journal of Applied Social Psychology* 36, no. 9 (September 2006), 2325–35.

a nurse in Minnesota invented a soft shirt: Herz, *The Scent of Desire,* 152–60.

"'Smell'—as the matter emitted from a thing, its being sensed": Anne F. Elvey, *Matter of the Text: Material Engagements between Luke and the Five Senses* (Sheffield, UK: Sheffield Phoenix Press, 2011), 110.

Mothers whose children have left for college: Trish Green, *Motherhood, Absence and Transition: When Adult Children Leave Home* (Burlington, VT: Ashgate, 2010), 80.

the "prayers of the saints" are, in fact, incense carried in golden bowls: Rev. 5:8.

Smells are hard to describe . . . described by "simile, metaphor, or metonym": Green, *Aroma of Righteousness,* 5.

"Prayers when they reach heaven become fragrant roses, pouring out": J. R. Miller, *The Blossom of Thorns* (London: Hodder and Stoughton, 1905), 236.

"And walk in love, as also the Christ did love us": Eph. 5:2 (Young's Literal Translation).

"a soothing aroma to God": Eph. 5:2 (God's Word Translation).

"But as Pomanders and wood / Still are good": George Herbert, "The Banquet," *The Poems of George Herbert* (New York: Oxford University Press, 1913), 188.

"'He gave himself for us, an offering, and a sacrifice to God, for a sweet smelling savour.' Not that": John Flavel, "Sermon XII," *The Whole Works of the Reverend Mr. John Flavel,* vol. 1 (London: D. Midwinter, 1740), 67.

"Christ is the flower of Mary, who sprouted forth": Ambrose of Milan, quoted in Susan Ashbrook Harvey, *Scenting Salvation: Ancient Chris-*

tianity and the Olfactory Imagination (Berkeley: University of California Press, 2006), 126.

The *"Fragrance of Life"*: Harvey, *Scenting Salvation,* 64.

a means by which the human and the divine could "intermingle . . . in a communion of being": Harvey, *Scenting Salvation,* 65.

Jesus breathed out the "fragrance of His life": Harvey, *Scenting Salvation,* 80–81.

"We are the aroma of Christ to God": 2 Cor. 2:14–16.

"And we, as often as we hear anything of good people": Gregory the Great, quoted in Harvey, *Scenting Salvation,* 126.

"A student of mine": The Reverend Kimberly Jackson, "The Smell of Christ" (Absalom Jones Episcopal Center: August 27, 2014), http://absalomjones .org/sermon-smell-like-christ/.

"The aroma of the knowledge of God comes from Christ and through Christ": Ambrosiaster, quoted in *Romans,* Bray and Oden, eds., 210.

the people in Philippi seem to be his friends: Justin King, "Philippians 4:10–20; Friendship, Thanksgiving, and a Superior World View," *Journal of Theta Alpha Kappa* 33, no. 1 (2009): 36–52.

"Paul was absent from the Philippians and he wanted to be present": Fred B. Craddock, *Philippians* (Atlanta: John Knox, 1985), vii.

Scholars have noted that Paul's expression of thanks is a little tortured . . . commercial metaphor: Craddock, *Philippians,* 76. The passage in question is Phil. 4:17–18.

"Not that I seek the gift": Gordon D. Fee, "To What End Exegesis? Reflections on Exegesis and Spirituality in Philippians 4:10–20," *Bulletin for Biblical Research* 8 (1998): 81–84.

"Here you come to the real secret of class distinctions in the West": George Orwell, *The Road to Wigan Pier* (London: Secker and Warburg, 1997), 119–20.

"Odors, whether real or alleged, are often used as the basis for conferring a moral identity": Largey and Watson quoted in Louise J. Lawrence, *Sense and Stigma in the Gospels: Depictions of Sensory-Disabled Characters* (Oxford: Oxford University Press, 2013), 83.

Now it carries a stench: Isa. 1:13.

"a stench in my nostrils, an acrid smell that never goes away": Isa. 65:5b (NLT).

saints were thought to have the smell of sanctity: Harvey, *Scenting Salvation,* 220.

a homeless man named Richard Kreimer . . . barring Kreimer and his stench was permissible: Alan Hyde, "Offensive Bodies," in Drobnick, ed., *The Smell of Culture Reader,* 53–57.

"Put an altar of incense in your innermost heart. Be a sweet aroma of Christ": Origen of Alexandria, "Homilies on Exodus 9," quoted in Gerald Bray and Thomas C. Oden, eds., *1–2 Corinthians* (Downers Grove, IL: InterVarsity Press, 1999), 210.

"*What do I love when I love Thee?*": Augustine, *The Confessions*, X.vi.8, in
Mary T. Clark, trans., *Augustine of Hippo: Selected Writings* (Mahwah,
NJ: Paulist Press, 1984), 126. I have changed Clark's "you" in the first line
to "Thee."

Bread and Vine

all those seed-bearing plants and trees with fruit in the garden of Eden:
Gen. 1:29.
"*There is communion of more than our bodies when bread is broken*":
M. F. K. Fisher, *The Gastronomical Me* (New York: North Point Press,
1954), x.
"*My flesh is real food and my blood is real drink*": John 6:55.
*pagans who overheard Christian worship and teaching accused Christians of
cannibalism:* To defend themselves, Christians reminded pagan critics that
Christians believed in a bodily resurrection—surely no one would eat flesh
he expected to be resurrected—and they insisted that they were eating only
"ordinary and harmless . . . food." Stephen Benko, *Pagan Rome and Early
Christians* (Bloomington: Indiana University Press, 1984), 70. Similar
polemics would crop up during the Reformation, when Protestants glossed
the Catholic doctrine of transubstantiation as cannibalism. Margaret
Owens, *Stages of Dismemberment: The Fragmented Body in Late
Medieval and Early Modern Drama* (Newark, NJ: University of Delaware
Press, 2005), 209; Lee Palmer Wandel, *The Reformation: Towards a New
History* (New York: Cambridge University Press, 2011), 137–38.
"*That he is There (oh heavenly themel)*": Elizabeth Seton, quoted in Christina
Mazzoni, *The Women in God's Kitchen: Cooking, Eating, and Spiritual
Writing* (New York: Continuum, 2005), 149.
"*So they said to him, 'What sign are you going to give'*": John 6:30–35.
"*Medieval artists depicted this narrative as if the manna raining down from
the clouds were round communion wafers*": Gail Ramshaw, "Reflections
on the Lectionary," *The Christian Century* 126, no. 15 (July 28, 2009): 20.
It was . . . "like coriander seed, white" . . . like "cakes baked with oil": Exod.
16 (KJV); Num. 11:8.
as Rashi, the eleventh-century interpreter: Chaim Miller, ed., *The Chumash
with Rashi's Commentary: The Book of Numbers* (Brooklyn: Kol
Menachem, 2009), 87.
"*Cinnamon has a naturally pleasing sweetness that delights the taste*":
Elizabeth of Schonau, quoted in Mazzoni, *The Women in God's Kitchen*,
55–56.
"*You prepare a table*": Ps. 23:5.
"*On this mountain the* LORD *Almighty will prepare*": Isa. 25:6 (NIV).
it's really bruschetta: Mazzoni, *The Women in God's Kitchen*, 27.

Nourishment, delight, power, gratitude—all those things and more are whipping around the seemingly simple task of serving dinner: On power and food provision, see Psyche Williams-Forson, "Other Women Cooked for My Husband: Negotiating Gender, Food, and Identities in an African American / Ghanaian Household," *Feminist Studies* 36, no. 2 (2010): 435–61; and Laurel Thatcher Ulrich, "It 'went away she knew not how': Food Theft and Domestic Conflict in Seventeenth-Century Essex County," in Peter Benes, ed., *Foodways in the Northeast* (Boston, MA: Boston University, 1983), 94.

"making jam" . . . *"there were several unopened jars":* Maxine Kumin, "Enough Jam for a Lifetime," in Molly O'Neill, ed., *American Food Writing: An Anthology with Classic Recipes* (New York: Library of America, 2007), 590–93.

people assumed that Jesus was using unleavened matzah *at the Last Supper:* Reginald Maxwell Woolley, *The Bread of the Eucharist* (London: A. R. Mowbray, 1913), 2.

"I am going to learn to make bread": Emily Dickinson to Abiah Root, September 26, 1845, in Emily Fragos, ed., *Emily Dickinson Letters* (New York: Knopf, 2011), 15.

"The prestige of white flour" . . . *"whiter than it had ever been":* Michael Pollan, *Cooked: A Natural History of Transformation* (New York: Penguin, 2013), 255–57.

"When he said, 'I am the bread of life,' he must have meant": Susan Springer, a sermon for Ascension Day, 2014, preached at the closing Eucharist for the Preaching Excellence Program, Richmond, VA (unpublished; copy in author's possession).

developments in "microbiology, cereal chemistry, climate control, and industrial design" . . . *"Whitewash is extremely moral":* Aaron Bobrow-Strain, *White Bread: A Social History of the Store-Bought Loaf* (Boston: Beacon Press, 2012), 23–24, 30–60, 64–65.

"Let the vineyards be fruitful, Lord": Offertory from "Holy Communion, Setting One," in *The Lutheran Book of Worship* (Minneapolis, MN: Augsburg Publishing House, 1978), 66.

"A loaf of bread is the bearer of at least four major narratives or histories": Norman Wirzba, *Food and Faith: A Theology of Eating* (New York: Cambridge University Press, 2011), 13.

who makes possible our immigration to the Kingdom of God: Daniel G. Groody, "Homeward Bound: A Theology of Migration for Fullness of Life, Justice, and Peace," *Ecumenical Review* 64, no. 3 (October 2012): 299–313; and Daniel G. Groody, "The Church on the Move: Mission in an Age of Migration," *Mission Studies* 30, no. 1 (2013), 27–42.

"Because there is one bread": I Cor. 10:17.

"Deep in our souls we know that we are the bread of life": Gunilla Norris,
    Becoming Bread: Embracing the Spiritual in the Everyday (Mahwah, NJ:
    HiddenSpring, 2003), 4.

"foodwork" or "foodplay": Michelle Szabo, "Foodwork or Foodplay? Men's
    Domestic Cooking, Privilege and Leisure," *Sociology* 47, no. 4 (2013): 623–38.

"Bread of Heaven, Bread of Heaven": William Williams, "Guide Me, O Thou
    Great Jehovah" (no. 127), in *The United Methodist Hymnal* (Nashville,
    TN: The United Methodist Publishing House, 1989).

"These trips took place during the fifties": Norma Jean and Carole Darden,
    *Spoonbread and Strawberry Wine: Recipes and Reminiscences of a
    Family* (Garden City, NY: Anchor Press, 1978), 246, quoted in Psyche A.
    Williams-Forson, *Building Houses out of Chicken Legs: Black Women,
    Food and Power* (Chapel Hill: University of North Carolina Press, 2006),
    116–19, 125.

Grant's parents *"often went to the Union Station not to pick up anyone but
    to feed their friends"*: Gail Milissa Grant, *At the Elbows of My Elders:
    One Family's Journey Toward Civil Rights* (St. Louis: Missouri History
    Museum, 2008), 179.

women . . . *have decreased the frequency with which they receive Communion
    because they fear the calories*: M. Anthony Graham, Wendy Spencer, and
    Arnold E. Anderson, "Altered Religious Practice in Patients with Eating
    Disorders," *International Journal of Eating Disorders* 10, no. 2 (1991):
    239–43. The same study showed that 65 percent of people of a variety of
    religious faiths who used to attend religious events where food was central
    now avoided things like "church suppers, feasts, Passover celebrations,
    weddings."

"What, for example, does it mean to celebrate the Eucharist": Patrick T.
    McCormick, "How Could We Break the Lord's Bread in a Foreign Land?
    The Eucharist in 'Diet America,'" *Horizons* 25, no. 1 (1998): 47.

" 'Breaking bread' means eating. 'Our daily bread' means food": Tamar
    Adler, *An Everlasting Meal: Cooking with Economy and Grace* (New
    York: Scribner, 2011), 79.

*In the Middle Ages, several female mystics compared the soul in union
    with God to bread*: Sister Jeremy Finnegan, "Idiom of Women Mystics,"
    Mystics Quarterly 13, no. 2 (1987): 70.

Jesus asks Mechthild to place in His left hand all her "pains and adversities":
    Mechthild of Hackeborn, *Selected Revelations of S. Mechthild, Virgin:
    Taken from the Five Books of Her Spiritual Grace and Translated from the
    Latin by a Secular Priest* (London: Thomas Richardson, 1875), 50.

"God comes near to us unendingly in the bread of life": Oliver Clément, *The
    Roots of Christian Mysticism: Text and Commentary* (New York: New
    City Press, 1995), 125.

"Dry is all food of the soul if it is not sprinkled with the oil of Christ":
Bernard of Clairvaux, quoted in Adolf von Harnack, *History of Dogma,*
vol. 6, trans. William McGilchrist (London: Williams and Norgate, 1907),
11. For emphasis, I have rearranged the order of the last three phrases of
the sentence.

Who will enable me to find rest in you?: Augustine, *The Confessions,* I.v.5,
trans. Henry Chadwick (New York: Oxford University Press, 1991), 5.

Jesus identifies His father as a vineyard owner, Himself as the true vine: For
a thought- (and prayer-) provoking consideration of the image of God as
vine, see part IV of Margaret Feinberg, *Scouting the Divine: My Search for
God in Wine, Wool, and Honey* (Grand Rapids: Zondervan, 2009).

*The prophets of the Hebrew Bible envision Israel as a vine or a collection of
vines:* See Jer. 2:21; Ez. 15:1–5, 17:1–21, 19:10–15; Hos. 10:1–2. For a
helpful discussion of the relationship between vine imagery in the Hebrew
Bible and the Gospel of John, see Marianne Meye Thompson, " 'Every
Picture Tells a Story': Imagery for God in the Gospel of John," in Jörg Frey,
Jan G. van der Watt, and Ruben Zimmermann, eds., *Imagery in the Gospel
of John: Terms, Forms, Themes, and Theology of Johannine Figurative
Language* (Mohr Siebeck: Tübingen, 2006), 273–76. See also Howard N.
Wallace, "Harvesting the Vineyard: the Development of Vineyard Imagery
in the Hebrew Bible," in Mark A. O'Brien and Howard N. Wallace,
eds., *Seeing Signals, Reading Signs: The Art of Exegesis* (New York: T&T
Clark, 2004), 117–29.

"What more could have been done": Isa. 5:4–7 (NIV).

"I am the true vine": John 15:1.

*"Good vines require cutting and more cutting. A mile of runners won't give
you one more grape, so get rid of branches"*: Sister Judith Sutera, *The
Vinedresser's Notebook: Spiritual Lessons in Pruning, Waiting, Harvesting
& Abundance* (Nashville, TN: Abingdon Press, 2014), 20–21, 70–71.

"In Bethlehem the slayers mowed down the fair flowers": Ephrem of Syria,
"Hymn 24," in *Ephrem the Syrian: Hymns,* 196.

Later in Isaiah, there is: Isa. 27:2–6 (NIV).

"reminding them that they all can make a great wine" . . . *"creates a new
experience of alcohol"*: Deirdre Heekin, *Libation: A Bitter Alchemy*
(White River Junction, VT: Chelsea Green, 2009), 73, 23–43.

"I will make [Babylon's] officials and her sages drunk": Jer. 51:57. See also
Jer. 25:15.

*Alcohol doesn't cause intimate partner violence . . . than a batterer who
doesn't:* Ryan C. Shorey, Jeniimarie Febres, Hope Brasfield, and Gregory
L. Stuart, "The Prevalence of Mental Health Problems in Men Arrested
for Domestic Violence," *Journal of Family Violence* 27 (2012): 741–48,

especially 746; Demetrious N. Kyriacou, et al., "Risk Factors for Injury to Women from Domestic Violence," *The New England Journal of Medicine* 341, no. 25 (December 16, 1999): 1892–98; and Catherine Carlson, "Three Essays Analyzing the Impact of Community and Neighborhood Factors on Intimate Partner Violence against Women in Uganda (dissertation, Columbia University, 2013).

The lovers in the Song of Songs are enjoined to drink: Song of Sol. 5:1.

"O God of too much giving": Jessica Powers, "But Not With Wine," in *The Selected Poetry of Jessica Powers,* eds. Regina Siegfried and Robert Morneau (Washington, DC: ICS Publications, 1999), 17.

The psalmist's cup . . . was the one Jesus drank from: Erasmus, quoted in M. A. Screech, *Laughter at the Foot of the Cross* (Boulder, CO: Westview Press, 1999), 111–12. Screech has rendered *praeclarus* "goodly"; I prefer "delightful."

the Flemish monk Louis de Blois considered the question: Louis of Blois, *Spiritual Works of Louis of Blois, Abbot of Liesse,* ed. John Edward Bowden (London: R&T Washbourne, 1903), ch. 14. Full text available at www.ccel.org/ccel/blois/spiritual.txt.

Ruusbroec speaks of "spiritual inebriation" . . . "his heart must break": John of Ruysbroeck, *The Adornment of the Spiritual Marriage,* trans. C. A. Wynschenk Dom (London: John M. Watkins, 1951), 69–70.

"Grant that my soul may hunger after Thee, the bread of angels": Kristen van Ausdall, "Communicating with the Host: Imagery and Eucharistic Contact in Late Medieval and Early Renaissance Italy," in Sarah Blick and Laura Deborah Gelfand, eds., *Push Me, Pull You: Imaginative and Emotional Interaction in Late Medieval and Renaissance Art* (vol. I) (Leiden: Brill, 2011), 462–63, including n. 35.

Blood of Christ, make me drunk: Mother Mary Francis, *Anima Christi: Soul of Christ* (San Francisco: Ignatius Press, 2001), 29.

Laboring Woman

an unprecedented number of men have participated in births: Judith Walzer Leavitt, *Make Room for Daddy: The Journey from Waiting Room to Birthing Room* (Chapel Hill: University of North Carolina Press, 2009).

At Christmas we read . . . pierced for our transgressions: Isa. 52:7–10, 53:4–5.

"Out of my womb before the morning star" . . . "that is, from his substance": Christian interpreters have often taken the first line of Psalm 110 ("The Lord says to my lord") to mean the father is speaking to Jesus. That is the framework through which Augustine and Cyril interpret verse 3, which in their Latin Bible read *ex utero ante luciferum genui te*—out of my

womb before the morning star (said the father to his son) I bore you. On this line of interpretation, and for Augustine and the Council of Toledo, see Rogers, *After the Spirit*, 114–16. For Cyril, see Daniel F. Stramara, *Praying—with the Saints—to God Our Mother* (Eugene: Wipf and Stock, 2012), 219–20.

John Calvin suggests that Isaiah is trying to tell us something about the "astonishing warmth of love and tenderness": John Calvin, commentary on Isaiah 42:14, in *Commentary on Isaiah, Volume 3: Isaiah 33–48*, trans. William Pringle (Grand Rapids, MI: Christian Classics Ethereal Library), 238. Full text available at ccel.org/ccel/calvin/calcom15.xi.i.html.

the laboring woman's cry is an angry shout: Robert Jamieson, Andrew Fausset, and David Brown, *A Commentary: Critical, Practical and Explanatory, on the Old and New Testaments*, vol. 2 (Toledo, OH: Jerome B. Names, 1884), 223.

the loud cries of God . . . required to "awaken a sleeping world" to the truth of itself: Matthew Henry, "Isaiah XLII," in *Commentary on the Whole Bible*, vol. 4: Isaiah to Malachi, http://www.ccel.org/ccel/henry/mhc4 .Is.xliii.html.

"Mooing was the only sort of deep moaning noise that made my whole body feel good": "Non-medication Coping Strategies," *Our Bodies, Ourselves*, April 13, 2014, http://www.ourbodiesourselves.org/health-info /non-medication-coping-strategies/.

"Deep guttural, almost animal-noises came from within me": "Giving Birth," *Our Bodies, Ourselves*, April 14, 2014, http://www.ourbodiesourselves .org/health-info/giving-birth/.

The Arabic means to "hiss": For the Arabic and Aramic cognates, see *Gesenius' Hebrew Grammar*, trans. Samuel Prideau Tregelles (Grand Rapids: Eerdmans, 1949), 684.

"Does the rain have a father?": Job 38:28–29. The translation follows Stramara, *Praying—with the Saints—to God Our Mother*, 83.

prays for us with deep groans: Rom. 8:26.

"The key to the patient's ability" . . . "a need for control": Priscilla Richardson Ulin, "The Exhilarating Moment of Birth," *American Journal of Nursing* 63, no. 6 (1963): 60–67.

"To the woman he said, 'I will greatly multiply your pangs in childbearing,'": Gen. 3:16.

"Now birds, by sitting on their eggs" . . . "In Ecclesiasticus it says": Gregory of Narek and Anthony of Padua, quoted in *Stramara, Praying—with the Saints—to God Our Mother*, 298, 390.

the parts of our life that bespeak our finitude and "misdirected desire": On sin as a misdirected desire, see Sarah Coakley, *God, Sexuality and the Self: An Essay "on the Trinity"* (New York: Cambridge University Press, 2013), 26, 51fn10, and passim.

*A sixteenth-century devotional text . . . "with deepe sighes and groanes
we greatlie long for":* Jennifer Wynne Hellwarth, *The Reproductive
Unconscious in Medieval and Early Modern England* (New York:
Routledge, 2002), 70–84.

*Midwife Ina May Gaskin likes to say . . . less likely that a woman will tear
and need stitches:* Ina May Gaskin, *Ina May's Guide to Childbirth* (New
York: Bantam Books, 2003), 178. See also Sarah Jobe, *Creating with God:
The Holy Confusing Blessedness of Pregnancy* (Brewster, MA: Paraclete
Press, 2011), 48–52.

"Loud moaning may convey a beginning plea for help": Diane J. Angelini,
"Nonverbal Communication in Labor," *American Journal of Nursing* 78,
no. 7 (1978): 1222.

the baby has an active role in labor and delivery: Beth Kephart, "A Baby's
View of Birth," *Parenting* 14, no. 2 (2000): 90–97.

"Sing to the Lord a new song": Ps. 33:3; 96:1.

*Medical practitioners in fields as varied . . . the lute to soothe the pains
of laboring women:* Sasitorn Phumdoang and Marion Good, "Music
Reduces Sensation and Distress of Labor Pain," *Pain Management
Nursing* 4, no. 2 (2003): 54–61; Caryl Ann Browning, "Using Music
During Childbirth," *Birth* 27, no. 4 (2001): 272–76; Penny Simkin and
April Bolding, "Update on Nonpharmacologic Approaches to Relieve
Labor Pain and Prevent Suffering," *Journal of Midwifery and Women's
Health* 49, no. 6 (2004): 489–504; B. M. Morgan and T. Goroszeniuk,
"Music During Epidural Caesarean Section," *Practitioner* 228, no. 1390
(1983): 441–43; S. B. Hanser, S. C. Larson, and A. S. O'Connell, "The
Effect of Music on Relaxation of Expectant Mothers During Labor,"
Journal of Music Therapy 20 (1983): 50–58; and Francine H. Nichols and
Sharron Smith Humenick, *Childbirth Education: Practice, Research and
Theory,* 2nd ed. (Philadelphia: W. B. Saunders Company, 2000), 259.

*As my friend Stina Kielsmeier-Cook ... Does God wonder if the labor is
working?:* Stina Kielsmeier-Cook generously talked to me about this point at
a writing workshop at the Collegeville Institute, summer 2014. I am utterly
influenced by, and here am drawing on and paraphrasing, her thoughts and
writing about this. I direct readers to her wonderful blog, where she explores
the point: https://stinakc.wordpress.com/category/god-is-a-laboring-mother/.

"[Christ] gives the analogy of bitter labor": Katharina Schutz Zell, quoted in
Teresa Berger, *Gender Differences and the Making of Liturgical History:
Lifting a Veil on Liturgy's Past* (Burlington, VT: Ashgate Publishing
Company, 2011), 87.

*"Suppose we admitted for the sake of argument that motherhood was
powerful":* Laurel Thatcher Ulrich, "Martha's Diary and Mine," *Journal
of Women's History* 4, no. 2 (1992): 159.

Underpinning the hard work is the profound strength of laboring: Biblical
scholar Katheryn Pfisterer Darr notes that while Isaiah 42 is the only passage
in the Hebrew Bible that likens God to a laboring woman, it is not the only
one to liken *someone* to a laboring woman. Darr says that in all the other
passages, the point of the simile is pain—the scriptures compare human
beings and other deities to laboring women to stress fear and anguish. But
in this Isaiah reference, Darr argues, the image might rightly be read as one
of strength. Here again, the key to the simile in Isaiah is the soundscape:
in verse 13, we hear God shrieking a battle cry, and then in verse 14 we
hear God groaning in labor—and then in the very next verse, we encounter
"cosmic upheaval. Mountains and hills will be desiccated . . . rivers will be
changed into islands." Darr argues that within the Isaiah passage "the simile
of a travailing woman is employed because the poet has perceived within the
exaggerated breaths which are characteristic of women in labor a striking
image by which to convey a sense of the force of the breath of God. Here the
simile 'like a travailing woman' . . . bespeak[s] power and might—an image
which is equal in intensity to the warrior image that precedes it. Yahweh
goes forth like a warrior shouting a war cry, and demonstrates power over
foes. Yahweh gasps and pants like a woman in travail, and the breath of
God desiccates the earth." Katheryn Pfisterer Darr, "Like Warrior, Like
Woman: Destruction and Deliverance in Isaiah 42:10–17," *Catholic Biblical
Quarterly* 49 (1987): 567–70, passim.

"I felt so strong": Gaskin, *Ina May's Guide to Childbirth,* 88.

"We tap on inner strengths . . . all sorts of situations": "What Happens
in Labor?" *Our Bodies, Ourselves,* October 15, 2011, http://www
.ourbodiesourselves.org/health-info/what-happens-in-labor/.

"The mystery I wish to explore": Ellen F. Davis, "Vulnerability, the
Condition of Covenant," in Ellen F. Davis and Richard B. Hays, eds.,
The Art of Reading Scripture (Grand Rapids, MI: William B. Eerdmans,
2003), 278.

"But I also need to enter again into the womb of my Lord": The Monk of
Farne, quoted in Stephen Gilbert Timothy Bulkeley, "The Image of God
and Parental Images: A Dialogue Between Theology and Psychology"
(dissertation, University of Glasgow, 1981), 211.

"We know that our mothers only bring": Julian of Norwich, *Revelations
of Divine Love,* trans. Elizabeth Spearing (New York: Penguin Books,
1998), 141.

"the body's availability is also its vulnerability": Beth Felker Jones, *Marks of
His Wounds: Gender Politics and Bodily Resurrection* (New York: Oxford
University Press, 2007), 105.

"God is vulnerable because God loves": William C. Placher, *Narratives
of a Vulnerable God: Christ, Theology, and Scripture* (Louisville, KY:
Westminster John Knox Press, 1994), 18.

"And in accepting our nature": Julian of Norwich, *Showings,* trans. Edmund
Colledge and James Walsh (New York: Paulist Press, 1978), 304.

Between 6 and 10 percent of women in American prisons are pregnant:
International Human Rights Clinic, CLAIM, and ACLU, "The Shackling
of Incarcerated Pregnant Women: A Human Rights Violation Committed
Regularly in the United States" (August 2013), 3, https://ihrclinic.uchicago
.edu/sites/ihrclinic.uchicago.edu/files/uploads/Report%20-%20Shackling
%20of%20Pregnant%20Prisoners%20in%20the%20US.pdf.

*forty thousand pregnant women are incarcerated each year in the United
States:* Vicki Elson and Marianne Bullock, "Adapting Birth Services for
Incarcerated Mothers," *Midwifery Today* 101 (2012): 20–23.

*A woman can labor for twelve hours in her prison cell before she becomes
convincing:* Jenni Vainik, "The Reproductive and Parental Rights of
Incarcerated Mothers," *Family Court Review* 46, no. 4 (2008): 670.

In some states, women are shackled during labor and delivery: Ginette G.
Ferszt, "Who Will Speak for Me? Advocating for Pregnant Women in
Prison," *Policy, Politics, & Nursing Practice* 12, no. 4 (2011): 254–56.

placing "belly chains, leg irons, belts, and handcuffs": Vainik, "The
Reproductive and Parental Rights of Incarcerated Mothers," 670–94.

Eighteen states have laws that restrict the use of shackles on laboring women:
International Human Rights Clinic, CLAIM, and ACLU, "Shackling of
Incarcerated Pregnant Women."

Some hospitals practice "medicinal shackling": Alice Edwards, "Supporting
Incarcerated Women," *Special Delivery* 27, no. 1 (2004): 32.

*Most incarcerated mothers are separated from their children within twenty-
four hours of giving birth:* Angelina N. Chambers, "Impact of Forced
Separation Policy on Incarcerated Postpartum Mothers," *Policy, Politics,
& Nursing Practice* 10, no. 3 (2009): 204.

"My sweet Lord . . . are you not my mother and more than my mother?":
Marguerite d'Oingt, quoted in Caroline Walker Bynum, *Jesus as Mother:
Studies in the Spirituality of the High Middle Ages* (Berkeley: University of
California Press, 1982), 153.

the fetal Jesus's devoting . . . The pressure lasts a long time: These two paragraphs
are inspired by—indeed, closely paraphrase—Kephart, "A Baby's View
of Birth," 95. My description of Jesus's birth is also inspired by Elizabeth
Gandolfo, "A Truly Human Incarnation: Recovering a Place for Nativity in
Contemporary Christology," *Theology Today* 70, no. 4 (2014): 382–83.

Mary's cervix needs the estrogen so that it may soften and dilate: Estrogen is
also needed for "the production of prostaglandin and oxytocin receptors.
Without these, vaginal childbirth would be impossible, for it's only after
estrogen makes the mother's uterus more susceptible to oxytocin—and
oxytocin and prostaglandin then stimulate the contractions of smooth

muscles in the uterine wall—that the whole choreography of labor can genuinely begin." Kephart, "A Baby's View of Birth," 95.

"How silently, how silently, The wondrous Gift is giv'n!": Phillips Brooks, "O Little Town of Bethlehem," *Lutheran Book of Worship* (Minneapolis, MN: Augsburg, 1978), 41.

in the centuries leading up to Jesus's birth, women often had four or five children: Elizabeth Ann R. Willett, "Infant Mortality and Family Religion in the Biblical Periods," *DavarLogos* 1, no. 1 (2014): 28.

Mary could have died in childbirth. Jesus could have died: Gandolfo, "A Truly Human Incarnation," 383.

"It came about" . . . she didn't need any assistance: Jennifer A. Glancy, *Corporal Knowledge: Early Christian Bodies* (New York: Oxford University Press, 2010), 81–136; and Denise Ryan, "Playing the Midwife's Part in the English Nativity Plays," *Review of English Studies* 54, no. 216 (2003): 435–48.

"[Joseph] went outside and brought to the Virgin a burning candle": Birgitta of Sweden, quoted in J. W. Robinson, "A Commentary on the York Play of the Birth of Jesus," *The Journal of English and Germanic Philology* 70, no. 2 (1971): 245.

In that psalm, we petition: L. Juliana M. Claassens, *Mourner, Mother, Midwife: Reimagining God's Delivering Presence in the Old Testament* (Louisville, KY: Westminster John Knox Press, 2013), 73.

"Yet it was you who took me from the womb": Ps. 22:9–11.

before Moses could act on God's behalf to deliver the children of Israel, the Hebrew midwives Shifra and Puah did: Exod. 1:15–21.

when Rachel laboring with Benjamin is in distress, it is her midwife who speaks words of reassurance to her: Gen. 35:17; Jennie R. Ebeling, *Women's Lives in Biblical Times* (New York: T&T Clark, 2010), 100.

in ancient Israel, midwives were often . . . women who were themselves barren: Ebeling, *Women's Lives in Biblical Times*, 100; and Carol L. Meyers, *Rediscovering Eve: Ancient Israelite Women in Context* (New York: Oxford University Press, 2013), 173.

"I asisted to Lay her out, her infant Laid in her arms": Laurel Thatcher Ulrich, *A Midwife's Tale: The Life of Martha Ballard, Based on Her Diary, 1785–1812* (New York: Knopf, 1990), 44.

"Can a woman forget her nursing child, or show no compassion for the child of her womb?": Isa. 49:15.

"What writers in the high Middle Ages": Bynum, *Jesus as Mother*, esp. 122–33.

"what am I but an infant suckling your milk": Augustine, *The Confessions*, IV.i.1.

"He has given suck—life to the universe": Ephrem of Syria, "Hymn 4 On the Nativity," *Ephrem the Syrian*, 100.

"If someone were to ask me" . . . "tired, frightened, or distressed": Elizabeth Gandolfo, "Mary Kept These Things, Pondering Them in Her Heart:

Breastfeeding as Contemplative Practice and Source for Theology,"
Spiritus 13, no. 2 (2013): 174.

"Wee are thy infants, and suck thee": Henry Vaughan, "Admission," *The*
Poetical Works of Henry Vaughan: With a Memoir (Boston, MA: James R.
Osgood & Company, 1871), 135.

"Here below, He who has promised us heavenly food": Augustine, trans.
Dame Scholastica Hebgin and Dame Felicitas Corrigan, "Second Discourse
on Psalm 30," *St. Augustine on the Psalms,* vol. 2 (Mahwah, NJ: Paulist
Press, 1961), 20–21.

"Through some secret aspirations the soul understands": Saint Teresa of
Avila, *The Interior Castle,* trans. Kieran Kavenaugh and Otilio Rodriguez
(Mahwah, NJ: Paulist Press, 1979), 179–80.

"The first time cost me $20,000 in savings to nurse her for six months":
Sharon Hays, *The Cultural Contradictions of Motherhood* (New Haven,
CT: Yale University Press, 1996), 77.

the *"good mother" is one who nurses:* Janet Lynne Golden, *A Social History*
of Wet Nursing in America: From Breast to Bottle (New York: Cambridge
University Press, 1996); and Amy Laura Hall, *Conceiving Parenthood:*
American Protestantism and the Spirit of Reproduction (Grand Rapids,
MI: William B. Eerdmans, 2008), 123–212.

working-class women have a much harder time nursing: Linda M. Blum,
At the Breast: Ideologies of Breastfeeding and Motherhood in the
Contemporary United States (Boston, MA: Beacon Press, 1999), 108–46;
and Jodi Kantor, "On the Job, Nursing Mothers Find a 2-Class System,"
New York Times, September 1, 2006.

The people have their manna . . . go ahead and kill him: Num. 11:4–15.

reading Numbers . . . the way breast milk nourishes: L. Juliana M. Claassens,
The God Who Provides: Biblical Images of Divine Nourishment
(Nashville: Abingdon, 2004), 3.

"all too often these babies did not survive": Meyers, *Rediscovering Eve,* 173.

"putting milk into babies": Winston Churchill, quoted in Rachel Muers, "The
Ethics of Breast-Feeding: A Feminist Theological Exploration," *Journal of*
Feminist Studies in Religion 26, no. 1 (2010): 17.

"And you, Jesus, are you not also a mother?": Saint Anselm, "And You, Jesus,
Are You Not Also a Mother?" in *The Prayers and Meditations of St. Anselm,*
trans. Benedicta Ward (Harmondsworth, UK: Penguin, 1973), 153–56.

Laughter

"fell on his face and laughed" . . . name his son Let-Him-Laugh, God is joining
in: Gen. 17:17; Mary Phil Korsak, "God's Laughter," *Yearbook of the*
European Society of Women in Theological Research 14 (2006): 166–67.

"The LORD *appeared to Abraham":* Gen. 18:1–10.

the communication to Sarah is indirect: My reading of this indirection
closely follows Rachel Adelman's brilliant article "On Laughter and Re-
membering," *Nashim: A Journal of Jewish Women's Studies and Gender
Issues* 8 (Fall 5765/2004): 230–32.

Rashi . . . said that Sarah's laughter was "inward" in two ways: Adelman,
"On Laughter and Re-membering," 233.

"The LORD said to Abraham . . . 'Oh yes, you did laugh' ": Gen. 18:13–15.

Rashi says . . . Sarah keeps her laughter to herself: Adelman, "On Laughter
and Re-membering," 235–37.

"Now Sarah said . . . 'in his old age' ": Gen. 21:6–7.

she is laughing at the limitations she perceives: This reading follows Adelman,
"On Laughter and Re-membering," 240.

"The wicked plot against the righteous": Ps. 37:12–13.

"They return at evening, snarling like dogs": Ps. 59:6–8 (NIV).

"the kings of the earth rise up in revolt": Ps. 2:2, 4 (BCP).

the psalmist's enemy is described . . . then eats them alive: Brian Doyle,
"Howling like Dogs: Metaphorical Language in Psalm LIX," *Vetus
Testamentum,* 54, no. 1 (2004): 77–79. See also Brian Doyle, "God as
Dog: Metaphorical Allusions in Psalm 59," in P. Van Hecke, ed., *Metaphor
in the Hebrew Bible* (Leuven: Leuven University Press, 2005), 49–53.

"As long as we are in the vale of tears we may not laugh, but must weep":
Jerome, quoted in Jacqueline Aileen Bussie, *The Laughter of the
Oppressed: Ethical and Theological Resistance in Wiesel, Morrison, and
Endo* (New York: T&T Clark International, 2007), 18.

"it is clear that there is never a time for laughter for the faithful soul": Benedict
of Aniane, quoted in Irven M. Resnick, " 'Risus Monasticus': Laughter and
Medieval Monastic Culture," *Revue Bénédictine* 97 (1987), 93. See also
Ingvild Saelid Gilhus, *Laughing Gods, Weeping Virgins: Laughter in the
History of Religion* (New York: Routledge, 1997), 60–63, 79.

*My favorite examples of this come from the women's suffrage movement . . .
"laughingly remarked that she had been afraid that the gentleman would
lose his head at some point":* Krista Cowman, " 'Doing Something Silly':
The Uses of Humour by the Women's Social and Political Union, 1903–
1914," *International Review of Social History* 52, no. S15 (2007): 259–74.

"We're dressed like clowns and you're the ones who look silly": "KKK
Confronted by Clowns," *The Jacksonville Free Press,* November 15, 2012.

*"Nothing undermines authority like holding it up to ridicule" . . . a reordering
might be possible:* Paul Routledge, "Sensuous Solidarities: Emotion,
Politics and Performance in the Clandestine Insurgent Rebel Clown Army,"
Antipode 44, no. 2 (Mar. 2012): 432–33.

*Laughter binds together oppressed people and expresses criticism of dominant
institution:* Nathan Wise, "Fighting a Different Enemy: Social Protests
Against Authority in the Australian Imperial Force during World War I,"

International Review of Social History 52, no. S15 (2014): 229; Sammy Basu, " 'A Little Discourse Pro & Con': Levelling Laughter and Its Puritan Criticism," *International Review of Social History* 52, no. S15 (2014): 98.

Laughter alleviates the stress and tension of political organizing and protest: Cowman, "Doing Something Silly," 269; and Marty Branagan, "Activism and the Power of Humour," *Australian Journal of Communication* 34, no. 1 (2007): 50.

Laughter . . . can "defuse threatening situations": Cowman, "Doing Something Silly," 266.

Costumes and funny songs also command observers' attention: Cowman, "Doing Something Silly," 271.

you might forget what was said in the speeches, but you remember the dramatic spectacles: Branagan, "Activism and the Power of Humour," 46.

laughter fosters (and proclaims) confidence: Marjolein 't Hart, "Humour and Social Protest: An Introduction," *International Review of Social History* 52, no. S15 (2007): 2.

"It is of course difficult to laugh in the face of danger": M. Lane Bruner, "Carnivalesque Protest and the Humorless State," *Text and Performance Quarterly* 25, no. 2 (2005): 149.

"The circus came to the State Capitol this week": Thom Goolsby, "Moron Monday Shows Radical Left Just Doesn't Get It," *Chatham Journal,* June 7, 2013, http://www.chathamjournal.com/weekly/opinion/myopinion/moron -monday-shows-radical-left-just-does-not-get-it-130607.shtml.

She holds a banner proclaiming, in purple letters, "Ladies for Justice": You can see Amy Laura Hall's banner on her blog: http://www.profligategrace .com/?p=1444. In that post, she explains the tea dress: "You might wonder why I bought a vintage tea dress and white gloves for a serious rally? Well, that was a bit of a Bridget Jones moment. Tim Tyson . . . suggested some of us dress up as if indeed for a 'Tea Party.' " See also her provocative essay "Why I Will Not Submit to Arrest, Or, the Problem With Moral Mondays," http://religiondispatches.org/why-i -will-not-submit-to-arrest-or-the-problem-with-moral-mondays/.

Also in attendance is a klatch of Raging Grannies: For more on Raging Grannies' history and their use of humor at protests, see Carole Roy, "When Wisdom Speaks, Sparks Fly: Raging Grannies Perform Humor as Protest," *Women's Studies Quarterly* 35, no. 3 (2007): 150–64.

"What a beautiful sight it is for God when a Christian mocks . . . the clatter of the tools of death and the horror of the executioner": Minucius Felix, quoted in Shane Claiborne, Jonathan Wilson-Hartgrove, and Enuma Okoro, *Common Prayer: A Liturgy for Ordinary Radicals* (Grand Rapids, MI: Zondervan, 2010), 475.

Rouault's contemporaries noticed resonances between . . . wrote novelist Francois Mauriac: Franco Mormando, "Of Clowns and Christian

Conscience: The Art of Georges Rouault," *America* 199, no. 17 (2008): 18; Nora Possenti Ghiglia, "Rouault's Faces of Christ: Notes for a Pictorial Contemplation," in Stephen Schloesser, ed., *Mystic Masque: Semblance and Reality in Georges Rouault, 1871–1958* (Boston: McMullen Museum of Art, 2008), 414; Soo Yun Lang, "A Spiritual Interpretation of the Vernacular: The Literary Sources of Georges Rouault," *Logos: A Journal of Catholic Thought and Culture* 6, no. 2 (May 2003): 115; and Hans Urs von Balthasar, *The Glory of the Lord: A Theological Aesthetics, Volume V: The Realm of Metaphysics in the Modern Age,* trans. Oliver Davies, Andrew Louth, Brian McNeil, John Saward, and Rowan Williams; eds., Brian McNeil and John Riches (San Francisco: Ignatius Press, 1990), 203.

the idea of Jesus as clown . . . speaks in riddles: Theologian Joas Adiprasetya says that, across many cultures, clowns share three characteristics. First, "Clowns cannot walk patiently in the world's path. . . . No one can fully understand their thoughts, sayings, and deeds; at one time they can be vulgar and rude but at another time they can be very unselfish and loving." Second, clowns practice "criticism and solidarity. . . . When society is in a chaotic situation, they respond to it boldly. Since each chaotic situation separates the oppressed from the oppressor, the clowns clarify their position by taking sides with the oppressed." Third, clowns are both "Victim and Healer." All three of these characteristics are exemplified in Jesus. Joas Adiprasetya, "Following Jesus the Clown," *Theology Today* 69, no. 4 (2013): 418–27. On the Holy Fool tradition, see also Peter C. Phan, "The Wisdom of Holy Fools in Postmodernity," *Theological Studies* 62, no. 4 (2001): 730–52; Charles L. Campbell and Johan H. Cilliers, *Preaching Fools: The Gospel as a Rhetoric of Folly* (Waco, TX: Baylor University Press, 2012); and Derek Krueger, *Symeon the Holy Fool: Leontius's Life and the Late Antique City* (Berkeley, CA: University of California Press, 1996), esp. 55–72.

that tradition goes all the way back to Paul: 1 Cor. 1:18, 1:21, 3:19, 4:10.

"One who is slapped": L. L. Welborn, *Paul, the Fool of Christ: A Study of 1 Corinthians 1–4 in the Comic-Philosophic Tradition* (New York: T&T Clark, 2005), 70.

parodic and ironic. . . . It was not the Romans who had the last laugh: Joel Marcus, "Crucifixion as Parodic Exaltation," *Journal of Biblical Literature* 125, no. 1 (2006): 73–87.

"Laughter makes it possible for us to make a negative judgment while yet remaining open": Ellen F. Davis, *Proverbs, Ecclesiastes, and the Song of Songs* (Louisville, KY: Westminster John Knox Press), 211.

There is a rabbinic tradition . . . until the end of days: Adelman, "On Laughter and Re-membering," 241. Adelman is drawing on Midrash *Tanhuma,* parshat *Hayei Sarah,* and *Yalkut Shimoni,* Proverbs. NB: The eschatalogical gloss on Prov. 31:25 cannot be directly inferred from

Proverbs, and, although most English translations render the verb in
question as "laugh," a more lexically precise rendering of the Hebrew,
vatishak, might be "rejoiced" (in contrast with *vatizhak* in Gen. 18:12).

"The mouth filled with real laughter": Avivah Gottlieb Zornberg, *The
Beginning of Desire: Reflections on Genesis* (New York: Schocken Books,
2011), 100.

"I try to give a pep talk you know": Kimberly Greer, "Walking an Emotional
Tightrope: Managing Emotions in a Women's Prison," *Symbolic
Interaction* 25, no. 1 (2002): 117–39.

Lord, to laugh in the midst: Claiborne, et al. *Common Prayer*, 73, 120.

Flame

"I came to bring fire to the earth": Luke 12:49.

Cyril of Alexandria . . . "'while he was explaining the scriptures'": Cyril of
Alexandria and Ambrose, quoted in Arthur A. Just, ed., *Luke* (Downers
Grove: InterVarsity Press, 2003), 217.

"I, the highest and fiery power, have kindled every spark of life": Hildegard of
Bingen, "The Book of Divine Works," in Owen Goldin and Patricia Kilroe,
eds., *Human Life and the Natural World: Readings in the History of
Western Philosophy* (Orchard Park, NY: Broadview Press, 1997), 82–83.

Fiery One . . . Burning Flame: Sebastian Brock, trans., *Bride of Light: Hymns
on Mary from the Syriac Churches* (Kerala: St. Ephrem Ecumenical
Research Institute, 1994), 47, 38, 71.

*"We can define fire as a self-sustaining, high-temperature oxidation reaction" . . .
"from cooling and 'going out'"*: Hazel Rossotti, *Fire* (New York: Oxford
University Press, 1993), 5, 21–22.

"a fire that devours fire; a fire that burns in things dry and moist": Eleazar
Ben Kaller, quoted at http://edgeofenclosure.org/pentecostabc.html.

*"Lie down in the fire and see and taste the flowing Godhead in your
being"*: Mechthild of Magdeburg, quoted in Carmen Acevedo Butcher,
Incandescence: 365 Readings with Women Mystics (Brewster, MA:
Paraclete Press, 2005), xvi.

the Word "opens up what was closed and sets fire to what was frigid":
Bernard of Clairvaux in Laura Swan, ed., *The Benedictine Tradition*
(Collegeville, MN: Liturgical Press, 2007), 40.

Often, in scripture . . . fire seems to stand principally for God's anger: See, for
example, Exod. 21:31; Deut. 32:22; Jer. 4:4, 15:14, 17:14, 21:11; Lam. 2:3–4;
Ezek. 36:5; Amos 5:6; Nah. 1:6; Zeph. 1:18, 3:8.

*"When, therefore, our God is compared to fire, is it only because of the more
terrible aspects of his nature"*: F. B. Meyer, *The Way into the Holiest*
(Grand Rapids, MI: Christian Classics Ethereal Library), 147. Full text
available at http://www.ccel.org/ccel/meyer/into_holiest.pdf.

Soil nourished by burned vegetation becomes more nutritious: "Benefits of Fire," Cal Fire website, http://www.fire.ca.gov/communications /downloads/fact_sheets/TheBenefitsofFire.pdf.

The seeds then find a congenial place to germinate in the beds of ash left after the fires have died down: Stephen F. Arno and Stephen Allison-Bunnell, *Flames in Our Forest: Disaster or Renewal?* (Washington, DC: Island Press, 2002), 53–58.

"God is not elementary fire, that heateth and burneth a body": Walter Hilton, "Treatise Written to a Devout Man," in *The Scale (or Ladder) of Perfection* (Westminster Art and Book Company, 1908), 336–37. For other passages where God's fire seems to refine, to destroy for the purpose of restoration, see Jer. 6:29; Eze. 22:20, 24:12; Zech. 13:9; Mal. 3:2.

"There is labour and great struggle for the impious": Amma Syncletica, in *The Wisdom of the Desert,* trans. Thomas Merton (London: Sheldon Press, 1960), 55.

the day was sometimes called Pascha Rosatum: David Lyle Jeffrey, ed., *A Dictionary of Biblical Tradition in English Literature* (Grand Rapids, MI: William B. Eerdmans, 1992), 598.

"Before them fire devours": Joel 2:3 (NIV).

"Barn's burnt down": Masahide, quoted in Christine Valters Paintner, *Water, Wind, Earth & Fire: The Christian Practice of Praying with the Elements* (Notre Dame, IN: Sorin Books, 2010), 57.

"For now is the axe put unto": Paul V. Marshall, ed., *Prayer Book Parallels: The Public Services of the Church Arranged for Comparative Study,* vol. 1 (New York: Church Hymnal, 1989), 212. See Matt. 3:10 and Lk. 3:9.

The people "have kindled a fire in mine anger, which shall burn for ever": Jer. 17:4 (KJV).

"The LORD once called you, 'A green olive tree, fair with goodly fruit'": Jer. 11:16.

"Our God comes and does not keep silence": Ps. 50:3.

"As wax melts before the fire": Ps. 68:2.

"Come, Holy Ghost, all-quick'ning fire": Charles Wesley, "Hymn to the Holy Ghost" in Wesley and Wesley, eds., *Hymns and Sacred Poems,* 184–85.

"Remember not, Lord, our offences": Marshall, ed., *Prayer Book Parallels,* vol. 1, 191, 193.

The rabbis note that it takes some time: Lawrence Kushner, *Jewish Spirituality: A Brief Introduction for Christians* (Woodstock: Jewish Lights, 2001), 23–24.

The miracle is that Moses paid attention long enough . . . who could really see: Ellen F. Davis, *Getting Involved with God: Rediscovering the Old Testament* (Cambridge, MA: Cowley, 2001), 45–49.

it almost seems a cliché: On burning with love as a "dead metaphor" in the medieval mystics, see Robert Glenn Davis, "The Force of Union: Affect and Ascent in the Theology of Bonaventure" (dissertation, Harvard University, 2012), 4.

Catherine of Siena wrote of her soul being set afire: Butcher, *Incandescence,* 14.

Gertrude the Great cried out, "Lord, how I want my soul to burn": Gertrude the Great, quoted in Butcher, *Incandescence,* 95.

Teresa of Avila described God's igniting a "fire in the heart": Teresa of Avila, quoted in Nicholas W. Youmans, "Haec Visio Rapit: Mystic Love and the Erotic in Bonaventure's *Sunday Sermons,*" in Timothy J. Johnson, ed., *Franciscans and Preaching: Every Miracle from the Beginning of the World Came About Through Words* (Danvers: Brill, 2012), 136.

"turned to slag": Isa. 1:22, in Brevard S. Childs, *Isaiah* (Louisville, KY: Westminster John Knox, 2001), 14.

"The bellows blow fiercely": Jer. 6:29–30.

a chemist can tell what elements are present in a solution by the color flame it produces: Rossotti, *Fire,* 159–61.

cell or cave of self-knowledge: Thomas McDermott, *Catherine of Siena: Spiritual Development in Her Life and Teaching* (Paulist Press, 2008), 281fn232; and *Saint Catherine of Siena, As Seen in Her Letters,* trans. and ed. Vida D. Scudder (New York: E. P. Dutton and Co., 1905), 141. See also Jane Tylus, "Mystical Literacy: Writing and Religious Women in Late Medieval Italy," *A Companion to Catherine of Siena,* eds. Carolyn Muessig, George Ferzoco, and Beverly Mayne Kienzle (Leiden: Brill, 2012), 168.

"Go sit in your cave" and "Go and sit in your cell and your cell will teach you everything": Christine Valters Paintner, *Desert Fathers and Mothers: Early Christian Wisdom Sayings, Annotated and Explained* (Woodstock: Skylight Paths, 2012), 91; and *The Sayings of the Desert Fathers,* rev. ed., trans. Benedicta Ward (Kalamazoo, MI: Cistercian, 1984), 138–39.

"When self-knowledge is rooted in the depths of divine love": Susan W. Rakoczy, "Transforming the Tradition of Discernment," *Journal of Theology for Southern Africa* 139 (March 2011): 98.

Amma Syncletica, preferred to speak of the cave as a nest: Mary C. Earle, *The Desert Mothers: Spiritual Practices from the Women of the Wilderness* (Harrisburg: Morehouse Publishing, 2007), 25.

"To contemplate is to look intently at reality": James W. Douglass, *Resistance and Contemplation: The Way of Liberation* (Eugene, OR: Wipf & Stock, 2006), 51.

a letter she wrote in September 1377 to Trincio dei Trinci: Catherine of Siena to Trincio dei Trinci and his brother Corrado, in Kenelm Foster and Mary Jane Ronayne, eds. and trans., *I, Catherine: Selected Writings of St. Catherine of Siena* (London: Collins, 1980), 154. For a discussion of Trincio dei Trinci and the context of the letter, see Suzanne Noffke, trans., *The Letters of Catherine of Siena,* vol. II (Tempe: Arizona Center for Medieval and Renaissance Studies, 2001), 422.

"You, God, light coals on fire with the love that eventually melts hatred":
Catherine of Siena, quoted in Butcher, *Incandescence,* xvi.

*"I AM BURNING MYSELF" . . . catalyzed Robert McNamara's turn against
the war:* Sallie B. King, "They Who Burned Themselves for Peace: Quaker
and Buddhist Self-Immolators during the Vietnam War," *Buddhist-
Christian Studies* 20, no. 1 (2000): 127–50; Douglass, *Resistance and
Contemplation,* 20–25; and Marjorie Hope, "The Reluctant Way: Self-
Immolation in Vietnam," *Antioch Review* 27, no. 2 (1967): 149–63.

*God determined that it would be impossible. . . . God came down to deliver
the people:* Davis, *Getting Involved with God,* 48–49.

*"If you will, you can become all flame": The Sayings of the Desert Fathers:
The Alphabetical Collection 1,* trans. Benedicta Ward (Kalamazoo, MI:
Cistercian Publications, 1975), 103.

"Finally I say . . . all right, it is improbable, all right, there is no God": Jeanne
Murray Walker, "Staying Power," *Poetry* 184, no. 2 (2004): 93–94.

In This Poverty of Expression, Thou Findest That He Is All

To a degree perhaps impossible to capture in the individual notes, my
overview of apophaticism is indebted to the work of Denys Turner.
Beyond Turner's general framework, my own thinking about and
attempts to practice apophatic speech (unspeech)—the implications of
apophasis for prayer and prayer for apophasis—is not my own thinking
at all, but that of Rowan Williams. I am particularly influenced by
Williams's sermon "A Ray of Darkness" and his treatment of negative
theology in *The Wound of Knowledge,* but lines of thought from his
other work have almost surely seeped into my discussion here. I am also
influenced by other readers of Williams, most especially Mike Higton and
Benjamin Myers.

*Maybe we would come closer to telling the truth if we said very little, or
nothing at all:* Rick McDonald, "The Perils of Language in the Mysticism
of Late Medieval England," *Mystics Quarterly* 34, no. 3 (2008): 45–70.

*This dark cloud, a cloud of unknowing, is taken as negating all sense, all
categories, all material analogies:* Denys Turner, *The Darkness of God:
Negativity in Christian Mysticism* (Cambridge: Cambridge University
Press, 1995), 16–18, passim.

To invoke apophatic theology is to imply that God is ultimately unknowable:
Turner, *Darkness of God,* 19–20.

It "first says something" about God, "and then, in the same image, unsays it":
Turner, *Darkness of God,* 21–22.

"If we attend to the Greek etymology": Turner, *Darkness of God,* 19–20.

*the "astringent" suggestion that God's unknowability demands we say nothing
of God:* Turner, *Darkness of God,* 210.

The Cloud of Unknowing: McDonald, "The Perils of Language," 55; and passim: *The Cloud of Unknowing*, trans. Carmen Acevedo Butcher (Boston: Shambhala Publications, 2009), 129–30. See also Turner, *Darkness of God*, 186–210.

"There is a sense in which any *writing or speaking about God"*: Slee, *Praying Like a Woman*, 127.

"Know this: The Lord himself is God" . . . *"can we live in safety"*: From the Jubilate (83), Canticle 8: The Song of Moses (85), and Suffrages A (97). All found in "Morning Prayer: Rite Two," *The Book of Common Prayer*, 74–102.

it could be nothing more than my own will I am speaking, my will iced and decorated with a lofty spirituality and an earnest mien: This insight comes from Rowan Williams, and my formulation is entirely indebted to the distillation of Williams in Myers, *Christ the Stranger*, 101.

We cannot really say that nearness; we can only gesture toward it: This formulation follows Mike Higton, *Difficult Gospel: The Theology of Rowan Williams* (New York: Church Publishing, 2004), 52.

God is nearer and more than I can say: Myers, *Christ the Stranger*, 103.

"In spite of everything . . . we go on saying 'God' ": Rowan Williams, "Trinity and Revelation," in *On Christian Theology* (Oxford: Blackwell, 2000), 131.

"Truly, you are a God who hides himself, O God of Israel, the Savior": Isa. 45:15 (NIV).

The self-hiding God is also, at the same moment, the God who self-discloses: Belden C. Lane, "A Hidden and Playful God," *The Christian Century* 104, no. 27 (September 1987): 812.

usually hide in the same places over and over again: I owe this insight to MaryAnn McKibben Dana, who made this point to me in a conversation in 2012.

"When you search for me, you will find me; if you seek me with all your heart": Jer. 29:12–13.

"God becomes all to thee; for He is to thee the whole of these things which thou lovest": Augustine, *Gospel of John, First Epistle of John, and Soliloquies*, ed., Philip Schaff (Grand Rapids, MI: William B. Eerdmans, 1978), 88–89.

When the construct fails us . . . maybe we will glimpse the God beneath the picture we had faithfully, longingly, lovingly made: Rowan Williams, *Christian Trial: How the Gospel Unsettles Our Judgment* (Grand Rapids: Eerdmans, 2000), 137; Myers, *Christ the Stranger*, 5, passim; Higton, *Difficult Gospel*, 49, 53, passim.

O the depth of the riches both of the wisdom and knowledge of God! how unsearchable: Rom. 11:33–36 (KJV).

A Short Note from the Women's Prison

This image haunts Isaiah and Jeremiah and Lamentations: See Isa. 3:16–17;
    Jer. 2–3, 13:20–27; Lam. 1:12–22.
*A staggering number of incarcerated women—over 90 percent, according to
    some studies—have been physically or sexually abused (or both) . . .
    perfectly reasonable responses to abuse:* Mary E. Gilfus, "Women's
    Experiences of Abuse as a Risk Factor for Incarceration," National
    Research Center on Domestic Violence, http://www.vawnet.org/applied
    -research-papers/print-document.php?doc_id=412.
"The LORD is acting as the witness": Mal. 2:14–15 (NIV).
*"'I hate divorce,' says the Lord God Almighty. 'But I also hate a man
    covering his wife with violence as with a garment.'":* Mal. 2:16; trans.
    Sarah Jobe.
intentionally omitted from Jewish public liturgy: Mishnah Megillah 4:10; cf.
    Johannah Stiebert, *The Exile and the Prophet's Wife: Historic Events and
    Marginal Perspectives* (Collegeville, MN: Liturgical Press, 2005), 18–19.
    Many thanks to my colleague Laura Lieber for helping me understand
    the nature of the rabbinic decision to omit Ezekiel 16 from the cycle
    of *haftarot.*
committed to wrestling with it: The literature that wrestles with the biblical
    trope of God as abusive husband is vast. My starting point for this
    wrestling was Renita Weems, *Battered Love: Marriage, Sex, and Violence
    in the Hebrew Prophets* (Minneapolis, MN: Fortress Press, 1995). Other
    studies that I have found instructive include Gerlinde Baumann, *Love and
    Violence: Marriage as Metaphor for the Relationship between YHWH
    and Israel in the Hebrew Prophets* (Collegeville, MN: Liturgical Press,
    2003); Julia M. O'Brien, *Challenging Prophetic Metaphor: Theology and
    Ideology in the Prophets* (Louisville, KY: Westminster John Knox Press,
    2008), 63–76; and the symposium on "Characterization of God in the
    Book of Hosea," presented at the 2007 meeting of the Society of Biblical
    Literature and published in Volume 30, Issue 1, of *Horizons in Biblical
    Theology.*
Almighty God, we pray for all victims of abuse: "Prayers for Domestic
    Violence Awareness Month 2011," the Metropolitan New York Synod
    Domestic Violence Awareness Task Force, www.mnys.org/assets/1/7
    /Domestic_Violence_Awareness_Month_Prayer_Calendar.doc; and
    "Prayer to End Domestic Violence," the Community of Our Lady of
    Perpetual Help, Salem, VA, http://www.olphsalem.org/ministries/justice
    _peace/domvioawa/text23.html.

Acknowledgments

As ever, a staggering number of people helped me write this book. More than I can express, I am grateful to and for:

Janelle Agius
Carla Barnhill
Lori Baron
Katie Benjamin
Elizabeth Berg
Debbie Blue
Claudia Boutote
Kate Bowler
Anne Marie Boyd
Luke Bretherton
Bill Brosend
Christine Brosend
Cathie Caimano
Chuck Campbell
Stephen Chapman
Robert Clark
Lil Copan
Sara Olson Dean
Diane Decker
Elizabeth Gandolfo
Paul J. Griffiths
Amy Laura Hall
Kathryn Hamilton
Esther Hamori

Melissa Harrell
Richard B. Hays
Joe Hensley
Judith Heyhoe
Josette Huntress
    Holland
Paula Huston
Sarah Jobe
Tim Jones
Tony Jones
Mari Jorstad
Juli Kalbaugh
Stina Kielsmeier-
    Cook
Adrienne Koch
Rebekah Latour
Terri Leonard
Randy Maddox
Carol Mann
Joel Marcus
Mickey Maudlin
Donyelle McCray
Brett McKey
Andy Meisenheimer

Shauna Niequist
Amy Peterson
Thea Portier-Young
Michael Reinke
Dan Rhodes
Patti Rieser
Sarah Ruble
Tim Sedgwick
Renee Senogles
Ann Swindell
Mark Tauber
Barbara Brown
    Taylor
Laura Turner
Isaac Villegas
Jeanne Murray
    Walker
Kaye Ward
Jo Bailey Wells
Alissa Wilkinson
Leslie Winner
Norman Wirzba
Greg Wolfe
Lisa Zuniga

I am also grateful to my students at the Collegeville Institute and the Seattle Pacific MFA program, who read and workshopped chapter drafts; to my students at the North Carolina Correctional Institute for Women (formerly Raleigh Correctional Center for Women); to my students and colleagues at St. Mary's School (and to the Rev. Ann Bonner-Stewart, for going on maternity leave so that I could fill in); to the congregation of St. Paul's Episcopal Church in Louisburg, North Carolina; and to the many church communities and groups of clergy that have listened to me ponder biblical images of God. I am especially thankful to Virginia Theological Seminary, whose podium first provided me the excuse to put some of these thoughts onto paper.

Thank you.

Also by Lauren F. Winner

HarperOne
An Imprint of HarperCollins*Publishers*

Discover great authors, exclusive offers, and more at hc.com